Dressing Smart

Doubleday

New York   London   Toronto   Sydney   Auckland

DRESSING

SMART

The
WOMAN'S
Guide To
STYLE

By Pamela Redmond Satran

PUBLISHED BY DOUBLEDAY

A DIVISION OF BANTAM DOUBLEDAY DELL PUBLISHING GROUP, INC.
666 FIFTH AVENUE, NEW YORK, NEW YORK 10103

DOUBLEDAY AND THE PORTRAYAL OF AN ANCHOR
WITH A DOLPHIN ARE TRADEMARKS OF
DOUBLEDAY, A DIVISION OF BANTAM DOUBLEDAY
DELL PUBLISHING GROUP, INC.

LIBRARY OF CONGRESS CATALOGING-IN-PUBLICATION DATA

Satran, Pamela Redmond.
    Dressing smart: the thinking woman's guide to style / Pamela Redmond
Satran.—1st ed.
        p.   cm.
    Includes index.
    1. Clothing and dress.   2. Fashion.   I. Title.
TT507.S27   1990   88-36610
646'.34—dc19   CIP

ISBN 0-385-24525-4
COPYRIGHT © 1990 BY PAMELA REDMOND SATRAN

DESIGNED BY DIANE STEVENSON/SNAP•HAUS GRAPHICS

ILLUSTRATIONS BY CHRISTINE CHANG

FOR MY MOTHER
A witty and opinionated arbiter of style

Acknowledgments

I would like to thank my agent, Molly Friedrich, for her boundless enthusiasm from the beginning and for believing, finally, in the marriage of substance and style. Enormous thanks too to my editors at Doubleday, Loretta Barrett and Kara Leverte, and to publisher Nancy Evans and art director Alex Gotfryd, for offering their many good ideas and for their generous consideration of mine. I'd like to thank the photography team: photographer Lynn Kohlman, for her energy and careful work, makeup artist Glenn Marzialli, hair stylist Michel, and dresser Clara Johnson, who all made everything easier. Special thanks to the women who triumphed over wildcat strikes, explosions, half-blind taxi drivers, economics papers, surgery schedules, and recalcitrant bosses to be profiled for this book. For their help in tracking down these wonderful women, thanks to Daina Hulet, K. C. Summers, Paula Span, Julee Spencer, Susan Kaiser, Valerie Monroe, Pat Mulready, Valerie Steele, Nancy Seller, Susan Gordon, Dale Venturini, and Lisa Lebowitz. Thanks also to Christine Chang and Sarah Micklem for contributing their talents to the art in this book and to Samantha Robbins, Jamie Luwenda, and The Diamond Information Center for information on the Bests. Extra thanks to the experts who brought their intelligence about clothes to this project, and to other projects in the past: Michael Solomon, Pat Mulready, Ellen Berman, Joyce Grillo, Vicki French Morris, Molly Mackenzie, Mary Gallagher, and Kim Bonnell, co-driver of the Fashion Ambulance. And thanks for various, nevertheless essential, help to Billie Fitzpatrick, Geraldine Stutz, Joanne Mattera, Maria Simson, Xanthipe Joannides, Rita DiMatteo, Marian Golan, Janet Chan, Mary Peacock, Margi and Katie Marshall, Evelyn Santana, and Dick and Rory Satran.

Contents

Contents

Contents

Contents

IV. GOOD LOOKS

Contents

V. STYLE

Introduction

In 1980, I found myself—a journalist by training and experience—with a job as a fashion editor at *Glamour* magazine. While I had always liked clothes, I had no professional background in fashion. Indeed, I had not the foggiest idea what a fashion editor did. I didn't feel on familiar turf until the fashion director called a meeting to discuss story ideas for future issues. Here at last was something that, from my years as a newspaper reporter and editor, I knew how to do. I scribbled down my proposals, culled from my own experience of buying and wearing clothes, and arrived at the meeting with a measure of confidence. One of the other editors spoke up first.

"My idea," she said, "is pink."

I waited, my interest piqued. What about pink? I wondered. Which shades of pink are most flattering to which types of women? How to wear pink for work? The feminist implications of pink? I kept waiting.

"Well," the fashion director said finally, "I like it."

I learned two important lessons from that exchange:

1. The fashion world is primarily interested in clothes as fashion—in whether they're attractive or not, whether they're in style or out.

2. I, as a "real" woman fresh to the fashion world, was vastly out of step with that world. My story ideas, which to my laywoman's viewpoint seemed supremely obvious (which clothes make you look thinner? how could you find style on a budget?) were viewed by my colleagues as nothing short of revolutionary.

Over the six years I spent at *Glamour*, I wrote and produced scores of those stories that seemed so radical at the start of my tenure: stories on how clothes are made, how they're priced, how they're sold, how to determine what's best and what's most flattering and how to get it at the best price, how clothes influence feelings and opinions and lives. Those stories kept me interested, but perhaps more to the point (or I wouldn't have been allowed to keep doing them), they kept the readers of *Glamour* interested.

While more magazines and newspapers are now publishing insightful stories about buying and wearing clothes (as opposed to primarily visual fashion layouts), these sorts of pieces are still not as prevalent as they deserve to be. The reason is simple: Most fashion editors are not journalists—the majority come from the fashion business itself—and most journalists are not experienced in writing about style. And many publications, loathe to offend all-important fashion advertisers, are reluctant to run stories that may be perceived as "anti-fashion."

I should say here that I'm as happy as the next woman (probably happier) to spend a rainy Sunday afternoon draped across the couch gazing at magazines full of gorgeous pictures of pink clothes. But to me, looking at clothes only as fashion is like looking at sex only as physical. Sure, I'm interested in the in-the-flesh reality, but I'm more interested in the ideas and feelings beneath it.

My guess is that your first reaction to this book will be, "That's different": a style book with few pictures and lots of words and no fashion guru's prescription for how you "should" dress. But I think your second rection will be, "Of course." Of course what you really need to know to make smart decisions about buying and wearing clothes is the kind of information you'll find here.

When I started writing this book, I thought I knew so much from my years of reporting and writing about clothes that, if I'd wanted to, I could have presented myself as an expert. And then I started talking to the real experts—retailers and designers and image consultants and personal shoppers and psychologists and academics and trend forecasters and personnel directors and dozens of women all over the country—and discovered a whole world of new insights.

I discovered, for instance, that there's a revolution brewing among working women concerning professional clothes—a new way of thinking about image and style that will have enormous impact on the way women dress for work over the next ten years. I heard dozens of emotionally wrenching stories of women's clothing fears and triumphs, and found out why the source of it all is often dear old mom. In one particularly illuminating tour through a store's designer department with an expert tailor, I got a vivid illustration of why some very expensive clothes deserve to cost hundreds of dollars, and why others aren't worth the price of the hangers they're displayed on.

These are the kinds of things you'll discover, too, in this book. The material is organized into five sections—Work, Money, Love, Good Looks, and Style—and each of those sections contains five different kinds of pieces:

• Reporting pieces that investigate various aspects of buying and wearing clothes: how to psych out different kinds of stores to get the best buys, for instance, or how to choose clothes most flattering to your body.

• Emotional Issues, which examine the feelings behind clothes: hating or loving to shop, why lingerie may (or may not) make you feel sexy, how clothes can be comforting to the soul as well as the body.

• Bests, which are detailed analyses of what makes an item the best of its kind: the best jacket, for example, or the best terry cloth robe.

• Lists designed to give you fast, efficient information: Eight Things Never to Wear Shopping, for instance, and Ten Pieces That Add Ten Pounds to Your Hips.

• Profiles of women who have great style, and how they got it. These are real women from all over the country of different ages, occupations, sizes, shapes, incomes, and ways of dressing.

Ironically, what I got from writing this book was that I became an expert—I mean an expert in shopping and dressing in my everyday life. I began shopping more efficiently, and with more pleasure, and when I bought, I found I got things I loved at fair prices every time. I developed a wardrobe that's supremely workable, that rises to every occasion, that's stocked with clothes that make me feel terrific and look my best.

After all these years of writing about the fashion business, I still consider myself an outsider, a woman who cares a lot more about whether a dress makes her look thinner than whether it's this season's hot color. The difference is that now I'm armed with an insider's knowledge about buying and wearing clothes—the kind of knowledge that can help every woman dress smart.

—*Pamela Redmond Satran*

WORK

Part I

Style

and the

Corporate

Woman

•

You work for a corporation. You need to buy some new clothes to wear to this corporation. In the store, you see a peach jacket. You love peach. You look great in peach. But maybe peach is too feminine? Navy is more serious. But you have four navy jackets. You're bored with navy jackets. You're bored with jackets, period. But jackets convey professionalism. Jackets provide the crucial third layer of authority. Jackets are what men wear. But you're not a man. But maybe you should pretend not to realize that. Maybe you should wear exactly what you want and see what happens. Maybe, just maybe, things have changed.

Things *have* changed. Or, more correctly, they're starting to change. Five years ago, there was not much point in talking to corporate women about what they wore to work, because almost all corporate women wore navy or gray tailored suits, white shirts, little ties, clear stockings, and plain pumps. Even two years ago, when many women were beginning to vary the corporate uniform, talk about work clothes was rife with references to "rules" and to "image," to following men's standards and not standing out.

Now, suddenly, many corporate women are talking about what they want to wear to work as opposed to what they should wear. They're talking about work clothes as expressing individuality rather than conforming to the corporation. They're talking about what looks good on them rather than what looks good to the chairman of the board; about indulging rather than hiding their femininity, about rediscovering the pleasure of clothes.

In the annals of work dressing, this is revolutionary. But it's a revolution that's still in its incipient stages.

"We're talking about the tip tip tip of the iceberg," says Dana Friedman, a senior research analyst for the Conference Board, who studies issues that relate to working women, including the history—and the future—of work clothes. "This [women expressing themselves through clothes at work] is a handful of very secure successful women."

One of those women is Dale Venturini, the general manager for a branch of a chemical manufacturing company in Cranston, Rhode Island. Venturini, the head and only female executive of a company in a male-dominated industry, says that working almost exclusively with men affects her way of dressing "not in the least."

"I do own a gray pinstripe suit," says Venturini, "and I've worn it maybe three times. I resent it when I have to wear that kind of outfit."

Instead, Venturini wears such things as a pale yellow dress that ends four inches above her ankle, has an eight-inch waistband and a fold-over collar. "It's very feminine and very simple," she says. "It doesn't look like a low-cut dress but it shows a little skin here and there." Venturini says she usually at least brings a jacket to work, but when she does, it's most likely to be pink or bright red.

"If I had to change the way I dress I wouldn't work for the company," says Venturini. "In this job I am me all the way. When they hired me they knew what they were getting—they called me at the last minute for the final interview, and I went in wearing what I'd put on that day, a light pink suit and a summery blouse. I wasn't worried about whether I'd be taken seriously."

Venturini wasn't always so confident about being accepted, no matter how she dressed. "In my last job I was a corporate vice president and I felt I had to dress to play the part," she says. "I hated every moment of it. I started to feel I had to dress like who I was. I'm extremely outspoken and very verbal, and now I dress to that personality."

Why can Venturini get away with dressing in a flamboyant manner that may make other corporate women shudder? "My personality fits my clothes. My clothes wouldn't hang right on someone else." And, perhaps most important: "I've already proven myself."

What Venturini is talking about is dressing to express her individuality as well as her femininity, which often amounts to the same thing. Underneath the changing styles of dress for corporate women are changing attitudes about women in the corporate world. If the old wisdom for women was to deny the ways in which they differed from men, the new way of thinking—at least for women who've established themselves—is to celebrate their distinctly female qualities.

"The change is something that's in the air," says Carol Sholler, owner of a fund-raising and marketing company. "It comes from a realization that while men and women can be equally effective, men and women are different."

"I think it's important to look like a woman instead of a man," says Judy Patrick, an Atlanta-based national account executive for Moving Systems Inc., a corporate relocation firm. "Women tried to look like men because they thought it was necessary for acceptance, but that's not true anymore. You can be very feminine but be knowledgeable. You can earn respect for having a brain and looking like a woman."

"We've pretty much figured out that no matter what we do, we can't be one of the boys," says Sheryl Spanier, a vice president of Fuchs, Cuthrell, a New York-based management consulting and corporate outplacement firm. "And by dressing like one of the boys, we hurt ourselves more than we helped ourselves. The risk you take in being feminine, or female, or attractive, is that someone will treat you in a less-than-appropriate manner, and we thought that if we dressed down and made ourselves invisible and unattractive, we would be avoiding sexual harassment. And I, frankly, think that didn't work. If you're going to get it, you get it, no matter how you're dressed."

Indeed, the male-inspired uniform was an attempt to avoid special attention of any kind, sexual or simply gender-related. The women who pioneered the upper echelons of male-dominated corporations were by definition "deviants," under close scrutiny and tremendous pressure to prove they could fit in. "If you have seven men and one woman, everything she does is going to be different, right?" says Ellen Berman, M.D., co-director of the Women's Center at the Philadelphia Psychiatric Center. "She breaks up the smooth flow of people who have a whole set of agreed-on norms and behaviors. So everything that person does you notice more. You have a woman who's a peer, by title, but who's supposed to be a subordinate, by gender, and so everybody's feeling really weird."

As more women moved up through the ranks, however, rules of behavior—and dress—had to change. "Once there are a group of women, the group culture changes," says Berman. "I mean, seven men and a woman is a group of men with an intruder. Four men and four women is a co-ed group in which everybody has to work together."

More women in high corporate positions also means that younger women new to the working world now have female role models for work dressing. "Ten years ago there were no women to look up to," says Ron Rau, director of personnel for a large Atlanta-based corporation. "Now young women can see successful women in business, even if it's just by walking into a bank and looking at the officers, and see what they're wearing."

"For many women [in the early seventies] the problem was that aside from their mothers there weren't any role models and they had to make it up as they went along," says Dr. Berman. "Now young women can look at other women who've been through that, who represent the options, instead of everybody starting from ground zero. Women who've made it to the top have the freedom to do whatever they damn well please."

In the professional world, these women now at the top have become fashion leaders, according to clothing psychologist Michael Solomon, head of the marketing department at Rutgers University. "The fashion leaders in a professional context are the older executives, because they're the ones who have internal self-confidence, they're the ones who are free to experiment. Who wears a dress to work? The senior women who've done well over the years. You never see them in those suits; those are for the junior to mid-level women. But now there's a greater and greater mass of women who five years ago were junior and now are mid-level to senior, and they're becoming role models and changing the standards of what's appropriate."

Some women who've moved up through the ranks over the past few decades say they remember the moment they realized dressing for success—in the classic terms defined by John T. Molloy's book *Dress for Success*—was no longer right for them.

"Five years ago or so I was wearing the version of the man's suit," says Claudia Rache, a loan officer for a Chicago mortgage company. "I would be wearing the actual button-down shirts with little ties. One day I was standing in line at the bank in my navy pinstripe suit with my light blue shirt and yellow tie and a man came up to me wearing the exact same outfit and said, 'I like your tie.' We could have been twins, and right there I said, 'Enough of this.'"

Other women say their move away from the corporate uniform and into more feminine, individual clothes was evolutionary. "There was a point at which I was traveling twenty or twenty-five weeks a year, which had a tremendous influence on how I dressed. A lot of my travel was to the Southwest, and the warm weather and more relaxed style was another influence," says Bonney Sevellon, the head of public relations for Potterhazlehurst, a Rhode Island advertising agency. "I found dresses traveled better than suits, and as my confidence grew, I began automatically buying clothes that had more appeal to me. So part of the change was practical, part of it was because I was bored with the uniform, and part of it came from self-confidence."

While the demise of the corporate uniform heralds a liberation from constricting rules of dress, it also means an end to easy answers about what to wear to work. Now, what's appropriate for the office depends not so much on the style of clothes themselves but on the particular corporate culture.

"It's critically important to read the corporate culture that you're in," says Bonney Sevellon.

"One male at this company wears too many power suits, and this is not a power suit agency. Whether he knows it or not he's making a statement to other people that he finds aggression and ambition terribly important in an agency that doesn't value those qualities."

How to read that corporate culture? "You have to be really observant," says Sevellon. "If there are men at the top you have to look at those men and interpret to a certain degree your style according to what you see in them, in their clothes as well as their behavior."

While that advice may sound like the old way of doing things, what's changed is how the male example is translated for women. "The correlation isn't pinstripe to pinstripe anymore," says Sevellon. "Now a very good dress with a high neck may go with a pinstripe suit. In a place where the top men wear slacks and tweedy jackets, women can wear separates. I see more men now with signature touches, and more women are doing that, too."

Dressing to conform to corporate culture is, however, a two-edged sword. On one side, it's undeniably a key to success, and it behooves any ambitious woman to take her dressing cues from the people above her on the corporate ladder. On the other side, however, if your style is too much at odds with that of your corporation, it could be a sign of trouble.

"It could be a big problem to deny, to say, 'Well, I can always change the way I dress,' or 'I'll put on the business suit, it's okay,'" says Margaret Newborg, vice president of Fuchs, Cuthrell and president of the Financial Women's Association. "It's really denying a whole piece of yourself. It's very important that you dress in a style you are comfortable with."

Newborg, a former banker, has personal experience with this phenomena. "I never ever wanted to wear a uniform, which made me stand out in the bank," she says. "It made me realize that in terms of environment I needed a place where I could be more creative. I needed a corporate culture that was a little more individual."

"I've known people who changed jobs they were so outraged by corporate clothes," says Joyce Grillo, president of Impression Management, a New York image consulting firm specializing in corporate clients. "If you hate the clothes you have to wear to work, you really need to think about that because it's telling you something about who you are. To buck the standard and dress how you want you have to be very confident, and you also have to be willing to lose everything."

In truth, not every woman in corporate America is bucking the standard, and it may not be because she lacks confidence or is afraid to take a risk. Some highly placed women believe the direction of corporate style in the future is not toward more adventurous clothes, but toward a bona fide uniform.

Diane Jones, manager of accounts payable for Xerox Corporation, based in Rochester, New York, is one woman who believes that the sensible thing for corporate women to do is forget about creating a distinctly female corporate style, forget about piecing together a replica of the male corporate style, and wear an executive uniform—standard suit, neutral shirt—issued to corporations through such firms as Coyne Textile Services in Syracuse.

"Trying to be unique can be a pain in the neck," says Jones. "When I saw those uniforms

I thought, Boy, wouldn't that be great. I'm so busy I don't have time to shop. It's hard to find basic styles in good-quality fabrics, and this place will even launder the garments for you."

The bottom line, says Jones, is the bottom line. "Women still earn less money than men, and then we have to spend more money on clothes just to go to work. I'd sooner be investing in stocks or real estate."

How to Invest Corporate Clothes with Personal Style

You're ready to leave the corporate uniform— the dark suit, the white shirt, the little tie— behind. Your only question is, What do you wear instead? How do you choose clothes that are appropriate for your job, yet reflect your personal style?

Elaine Mack, Bergdorf Goodman's personal shopper, says she advises corporate clients who want to break out of the mold to first experiment with a few bolder pieces, rather than to overhaul their entire wardrobes. "What a woman tries depends on how self-confident she is," says Mack. "Many women have been programmed for so many years that they should not stand out that it can be difficult to try something brighter or more feminine or stylish."

What happens when a woman does take a risk with a new, more adventurous piece? "I've never had anyone come back to me and say, 'What a mistake,'" says Mack, "but I have had women come back and say, 'Let's do more.'"

Mack says she always gives clients one good-looking suit they can rely on for even the most conservative of occasions, and then may recommend a range of blouses—from neutral and tailored to bright and adventurous—that can be worn underneath.

Also, Mack encourages corporate women to experiment with brighter colors, to mix colors and patterns, and to try new accessories. "Accessories are a very important way to develop personal style," says Mack. "You can try an interesting pin, a scarf at the throat, a wild-color hanky, one belt that's a knockout."

While more color and bolder accessories can be good ways to inject style into a corporate wardrobe, there are no absolute guidelines as to which colors or what accessories are best for you and your job. In fact, the most successful way to strike out in a new direction is to pay attention to your own tastes and preferences.

"It's best if it evolves naturally," says image consultant Joyce Grillo. "Some people like loose-fitting things or have a preference for a certain color or fabric, or some women like pins or antique jewelry or pearls. You also have to take into consideration your coloring and your body and what works well for you. If you've got a nice, long neck and you always wear a pearl choker, that's a personal statement."

Playing up your best features and choosing signature pieces can pay dividends in the corporate world, says Vicki French Morris, owner of French-Haines, a wardrobe consulting firm in Chappaqua, New York. "I would tell a client to dress in a way that enhances her eyes, her face, and her figure, not in a sexual but in an attractive way, because that will enhance her ability to communicate and make her job easier as well as make people more aware of her," says Morris. "I also recommend that people dress with a certain signature because in the corporate environment people are dying to get a handle on who you are. If there are colors you like, certain accessories or a style that appeals to you, I recommend that you go with that."

Often, says Morris, putting more style into your work wardrobe involves not radical changes but subtle variations. "I had a client who was athletic, with short hair, who was told in her performance report that people found her very unapproachable and formidable, but underneath she was very shy and young and was the only woman at her level," says Morris. "We took her very severe classic style and softened the edges. Instead of a severe gabardine suit, we got her a woolen silk gabardine, and added some signature accessories. Just doing a little bit can make it work."

Sometimes what's required, according to Morris, is not a change of style but an upgrade in quality. "People respond to quality, to good fabric and workmanship, rather than necessarily a designer item."

An awareness of quality is also something Susan St. Charles, an Atlanta image consultant, stresses with her corporate clients. The aim for working women, says St. Charles, is to balance personal style with appropriateness. "You might be really artistic and creative and want to use colors in accessories. If you use suiting as a style identity, it doesn't have to be a little conservative suit; you can go with a fuller jacket and a shorter or a longer skirt."

The most important thing, says Joyce Grillo, is not to get mired in details and dictums but to follow your instincts. "People get so hung up on the earrings and whether it's a dress or a suit or the color or the shape of the lapel, but that's not what really matters," Grillo says. "Unless you're totally outlandish or cheap or haughty or dowdy, you can wear just about anything as long as it's well put together, the whole thing works, and you look great in it. That's what people look for."

Nine Business-Dressing Rules to Follow

While many of the strict Dress for Success rules established in the seventies no longer apply, there are some guidelines for corporate dressing that remain valid. Here, the rules that still should be followed:

1. **BUY THE BEST QUALITY YOU CAN AFFORD**—Nowadays, quality can be more important than style in choosing clothes that are right for work. Quality affects not only how clothes look but how they move and how they fit, and high quality can often make the difference in whether a particular style—a slim skirt, say, or a knit jacket—looks professional, appropriate for work.

2. **DON'T WEAR ANYTHING SEXY**—Feminine and stylish do not equal sexy. Still absolutely *verboten*, according to businesspeople, personnel directors, image consultants: see-through fabrics, miniskirts, body-hugging clothes, necklines that reveal cleavage. Even clothes that

seem properly businesslike can fall over the edge into sexiness: the high-collared white blouse sheer enough to reveal the lace bra beneath, the glen plaid straight skirt that hugs your bottom, the plain black pumps with heels just a millimeter too high for business.

3. **DRESS MOST CONSERVATIVELY WHEN IN A NEW SITUATION**—This holds true for an interview or a visit to a new client or an initial sales pitch. It all goes back to corporate cultures: If you're not sure of the one you're stepping into, it's best to err on the side of conservatism.

4. **DRESS FOR YOUR BODY AND PERSONALITY**—Don't let advice or rules dominate what's right and comfortable for you. If you've heard you should wear red when making a presentation, and yet red makes you feel like a neon sign, don't wear red. Conversely, if wearing a navy suit on an airplane makes you feel as if you're bound in chains, wear that knit dress. Clothes that make you feel comfortable, flatter your outer self, will boost your inner confidence.

5. **DON'T WEAR ANYTHING SLOPPY**—I'm not talking about ketchup stains on the sleeves of your dress. I'm talking about subtle kinds of sloppiness—worn-down heels, roaming shoulder pads, a slip that peeks from the little slit at the back of your skirt—that can undermine what may in all other ways be a great look.

6. **DON'T WEAR ANYTHING TOO CASUAL**—While jeans and a T-shirt may be your dream work outfit, they're not appropriate at even the most casual of companies. You shouldn't, in other words, look as if you rolled out of bed and into whatever was lying on the floor, but as if you took some care with what you put on.

7. **ALWAYS WEAR STOCKINGS**—Okay, maybe not in Florida in July, maybe not every day to every office, although many businesswomen and clothing experts would disagree. Always controversial, but still sacred among most executive women is the rule on always wearing pantyhose. Hose mean that you're fully dressed; they make anything look more formal; they're as essential in most places as socks for men. But please, no sheer black with little flowers up the seam.

8. **TAKE YOUR CUES FROM YOUR BOSS**—Sometimes corporate style is set by the person at the top; most often, however, you should pattern yourself after the person directly above you, says image consultant Joyce Grillo. "Their style may be from zero to ten," says Grillo, "but they're the ones who are judging your appearance and performance." Does this mean that if your boss's style is a zero yours has to be, too? Of course not. But it may be a sign

that clothes are not that important at your company, and that your boss won't put great stock in yours, no matter how terrific.

9. **KEEP YOUR CORPORATION'S CULTURE IN MIND**—Your clothes can communicate effectively only when they speak the same language as that of what everyone else—especially everyone above you—is wearing. If everyone at your company wears tweed jackets and dowdy skirts to work, your incredible Donna Karan number will say nothing to them, at least not anything meaningful. The lesson: modify your dress to fit in with that of others at your company, and if your styles are wildly incompatible, give some thought to what that may say about your career goals vis-à-vis the goals of your company.

Eight Business-Dressing Rules No Longer in Effect

Some business-dressing rules that were almost sacrosanct a few years ago no longer apply. While your company's dictates, or your own style, may lead you to follow some of these rules (and really, there's nothing intrinsically wrong with doing so), the point is that you no longer have to, just because. The rules you may now feel free to break include:

1. **SUITS SHOULD BE MATCHED**—The rule about wearing matched suits started because, when proper business clothes for women were first being manufactured, the unmatched alternative was the equivalent of a man's sport coat and golf slacks. Now, with a wider range of better-designed options, suits don't necessarily have to "match"—in color or fabric or even pattern—to look just as pulled together, as formal, and as professional as his blue pinstripes.

2. **CHOOSE MENSWEAR TAILORING**—As with the rule above, the old alternative to menswear tailoring was frills or glitz. Now, clothes can be softer, more shaped, more detailed than a man's tailored suit, and be just as appropriate.

3. **STICK WITH DARK, NEUTRAL COLORS**—They may mimic men's clothes and make you fade into the boardroom walls, but then those aren't the aims of most professional women anymore. While some women still counterbalance style and color—choosing dark neutrals for dresses, for instance, and brights only for tailored jackets—many are looking to color in all kinds of business clothes to make them look better, feel better, and stand out in the crowd.

4. **WEAR ONLY UNOBTRUSIVE, REAL JEWELRY**—The old thinking: jewelry should be unobtrusive because you don't want to call attention to your femininity; real because, if

men wear any jewelry at all, it is never costume. Now, women are looking to bigger, often frankly fake jewelry for fun, for flattery, for a signature.

5. **CARRY A STANDARD BRIEFCASE**—Once upon a time, all serious women lugged around leather boxes, or at least soft-sided but quite standard briefcases. Often, they carried a purse, too, until they figured out that not only was this damned awkward, but it looked stupid. Then they started carrying the purse inside the briefcase. Then they started carrying the briefcase plus a gym tote. Then they—at least the smart ones—gave up and bought one big, soft leather tote in which to cart everything, or one good-looking small bag and to hell with the rest.

6. **ALWAYS WEAR A JACKET**—This rule postdates the "always wear a matched suit" one, but it became, if anything, more strict. Jackets provided that crucial "third layer of authority." Jackets defined your shoulders and hid your curves. Jackets were the one thing men wore that women could copy most successfully. Well, maybe you still like to wear a jacket, or maybe you feel as if you still have to, which is fine. Jackets are nice. But in general, they're no longer as crucial to a professional woman's attire as, say, shoes. You can wear a dress or a knit ensemble without a jacket and it won't look as if something's missing.

7. **WEAR ONLY PLAIN, NEUTRAL SHOES**—I have a personal bias about this one. I like plain, neutral shoes. I think plain, neutral shoes—black suede pumps, for instance, or navy leather slip-ons—are wonderful things to have in your wardrobe, making life infinitely simpler, looking right with everything you own. But again, they're no longer the only way to go. Red pumps? Fine. Spectators? Great. Fuchsia high heels with aqua piping and yellow bows? Okay, maybe there I'd draw the line.

8. **AVOID ANYTHING FASHIONABLE**—Only women were interested in fashion, the thinking went, and so fashion was out. Not serious. Fluffy, frivolous. Well, now that it's okay again to be a woman, it's okay again to be fashionable, within limits and without becoming a slave to it, which has never been truly in style anyway.

• *Style Analysis* •

LUCILLE CORRIER *is director of marketing communications at Touche Ross Financial Services Center in New York. Corrier was photographed in an Oscar de la Renta wool double-knit suit, something she'd wear to work and then out to dinner, that she bought at Loehmann's for about $400. Her dressmaker tailored the suit and moved around some buttons on the cuffs, because two had been destroyed. Corrier's patent leather pumps are Amalfi, on sale at a New York specialty store for about $50; her earrings are pearls bought in Hong Kong; her lucite bracelet a gift from her sister. The occasion? Happy October 2.*

I'M INTERESTED IN HOW WORKING AT A LARGE ACCOUNTING FIRM AFFECTS THE WAY YOU DRESS.

I feel that the way you dress has to make the other people around you feel comfortable. Even if a Patti LaBelle haircut and Christian Lacroix clothes were my best look, there's no way I would come to the office that way, because people here or in any office would get the wrong idea about what was going on in my head. Women who are feminine and feel feminine should dress in a feminine way. That doesn't have to mean ruffles and bows. There are lots of women around who aren't terribly feminine. They feel more comfortable in tailored clothes and I think they should wear them if that's what they truly feel more comfortable wearing.

WHAT WOULDN'T YOU WEAR TO WORK?

I don't wear sleeveless dresses to work, unless I wear jackets over them. I don't wear plunging necklines. I don't wear skirts with slits up the front or the back. I wouldn't wear minis,

even if I were ten pounds lighter. I don't like clothes that look like costumes. I wouldn't wear something that might be a wonderful cut but an outrageous color. I found a piece of silk and wool that I was crazy about, and it was in a really bright orange, and my first consideration was where could I wear it? I couldn't wear it to work, because the color was far too bright. Even if I had a very conservative blazer made out of it, it was a color that would cause comment. I'm not afraid of that, but I think it's unnecessary.

DO YOU WEAR PANTS TO THE OFFICE?

I have a pants suit I picked up at Syms that I absolutely adore, and I did wear it to the office a few years ago—it's cut like a man's suit and I wear it with silk blouses—but I decided not to do that anymore. Because of what I do here, I can sort of get away with it a little more than other people, but I feel that I really have to set an example. I don't like pants worn to the office unless it's a really nice pants suit, but you can't tell people, 'Your pants suit isn't nice,' so I just feel, don't do it at all.

DO YOU EVER TALK TO JUNIOR WOMEN ABOUT THEIR CLOTHES?

If they ask me. I certainly wouldn't impose my feelings about it. I definitely believe in a dress code for the office. I can't see how women can come to the office looking like they're going to the beach. What they do is retard their own progress if they dress that way. It gives off the wrong message.

I wasn't always this way. For a while I thought, If you're really good at your job, you should be able to wear what you want. I used to work in an agency where you could wear what you want—the creative advertising–public relations–marketing communications–business style that lends itself to a creative way of dressing. Here, in an accounting firm, not so much. Women here are wearing different-cut suits or suits with different kinds of blouses and more and more women are wearing dresses here, or blouses and skirts that have a dress effect. I see, not real frill, but less severe I-have-to-look-like-a-man-to-get-the-job-done.

WHAT'S YOUR PRIME MOTIVATION FOR GOING TO A DRESSMAKER?

It's a creative outlet for me. I have sewn, my mother has sewn, my mother had dressmakers and milliners. The idea of creating what you want, the idea of an original, that you don't see yourself coming and going, really appeals to me. I like the process and I like knowing this is something I came up with—the fabrication, the colors, the idea of using a particular kind of fabric you wouldn't expect. I got a gorgeous piece of gray flannel and made a turtleneck straight dress with shoulders—I have shoulders in everything—and then I had a jacket made of gray and blue and silver cashmere, and had a collar made of the same fabric for the dress. That's the kind of touch you don't see on clothes in the store.

HOW DID YOUR INTEREST IN CLOTHES BEGIN?

I'm a native New Yorker, and my mother was very fashion-conscious. To this day, I can still remember some of the outfits she wore when we were growing up and even some of the outfits that she would describe to my sister and me that she wore to dances. I have her engagement dress and my sister has her wedding gown. Her engagement dress is a stunning little black lace dress and it has big puff sleeves and it's inset with a beautiful georgette flower and it's fitted and has velvet bows down the front and a flowing skirt. I had the dress reconstructed—I had a lace border put on the bottom to match the lace because I needed the length—I'm taller than she is—and I had new velvet bows put on, and I had the lace all tacked together. I've worn it, and I love it. My sister's been asking me for it for years, but no dice.

I can remember the black patent leather high-heeled shoes with the cutouts around the edge. To this day, I could draw those shoes. If I were having my shoes made, I would have those copied. I loved her wedding shoes—they were satin T-straps—and I've always had a T-strapped shoe in my shoe wardrobe.

My mother used to sew a lot and was very interested in fabric. Starting when I was seven or eight years old we used to go to the fabric markets down on Orchard Street and Hester Street. I learned how to sew and knit when I was eight or nine years old. I'm not saying at the age of eight that I sewed like a dressmaker, and of course at school I took sewing. The first thing I ever made totally that I wore was my eighth grade graduation dress. It was kind of a cotton batiste, V neck with a cap sleeve, what *Vogue* would call very very very easy. We handwove the neckline. God, was that a horror.

WHAT KINDS OF THINGS DO YOU HAVE A PASSION FOR—COLORS, STYLES?

I love blues. Blue is really my favorite color. I love pastels. I love detail on a jacket or a coat or a suit, maybe in the cut or the seaming or the topstitching. I'm neurotic about having sleeves finished off well. There are so many beautiful blouses in the stores and you look, and the cuff is just turned up. I don't like that; it's a cheap way of finishing it off. I like handbound buttonholes when I can get them, but I can't even get them from my dressmaker anymore.

Shoes are another passion. I've probably got over a hundred pairs of shoes. Unfortunately, I have a long, narrow foot and I wind up having to get expensive shoes. I'm cursed with a Charles Jourdan foot, but Jourdan you can get at discount at a number of places. Although my favorite play shoes this summer were $7 at Marshall's in New Jersey.

TO WHAT EXTENT ARE YOU INFLUENCED BY FASHION?

I enjoy it; to me it's entertainment. But of course I'm influenced by it. Giorgio Armani is one of my favorite designers—what can you find wrong with anything he does? I also like Azzedine Alaia, because he's extremely creative with the seaming, although I'm not built for that anymore. I don't rush out and slavishly copy; I adapt more than copy. If I walk into Loehmann's or Syms and see an Armani for half price or less, I'll buy it in a second, because I really love his workmanship and his fabrics, but I don't go out to buy an Armani or to buy a Kenzo or to buy Courrèges. When I do shop for clothes, my number one rule is that it has to be marked down or else I don't even want to know, I won't even shop. I don't have time anymore to go to the stores and see what's there and then go track it down. Whatever's in Loehmann's, that's what I'll buy.

DO YOU PLAN A WHOLE DAY AROUND GOING TO LOEHMANN'S?

*W*ell, I don't plan a day. It turns into a day. I buy whatever appeals, although there's lots of stuff I don't buy because enough is enough and there's a budgetary limit as well. I'm not as much of an impulse buyer as I used to be. If I see something I think of what I have that will go with it or where I can wear it. But if I see something I can use and the price looks right I buy it.

WHAT'S THE PSYCHOLOGY FOR YOU BEHIND THE DISCOUNT?

I know I'm getting a better value, because I know what the markups are. I also know how things are constructed. It's amazing to me to go into a store and see a suit for $1,200 with buttons that are worth 89 cents. If I can get a suit for $400 that's in the store for $1,000, you don't even have to explore the psychology.

Women at the Bottom: A Different Set of Rules?

You think it's great that confident, accomplished women at the top are throwing off the yoke of the tailored business suit and setting new, more feminine, more relaxed standards for work dressing. When you make it to the top, you're going to wear red knit dresses and flowered blazers, too. For now, however, you're still at the bottom, way at the bottom. Maybe you're in an entry-level corporate job, or maybe you're a secretary. The question is, Have the rules for what women can wear to work loosened for you, too, or do you have to make up for your lack of experience with a uniform?

In fact, personnel and management experts are divided on whether corporate dressing rules are different for young women than they are for those with more of a track record.

"If I see someone junior, and by junior I mean someone with less than five years of experience, I expect to see them in more of a uniform, a dark suit and white blouse," says Lisa Lang, managing partner of the Rhode Island branch of Dunhill Executive Search. "They don't have enough credibility to make a lot of statements with their clothes. I deal a lot with financial companies that are very conservative, and for somebody who doesn't have much of a track record it's safest to start off with a dark suit and white blouse. If a woman dresses flamboyantly and she's twenty-one years old, there's no way she's going to be asked back after the first interview."

Psychologist Michael Solomon has posited that the standard business suit has become what he calls a "totemic emblem" for women (as well as men) starting out in the business world. With the uniform comes all the other qualities of the professional role—authority, maturity, propriety—that the young person has yet to acquire through experience.

"The suit becomes a lucky charm that gets the job and gains the person entrée into the business world," says Patricia Mulready, a home economics professor at New York University who specializes in the social psychology of clothing. The exception, says Mulready, is at more creative kinds of firms. "My students who went for interviews dressed in blue suits

at department stores in Delaware, in '76 and '77 when standards were a lot more conservative than they are now, didn't get second interviews. The ones who went in dressed more creatively did get hired."

In fact, not all managers, including those at more conservative companies, consider the suit-shirt-and-tie preferred business dress for entry-level women.

"I would not agree that the uniform is more necessary for younger women," says Ron Rau, director of personnel for a large Atlanta-based corporation. "If a young woman came in wearing a little suit I'd question where has she been that she's coming in dressed like that. I would feel as if she hadn't done her homework."

Whether a young businesswoman chooses to play it safe or be more adventurous in her way of dressing, the absolute is that she should wear clothes designated as professional as opposed to secretarial. In most corporations around the country, there is a very real, if sometimes subtle, difference. Secretaries interested in moving into the managerial ranks must, to some extent, switch fashion allegiance from their own group to that of the professional women.

"There's a real distinction here between the way secretaries and women on staff dress," says advertising executive Bonney Sevellon. "The secretaries wear a lot of skirts and blouses, or slacks, and some of them dress very casually. The secretaries that have any ambition to move up, and in this industry it's possible, dress more like what they aspire to."

Sevellon says she's bothered by the style gap between secretaries and professional women. "I'd like to see that whole category of women in support functions elevated and recognized, but when they differentiate themselves through their clothes, they hold themselves back a little bit. I don't think it's unreasonable to say part of it is budget, but a lot of it is self-image. It's a deep issue."

While many executives have trouble understanding why secretaries deliberately undermine themselves by not "dressing up" in managerial clothes, secretaries themselves say it's not as easy as simply changing outfits.

"I was lucky to have a woman boss who really believed in me and helped me change the way I looked," says one secretary who has moved into junior management. "But it was horrible when I started to wear those new clothes to work. My parents teased me, my friends teased me, and the other secretaries at work teased me. It was hard to keep my mind on where I wanted to go when I was constantly being reminded of what I was leaving."

In fact, says Stephanie Miller, a licensed certified social worker and executive director of the Women's Counseling and Psychotherapy Service in Columbia and Towson, Maryland, people dress for the group to which they care most about belonging—and, for a secretary or junior manager, that may not be the executives at her corporation but her friends from school or her family and friends in her neighborhood. "People only want to connect with the peer group they care about," says Miller. "If they don't care about impressing a group, they can dress differently and feel completely comfort-

able. If a secretary dressed in a way an executive woman deemed 'right,' her friends would think she was uppity."

Still, it's a fact of corporate life that the secretary who dresses like a professional woman has a better chance of actually becoming one.

"The way you dress is very revealing of your attitude toward work, and for secretaries it's very critical because they're at that crossroads of deciding whether they're going to be secretaries all their lives, or whether the job is a stepping-stone," says Lisa Lang. "The secretaries who claim to want to go ahead but dress primarily for comfort or for convenience put no commitment behind that claim, versus the person who is determined to get someplace and knows that the way you dress is part of the element required to move up."

"If you dress the part it helps you move into management. That's definitely true," says Susan Karp, a personnel director for Citibank. "The secretaries who present themselves in a professional way are given the opportunity to move into officer-level jobs. The clothes show that they're interested."

Karp cites the case of one secretary who recently moved into the executive ranks. "She got the opportunity to do this job, which involves dealing with a lot of people, because she looked right and she talked right," says Karp. "If she was the kind of person who was hanging around in jeans, as smart as she was nobody would have asked her."

Excuse Me, But Your Lack of Sophistication Is Showing

You've been out of college only a few years. You're not supposed to be sophisticated. Oh, yes, you are. Or your brain's working too hard on important things to worry about whether your clothes look dumb. That's no excuse. Even if most of the other corporate dressing rules fall by the wayside, the one that will remain in effect is: look sophisticated.

The whole trouble with this is that "sophisticated" is such a terrible word. It calls to mind Ladies in tight, black cocktail dresses, wearing pearls and red lipstick and waving cigarette holders. This is not what I mean.

Looking sophisticated in business-dressing terms means looking like a grown-up, someone capable and savvy. Like someone who's been at least partway around the block, someone who knows enough not to answer the phone with a "Hi, there!" and not to say, "Have a super day!" when she hangs up and who doesn't dot her *i*'s with little happy faces. If you do any of those things, stop. And if you wear any of the following unsophisticated but often-seen items to work, stop that, too.

A Sweet-looking Flower-sprigged Dress—You know the kind I mean. It's got semi-puffed sleeves and elastic at the waist and a self-belt and, in its worst incarnations, a lace collar. Many women, when they want to "branch out" from suits to dresses, choose this one. Big mistake. This dress is so ubiquitous, and so offensive, that several headhunters and

businesswomen put it first on their lists of pet peeves. One highly placed woman even told me she'd like to round up all of these dresses, take them out behind a barn somewhere, and shoot them. Don't you be wearing one when she does.

A Simple Shirt and Skirt—What's wrong with that? you want to know. It's tailored, appropriate, and I thought you said I didn't always have to wear a jacket anymore. Yes, but, a shirt and skirt—I'm thinking of such combos as a cotton turtleneck and a plaid skirt or a striped oxford shirt and a chino skirt—are what girls wear to high school. At least what they wore when your boss went to high school. Make a little more effort.

All-matching Jewelry—Well, some women can pull this off, if it's a trademark or it looks like they did it by design. Most people, though, when they're wearing a gold X pin and gold X earrings and a gold X necklace, look like they walked up to some department store jewelry counter and said, "I need some accessories and I don't know what I'm doing." What if you really don't know what you're doing and you're afraid, if you attempt to pick and choose, that you'll end up looking like a clown? Focus on the single item to which you're most naturally attracted—earrings, say, if you've had pierced ears since you were twelve—and walk up to a department store jewelry counter and say, "I need some earrings and I don't know what I'm doing."

Dress Pumps with Chunky Rubber "Walking Bottoms"—They're comfortable, you say? They're better than jogging shoes? That's debatable. You won't fool anyone with shoes that look semi-professional on top, like moon boots on the bottom. These shoes make it look as if you didn't know that there are now in the marketplace many perfectly presentable and extremely comfortable styles of women's dress shoes, even some engineered for walking. And maybe you didn't. But now you do.

A Briefcase with Protective Hardware on the Corners, Other Decorative Metal—The most unsophisticated versions are imitation leather, but lots of metal ruins the look of even a good leather briefcase. To understand why little metal corners look so dopey, think of them as analogous to those plastic penholders worn in the shirt pockets of supernerds. They say, "Save me from my clumsy self," as well as, "If this briefcase wears out, I won't be able to afford another one." Eeek! And any kind of decorative hardware—buckles that don't buckle anything shut, rings holding straps together, big shiny zippers—tends to cheapen what it's on, whether briefcase or purse or even clothes.

"Dress-up" Clothes—Many young women, when first attempting to "dress up" for work, choose clothes more appropriate for a cocktail party or a church social than a 10 A.M. meeting. These include shiny, neon-bright dresses (even conservatively cut ones); clothes with such peekaboo features as keyhole backs and lace insets; black-patterned stockings; white high heels with bows in front or pink dresses with bows in back. The irony is that, instead of making you look like a grown-up, these kinds of clothes make you look like an unsophisticated kid who doesn't know the ropes.

Anything Ill-fitting—Whether it's a skirt that's too tight, a jacket that pulls at the buttons, sleeves that hang down to your knuckles, or a coat that's an inch shorter than all your dresses, ill-fitting clothes seem to say that you don't know how to dress yourself, which is okay only if you're a six-year-old boy.

Dumb Work Clothes—These are usually found in a musty department store, in the section called "Career Dressing." They are prim, little matched suits—the kind where you have to buy the top and bottom together, so that one half never fits quite right. They are blouses with always-too-short sleeves and already-tied bows. They are blazers fit for a bank security guard and skirts we used to call "A-line." They may be the least sophisticated work clothes of all, because they showed you tried to do it right, but you had no idea what right really was. Before you buy stodgy "career clothes," look in the designer departments. You'll most likely be able to buy as-appropriate clothes . . . and surprisingly, for less money.

The Best: Jacket

Soft, Rounded Lapels—Lapels that feel stiff or are pressed flat indicate inferior quality.

No Topstitching!—In general, avoid jackets with topstitching (a line of stitching, along the edge of the lapel, for instance) as this can also indicate lower quality.

Soft, Invisible Shoulder Pads—Shoulder pads, no matter what their size, should feel natural, not be visible through the fabric of the jacket. The point: no one should be aware that they're there, including you.

Smooth Seams—Beware of puckering at seams or darts.

Full Lining—Not all good jackets demand full linings to hang correctly or feel comfortable, but most shaped wool ones should have it. The best lining fabric: silk, although many exquisite jackets are lined with rayon or a synthetic such as acetate, which can be more durable than silk.

Lining Sewn Down at Hem, Cuffs, Vents—Also, all stitching should be invisible.

Pleat in Top Back of Lining—For fullness, comfort across the back when you move your arms.

Real Opening at Cuff—If a cuff has buttons, even ones that don't actually unbutton, it should have a true vent. Buttons sewn onto a closed seam cheapen a jacket's look.

Neat Buttonholes—No loose threads or scraggly edges.

Single-Breasted—Whatever the style of the jacket, a single-breasted one (with only one row of buttons, closing front and center) will usually be more flattering than one that's double-breasted.

Single Vent—A jacket with a single vent (the slit in back) tends to be more comfortable and flattering than one with double vents. The vent should always lie closed and flat; if it pulls apart, the jacket's too small across the hips.

Notes on Style, Fit, and Fabric: The most classic jacket shape is that modeled on a man's: hip-length, single-breasted, with lapels. Is this still the "best" style, in terms of appropriateness, versatility, comfort, and flattery? It can be, if it looks good on your body. For

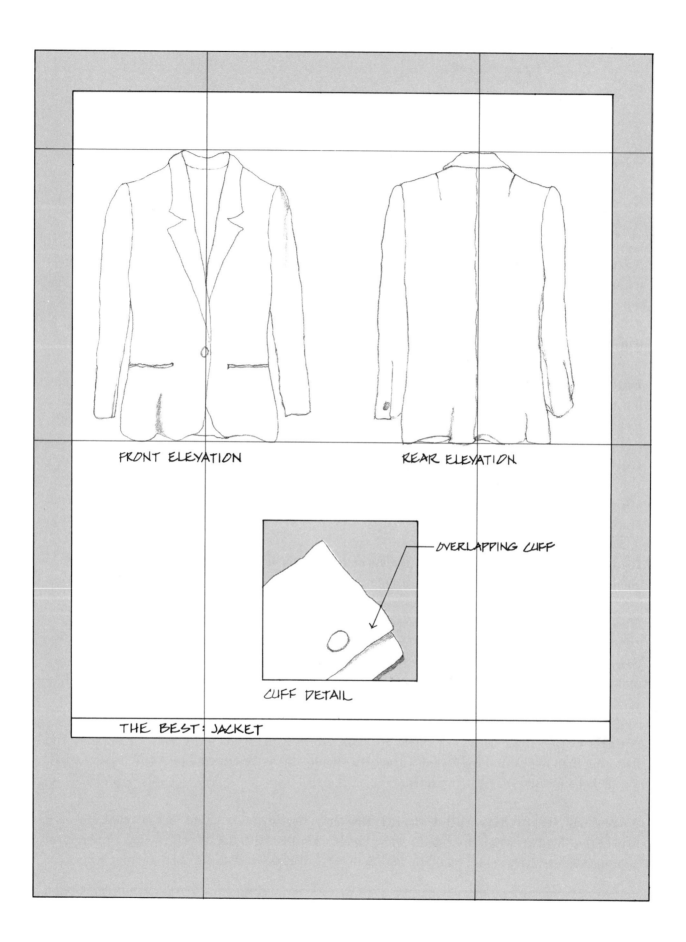

FRONT ELEVATION

REAR ELEVATION

OVERLAPPING CUFF

CUFF DETAIL

THE BEST JACKET

most women, that means a jacket that's cut a little longer than the broadest point of your hips, with some shaping at the waist. However, the best jacket for you may be one without lapels, or one that's fuller, or one that ends at the waist.

Double-breasted jackets are classics, too, and can be great-looking alternatives to the standard single-breasted style. Double-breasted jackets, however, tend not to be flattering if you've got a large bust, wide hips, or a boxy shape; and they don't look right on anyone when worn unbuttoned.

On fit, make sure the jacket doesn't pull across your hips or bust, gap at the buttons (they all should close and the jacket should lie flat, even if you intend to wear it unbuttoned), or tug across the back when you cross your arms. The jacket's waistline should fall at the same place as your own, the collar should lie flat against the back of your neck, and the front should not fold or gap. A good-fitting jacket will lie comfortably across your shoulders, your back, your waist as if it were cut for your body. Try on some very expensive, well-cut ones (by Armani, for instance, or Calvin Klein) to get a feeling for great fit, then try to duplicate that in your price range.

There are several good fabrics for jackets that can all be considered rivals for the best: wool gabardine, wool crepe, flannel, silk and wool or silk and linen blends are all terrific.

The Best: Silk Shirt

Soft Collar—Collar should not be stiff or heavily pressed, as this will cause fabric to wear over time.

Loop for Top Button—More comfortable when closed, neater looking when open.

Pearlized Buttons—Plastic may hold up better to wear and cleaning than real mother-of-pearl.

Neatly Finished Buttonholes—No stray threads!

Lots of Topstitching—Around edges of collar, cuff, shoulder seam, yoke, placket (sharper line and silhouette).

Well-finished Seams—Ideal are French seams; edge finishing is essential.

Back Yoke—Better fit across shoulders, and a nice style detail.

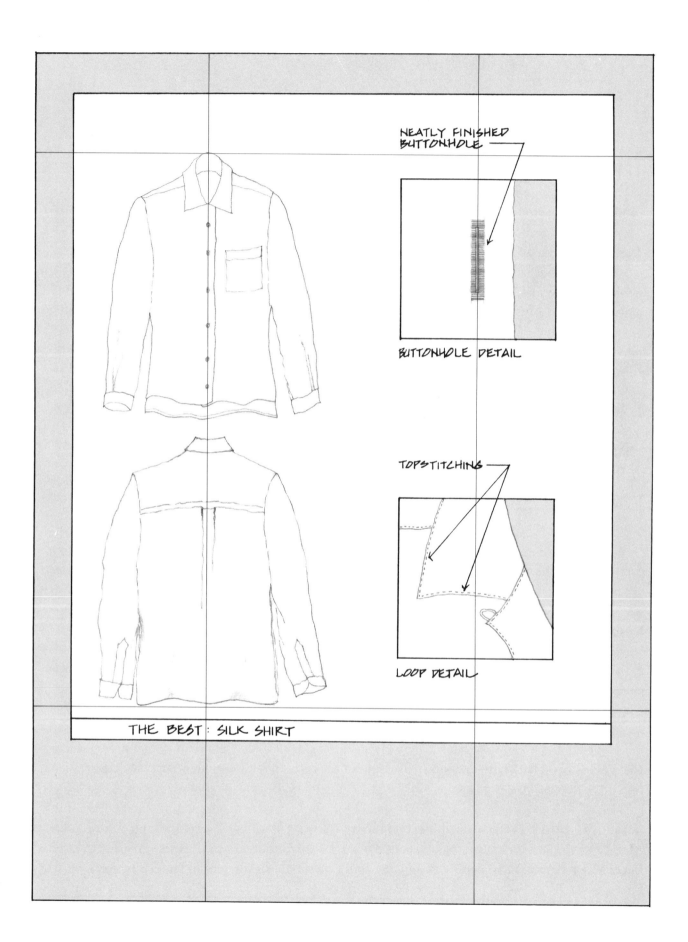

NEATLY FINISHED
BUTTONHOLE

BUTTONHOLE DETAIL

TOPSTITCHING

LOOP DETAIL

THE BEST: SILK SHIRT

One Breast Pocket—Not a must, but a nice extra.

Deep Armholes—The easier to raise, move your arms.

Soft Cuff—Should not be stiff, as this can cause silk to wear around edges of cuff.

Extra Button(s)—For obvious reasons.

Shirttail or Long Hem with Slits at Side—So it will stay tucked in.

A Note on Fabric: Silk comes in many permutations and grades; best for shirts are broadcloth or medium-to-heavy crepe de chine. Lighweight crepe de chine or tissue silk will wrinkle easily, water spot instantly, show underarm stains after the first wearing. In the store, squeeze silk down at the hem of the shirt: it should come away from your hand with minimal (or no) wrinkles, creases, discoloration. The new washable silks are worth a look (although most silk is hand-washable, even if it doesn't say so on the label), as are such blends as silk and wool.

Working the Room

Your company is having a party. Not a run-of-the-mill office party but an evening event to be attended by all the top executives of your firm as well as a select group of clients. The appropriate clothes are not what you'd wear out dancing with your beau, but not what you'd wear to work plus a nice pair of earrings, either. Which clothes, then, successfully straddle the line between business and socializing, which stray too far over it in either direction?

Dressing for business socials is a thorny enterprise, replete with its own set of complex rules. What's right for the office may not be the same as what's right for dinner with a client which may differ from what's right for a company party which can be different from what's right for a black-tie business event which is not the same as what's right for any of the above occasions when they're purely social. And then there are the "casual" business parties that may require different clothes from those you'd wear to a friend's barbeque.

Here, from women whose jobs require that they attend an array of social events, what works for each occasion, what doesn't.

Formal Business Events—When the invitation reads "black tie," formality reigns. Black tie does not necessarily (but may) mean a long dress; also appropriate are some street-length dresses and sometimes pants. Even when the occasion is not explicitly black tie, a late-night business social event calls for dressed-up clothes. The real difference between what's right for a business formal and a social one is in the details. Out are things overly sexy, overly glitzy, overly outrageous, but also out are clothes that make you look like a big stiff.

"I bought this dress that looks like something my mother-in-law would wear because I thought I should have it," says Paula Golden, executive director of the Massachusetts Seatbelt Coalition and the wife of a state senator. "It makes me look five or ten years older and I can't stand it."

Instead, Golden prefers evening clothes that are "fun and comfortable." "I don't have the guts for sexy clothes and senators' wives shouldn't look real sexy," says Golden, "but I will throw on black silk pants and a crazy top with a big, wild print and rhinestone shoes."

Claudia Rache, a loan officer for a Chicago mortgage company, has two dresses she reserves for black-tie business events: both simple, both mid-calf, both beaded, one black and one white. "The design is stark but the beading is attractive," says Rache. "I wear the black one with black hose and shoes and no other jewelry except elegant earrings."

Rhode Island advertising executive Bonney Sevellon has a single favorite dress for business parties: it's simply cut, black and somewhat sheer, with long, full sleeves and a high neck, which she wears with a bare, black slip underneath. "It's great because the slip is very sexy and low-cut and the dress isn't, so if people go naked I don't feel out of place and if they go conservative I don't feel out of place either," Sevellon says. "It's the kind of thing I can dress up with splashy jewelry or wear with just pearls."

Jody L. Serkes, the St. Louis-based co-owner of Voice Technologies, a voice-mail company, says she likes to get away from anything that resembles a suit when dressing for business formals. "I usually wear a three-quarter-length dress, in silk or jersey; something fun and pretty," says Serkes. "I always wear a lot of silver jewelry, big chunky jewelry, but elegant and not real glitzy."

While women agree that formal events are an opportunity to show another side of yourself through your clothes—a side that's fun and relaxed and attractive—they also caution that business formals can be a prime arena for making bad fashion mistakes. The reason: because they're special events, people's clothes are spotlighted, and a wrong move can be remembered for years.

Claudia Rache says she's seen some "interesting mistakes." "I constantly see stripes, puffy sleeves, and too much jewelry, which goes against my grain in a serious way," she says. "The person gets lost in all the chains, patterns, and puffiness. Also, very young women tend to dress too sexy, in something like a strapless minidress." If in doubt, says Rache, dress down and not up.

"People are always waiting to see your flaws," says Jody Serkes. "It's like drinking—I like to drink, but I don't do it at business events. If you make a jerk of yourself by how you act or what you wear, it will be in people's minds for a long time."

After-work Cocktail Parties/Business Dinners—The place and the people often dictate what's appropriate for business socials that begin where work leaves off. Usually what's called for are clothes that diverge somewhat from your usual work style, but not so radically that they would be totally out of place in the office.

Judy Patrick, an Atlanta-based executive for a corporate relocation firm, says that what she wears to a business dinner depends largely on "where the client wants to go." "Normally for dinner I'll wear a dress that's not quite as tailored as what I'd wear to work, something draped and more feminine," says Patrick. "If I'm meeting a client I've been working with for some time I feel I can dress not necessarily sexy but more relaxed, if I feel that they know me and know I'm there for business. But when I'm first getting to know someone I don't want them to get the wrong idea at all."

When Claudia Rache has to attend an event directly from her office, she wears a special white suit to work, and depends on "jewelry and a little scarf or some other little touch to bring it up to an evening level."

As with formal business parties, dinners and cocktail parties are opportunities to let clients see more of your personal side than they might in an office setting, and the right clothes can make you look fun, approachable, interesting, without crossing the bounds into strictly personal territory.

Lisa Amos, owner of ABT, a New Orleans management consulting firm, says a feminine dress she wore to a cocktail party launched her teaching career at Tulane University. "The dean of the business school was there, who'd only seen me in work clothes, and he came over to me and said, 'I've never seen you wear anything like that,'" Amos remembers with a laugh. "During that conversation I hooked him into saying he'd send me a contract to teach, and I've been teaching ever since."

Informal Office Parties—For the cookout at your boss's house, the terrace party at the island sales meeting, or the office picnic, do casual clothes really mean cutoffs and a T-shirt, or a dressed-down version of what you'd wear to work?

Decidedly out are the grubby tan shorts, black flip-flops, and husband's old oxford shirt that may be perfectly fine for a friend's afternoon lawn party. "For a long time I didn't own any nice casual slacks, just old jeans," says Paula Golden, "but I'm finally grown-up enough that I bought some slacks and tops that I can wear to casual business parties with a nice belt and some jewelry that's sort of different."

"At informal business events, I wear a lot of black and white, businesslike but fun clothes— maybe black shorts and a nice blouse and flats and, depending on what it is, possibly a jacket," says Jody Serkes. "But I dress conservatively and stay away from anything flamboyant—no Hawaiian shirts and no T-shirts. You just can't look like you're having too much fun even when you're supposed to."

Neither can you look like you're incapable of having any fun at all. "It's a mistake to wear a skirt," says Bonney Sevellon. "Again, it really has to do with reading the occasion and your company. There's a very strong boating influence in this agency, and when I first got here a few years ago, as a summer gift to the employees they gave us gift certificates to the Lands' End catalog. That made it very easy to decide what to wear to the company picnic."

Echoes Judy Patrick, "I wouldn't want to go to a sport function in a dress when everyone else was wearing shorts and slacks. I don't want to stand out other than that people think I look nice."

EMOTIONAL ISSUE:
CAN I WEAR A SWEATSUIT IN THE SWIMMING POOL?

Your boss, to make up for the late hours he's demanded of the staff all summer, has invited everyone to his fabulous country house for a big party. There will be food, there will be beer, there will be music, there will be swimming. Wait a minute, did he say swimming? That activity that all but requires the wearing of a swimsuit? The idea of stripping down to a twelve-inch-long, underwear-thin piece of latex in front of fifty of your closest co-workers strikes terror in your heart. You consider forgetting your swimsuit. You consider feigning illness. You consider jumping in the pool wearing a sweatsuit.

You're not alone. If there's one thing that can make even the most imperturbable businesswoman quake in her Amalfi pumps, it's the idea of wearing a swimsuit at a corporate function. Most women feel that if everyone is swimming, swim they must, however reluctantly; a few, though, down-and-out refuse.

"The owner of a company I worked for had pool parties all the time, and I felt really uncomfortable," says St. Louis business owner Jody Serkes. "I preferred to sit on the sidelines and drink iced tea and talk and not jump in the pool. I would love to swim, but I don't like the idea of someone remembering how I look in a bathing suit from then on in."

"I avoid swimming like the plague," says Bonney Sevellon, a Rhode Island advertising executive. "Sometimes I do swim, and wear a swimming suit reluctantly, but I'm uncomfortable with the whole idea in situations with clients."

Paula Golden's solution to the swimsuit dilemma is to wear one, again reluctantly, but always with "a towel around my buns."

Says relocation executive Judy Patrick, "I was just at a convention in Florida where there were a lot of prospective clients around the pool, so I put on my bathing suit and went to the pool, too. But people look at you differently when you're wearing a bathing suit. I felt a couple of times like I wanted to grab a blanket."

While looking bumpy, lumpy, or generally out of shape is the prime bathing suit fear of many women, looking terrific in a bathing suit can also present problems. "I'm slim and in shape, which can make some people resent you," says Judy Patrick. "Sometimes when I'm wearing a swimsuit in a business situation, I wish I weighed thirty pounds more."

On the Road

You are going on a business trip. Spread out on your bed is what looks like the contents of your entire closet. You tried making a list, but you've already gone far beyond it, throwing in your most comfortable pair of sneakers you might need if you want to take a walk in the early morning, your sweatpants you might want to wear if you're up late reading, the green silk blouse that will come in handy if your client wants to go to a fancy restaurant, the velvet skirt that goes with the green silk blouse . . . As you attempt to cram everything into your suitcase, you think of all the high-powered well-traveled businesswomen out there who surely have packing and travel dressing down to a science.

Well, not really. Often, because of time pressures and imprecise schedules and uncertain weather forecasts and plain old emotional reasons, even the most seasoned business travelers have developed decidedly unscientific, if effective, methods of getting their clothes together and taking them on the road.

"I'm a slam packer," says Jody Serkes, who travels constantly selling her company's voice-mail service to corporations. "I take everything to the cleaners, pack it still in the cleaning bags, and then pray that I've remembered to bring underwear and shoes."

"I keep saying I'm going to get it all down to a science and take three or four dresses and one pair of shoes," says Judy Patrick, who covers the Southeast territory for a relocation company, "but lots of times I also have dinner appointments with clients and need different clothing for that, and I usually end up carrying way too much."

For shorter trips, Patrick attempts to keep extras to a bare minimum: all the clothes she packs work with the same shoes, same accessories, and same makeup.

Linda Nicholas, a New York hair and makeup artist who travels constantly to out-of-town locations, says she packs one bag with her equipment and a few bulky cardigans, and another bag with "a lot of cotton pants, shorts,

and tops; a couple of layers of sweatshirts, quite a few T-shirts, a jeans skirt, a dressier black skirt and jacket, one or two long skirts, socks, flats, boots and sneakers, and tons of underwear." The underwear, for the most part, is packed for emotional rather than practical reasons. "I love lingerie, and I bring lots of it along even if I don't need it all," says Nicholas. "It's a part of home."

There's a method behind Nicholas's wide assortment of travel clothes: on location, she works long hours, and often travels to places where the temperature varies widely throughout the day. "In Arizona or California, it's very cold in the morning, so I wear a T-shirt, a sweatshirt, and a cardigan, and then by mid-afternoon I'm down to the T-shirt because it's eighty or ninety degrees, and then at night it's cold again," says Nicholas. "I like clothes that work in all climates, that can work when it's really hot or really cold depending on what's underneath."

In winter, when she usually travels from New York to warmer climates, Nicholas relies on layers so she doesn't have to lug along a winter coat. Her airplane clothes combine what's most formal and what's most comfortable in her wardrobe: "On the plane I wear a jacket or sweater, cotton knit pants that are both baggy and neat-looking, a knit top tucked in, and always a belt."

Judy Patrick, whose job demands more formal clothes, and often heads to an appointment right after her plane lands, travels in the suit or dress she'll wear through the business day.

For longer flights, traveling women are divided over whether it's best to dress down or up, and each pose their own, more psychological than practical, arguments.

One woman, a systems analyst for a Florida-based manufacturing company, wears the next day's business clothes on her frequent flights to Europe. "I used to wear something comfortable, telling myself I'd sleep," she says, "but I finally came to terms with the fact that I never really sleep anyway. I've tried all sorts of techniques to deal with jet lag—sleeping at home the day before, napping once I get there— and for me what works best is to just forge on, to go right to work when I arrive and pretend it's just another day. Wearing business clothes for traveling puts me in the frame of mind to do that."

Another woman, an accessories designer who travels to Europe several times a year, says she wears "nice" clothes on the overnight flight, but not necessarily those she'd wear to work. "I might wear an easy cashmere sweater with a cashmere cardigan over it, flats so I can run through the airport, cozy socks so I can take off my shoes on the plane and try to sleep, and always pants."

Why always pants? For one thing, she can curl up her legs for a nap with impunity. And for another: "If the plane crashes, it's better to be wearing pants in case I have to crawl out on the wing."

EMOTIONAL ISSUE:
IT PLAYED IN OMAHA, BUT WILL IT MAKE IT IN NEW YORK?

You are the vice president of a corporation in Omaha. You are going on a business trip to New York. You are happy with your work wardrobe; that is, you were happy with it in Omaha, but now, imagining how your clothes will look in Manhattan, you're full of insecurity. Will the suit that makes you feel sophisticated on home base make you feel like a yokel in New York? Will the clothes that look stylish in Omaha look hopelessly dowdy in Manhattan?

The question is, When you're traveling on business between cities with highly disparate styles, do you rely on what works at home, or do you attempt to dress for the city you're visiting?

Traveling from just about anywhere to New York seems to cause the most concern among professional women.

"When I'm going from Pittsburgh to New York, I pack two or three times, and change my mind a hundred times about what I'm going to wear," says Teresa Sokol, who does public relations for the graduate school of business at Carnegie-Mellon University. "I don't want to walk into a New York newsroom and have people know immediately that I'm from Pittsburgh. It's only New York that incites this panic; it seems like fashion central."

What's scary, says Sokol, is going into a different culture. "It's not that the clothes are so different," she says. "You do see people on the street wearing clothes that would cost my year's salary, but the women with comparable jobs and salaries to mine wear comparable quality and style."

How Sokol copes with dressing for New York: "I always go back to the things that make me feel good, because if I feel good I know I look good. But what I try to do for New York is go into high-powered accessories and make sure everything is more pulled together. I put more stock in that when I'm in New York than I do in Pittsburgh."

It's not only going to New York that can cause fashion problems; it may also be going from New York to a city with a very different style. A New York retail executive describes her first trip to Dallas: "I breezed in there all confident of my New York style: head-to-toe black, understated lines, minimal makeup and natural hair," she says. "I thought all these women in their bright silk dresses and high heels and exaggerated makeup, who I saw as tacky, would see me as chic, but they thought I looked like a bag lady. One person actually asked me if I had to attend a family funeral. By about the third day, I was feeling pretty drab myself. All that black just didn't look as good in the sun, and I ended up going to a local store and buying a couple of bright knit T-shirts—colors like hot pink and yellow that would never appeal to me in New York—and actually loved wearing them."

St. Louis-based Jody Serkes, who travels frequently selling her company's voice-mail systems, says she actually has different outfits for different cities: a New York outfit, a Chicago outfit, and so on.

After ten years of business travel, says Serkes, she has the different climate and style requirements down pat.

"California's a lot looser and you can wear a light, airy linen, while in New York that just dies," she says. "In New York you can get away with a lot more creativity, bolder colors and bigger earrings and great shoes and more fun. If I try that in St. Louis they're going to think I'm a clown. People in St. Louis are used to seeing clothes with very conservative lines: lots of glen plaid, double-breasted jackets, straight skirts."

If you travel on business to very different cities, you may not need different wardrobes for each, says Los Angeles image consultant Andrea Sells, but simply one all-purpose traveling wardrobe and a range of accessories.

"In New York in the fall you can't wear an ivory suit and a lavender blouse, not because there's anything wrong with that but because you'll stand out where the streets and buildings are gray and everyone else is dressed in gray and navy and black," says Sells. "If you travel a lot you should stay away from fabrics that are very flimsy or very heavy; rely on medium-weight knits, cottons, silks, and gabardines; choose neutral colors and use different kinds of colors for accents; change your accessories; add or take off a jacket."

In general, says Sells, corporate guidelines are the same everywhere, and if you tread a middle fashion ground when traveling, you can't go far wrong. Many women, who don't want to spend the time or money or energy to vary their wardrobes for business trips, agree.

"I'm getting involved now in advising a small hotel chain that's trying to attract executive women travelers," says Margaret Newborg, vice president of Fuchs, Cuthrell, a New York management consulting firm, and president of the Financial Women's Association. "I pretty much dress the same no matter where I am if I'm meeting businesspeople. I know I'm going to fit in, and even if they say, 'Oh, that looks a little modern,' it really does not matter because I know I'm not dressing outlandishly."

What One Woman Packs

As vice president of operations for Caressa Shoes, working half the time in New York, half the time in Fort Lauderdale, Florida, Rita DiMatteo's work life is travel. In addition, DiMatteo travels frequently for her job to Europe and around the United States.

While this sort of travel schedule isn't new to DiMatteo—she's traveled around the world for various footwear companies for over a decade—she confesses she still doesn't have her packing strategies down pat. "Especially with going back and forth between Florida and New York every week or two," she says. "I'm constantly finding I've left the shoes that go with the dress in the other place."

Even so, DiMatteo's packing techniques are more organized than those of most women. Her routine: "I lay everything that folds (or gets put into compartments, such as cosmetics) on the bed, and I hang everything that hangs on the hook on my bedroom door. Then I can stand in one place and look at everything I'm taking to see if something's missing. I also try to fast-forward myself through the days or weeks I'll be away to be sure I have the right things to wear."

When possible, DiMatteo packs everything in one soft-sided (for easier stowing) suitcase she carries on the plane, and also brings along a flat tote bag that slips easily under an airline seat. Her packing list? Cribbed from a 1982 New York *Times* article by author Rona Jaffe, DiMatteo has found the following list to offer good general guidelines for a week-long business trip to a city, or cities, with variable climate.

"I don't necessarily pack every item on this list; I may take a few dresses instead of skirts and shirts, for example," says DiMatteo, "but I always go over it before I put everything in the suitcase, just to make sure there's no category I've missed."

Here, as interpreted by DiMatteo, the list:

- 5 silk shirts
- 2 cotton shirts
- 4 short-sleeved cotton T-shirts
- 2 long-sleeved turtleneck sweaters (for maximum warmth, minimum volume: silk-and-cashmere blend)
- 2 wool skirts
- 2 cotton skirts
- 1 pair trousers
- 1 pair comfortable cotton knit pants
- 1 cotton jacket
- 1 wool jacket
- 1 raincoat with zip-out lining
- 2 pairs flat shoes (comfortable enough for walking, dressed-up enough for business)
- 1 pair boots
- 2 belts
- 10 pairs pantyhose
- "lots" of underwear
- 1 pair knee socks
- 1 nightgown
- 1 robe
- 1 bathing suit (if your hotel is likely to have a pool)
- 1 large handbag
- small hair dryer
- Tylenol/medications
- manicure equipment
- a tiny sewing kit
- bandages

- a small clock radio
- book

Dark colors are hardier than light; solids more versatile than prints. Hang everything you plan to wear immediately upon arrival, as hanging takes out the wrinkles. Obviously, the coat and boots are optional, depending on your destination. Layering can help cope with weather changes: if it turns frigid, you can wear the T-shirt under the turtleneck under a silk shirt under the wool jacket; pantyhose and knee socks under pants.

WORK

·2·

The

Professional

Image

·

You know all about image and business clothes. By this time, every professional woman does. You've heard about corporate image consultants, maybe even attended an image seminar at your company or businesswomen's club, maybe even been to a consultant for a makeover. You've read the articles about how to create and maintain a professional image, and if you haven't actually read *Dress for Success*, you've certainly heard about it.

But what you may not yet know is that the importance of image, at least the rigid brand of image that draws exact equations between specific items of clothing and specific messages, is waning, and may disappear entirely over the next decade. Rather than wearing clothes that deliver a generic image of power or authority or professionalism, corporate women will increasingly look to clothes to present an individual image, to express who they are as people rather than where they stand in the organization.

To understand how radical a change this is for the whole concept of image, you have to understand where it started: at the opposite end of the scale, with the idea of absolute conformity, down to the number of buttonholes in the cuff of a jacket. To understand how radical it is for an executive woman to say she wears a yellow dress and blue high heels and a three-inch-wide flower pin to work at her all-male corporation because she likes to express herself and her femininity, you have to understand where she started: in a man-tailored dark suit, a starched white blouse, and a bow tie chosen because it matched what her male colleagues were wearing.

The idea that clothes projected an image—and that creating the right image was crucial to success in the corporate world—was popularized by John T. Molloy in his book *Dress for Success*, and its companion edition aimed specifically at women. It was an idea whose time had come.

Through the 1970s, legions of women were entering the professional and corporate world, intending not just to work for a few years, until they got married, but to establish careers. Initially, these women wore to work what they'd been wearing on campus or in the playground or to tea: miniskirts and pants suits, "ladies' " dresses and jeans. Women soon realized that these clothes and their ambitions to move up through the corporate ranks didn't jibe.

This first wave of female corporate pioneers was ripe, then, for prescriptions such as Molloy's for what to wear—and in a larger sense, how to make it—in a man's world. Traditional sources of fashion guidance—Paris trends and designers' shows and magazines such as *Vogue*—simply weren't relevant to corporate dressing. Where your hemline fell or what color blouse you wore was determined not by any designer's inspiration but by what your (male) boss was wearing.

It was the feminist movement that, ironically, promoted the effort of women to mimic men in the first place. "Women were attempting to be treated fairly, and the idea was no special treatment, which meant in the minds of men and women that women had to be accepted as men, hence the little suit and the bow tie," says Dana Friedman, senior research analyst at the Conference Board.

While women may have been entering the work force en masse, they were still invading what had been male, and thus foreign, turf. "In any ambiguous new context your first job is to figure out what the context of the situation is, so you're going to hear a lot about rules, because that's what those women had to figure out," says Ellen Berman, M.D., co-director of the Women's Center at the Philadelphia Psychiatric Center. "Once everybody knows that women are there, and that they know what the rules are, then they can begin to decide how much they can bend them. But they couldn't do that until people stopped worrying about the fact that they were there, until people stopped waiting for them to do stupid things."

While corporate women had their own myriad reasons for embracing the Dress for Success concept, the mood of the country was also compatible with the notion of image dressing. Reagan was president, and suddenly style was at least as important as substance. Status and money were the acknowledged goals of the 1980s, and reaching them often had more to do with how you looked than with what you did. To get rich, went the common wisdom, you had to look rich; to become powerful you had to dress powerfully; to break into the white male ranks you had to, well, look like a white man.

The year that consumer psychologist Michael Solomon did his first survey on women's business clothes in *Savvy* magazine, 1983, "was the height of image consciousness," says Dr. Solomon. "The women who answered the survey were crazed about it. At the time it was a new weapon, like crystals or channeling."

From Solomon's viewpoint, Molloy's rigid brand of image dressing has about as much credence as such otherworldly fads as crystals and channeling. Says Solomon, "Molloy's whole approach—that there's a set of rules that are constant and that if you don't conform you're dead meat—runs contrary to everything I've ever found."

Today, most image consultants, who owe the very existence of their industry to the theories popularized by Molloy, also roundly reject his concepts.

"Whenever I hear people use that phrase, Dress for Success, I have a negative association. I don't associate it with what I'm doing," says Joyce Grillo, president of New York's Impression Management. "I know it doesn't work and people balk at it. What he said or what was originally dictated was never really true and it's certainly not valid or necessary anymore. I kind of resent it that it was ever out there."

While Los Angeles image consultant Andrea Sells calls Dress for Success "terrible," she says, "When it first came out it was right. It was the only way women could feel comfortable, compete with men and not stand out. But the navy or gray suit Molloy recommended was extremely boring, it showed no taste and no creativity and didn't work on every figure. Now that concept has been put to bed. Today, women are women, they have a major part in the work force, and they don't have to give up their femininity."

"A lot of people have used *Dress for Success* as a bible in the corporate world, but those concepts are really limited," says Susan St. Charles, an Atlanta image consultant. "It isn't accepted anymore except at the entry level. You don't find executive females wearing that suit, white blouse, and little tie. The rebellion has become the standard."

Indeed, what these image consultants say is backed up by personnel directors at large, conservative corporations. Where the tailored suit was once a symbol of professionalism and authority, it has come to signal immaturity, a lack of sophistication and creativity. Rather than providing an entrée into the business world, the little suit may actually close some corporate doors.

"If I was interviewing somebody and she was well spoken and articulate, I wouldn't care if she was wearing a gray suit and a white shirt and a bow tie," says Susan Karp, a personnel director at Citibank in New York. "After she came to work here she'd figure out you don't dress like that."

The *Dress for Success* book, says Karp, "did more damage to women. Maybe it came out at a different time, but people still buy that stuff. It's outdated; you just don't look like that anymore."

One reason the Dress for Success uniform gained so much credibility in the first place was that Molloy claimed his prescriptions were backed up by empirical evidence. According to Michael Solomon, however, none of this evidence has ever been documented.

In fact, says Susan Kaiser, an associate professor at the University of California at Davis and author of *The Social Psychology of Clothing* (Macmillan, 2nd ed., 1989), the findings of any clothing research are somewhat suspect. "The problem with the research is that you're dealing with stimuli, pictures of a suit versus a dress, and asking which one looks more appropriate for a job interview or a woman in management, and you're looking at a figure in the ether," Kaiser says. "In real life you have people and personalities, and who can carry off what, and especially if women have been in their jobs for a while, they're not going to feel like they need that prop any longer."

Does all this mean that the entire concept of professional image is dead?

Hardly.

Molloy's legacy is a widespread awareness that clothes are communication, that image is, indeed, important. What's changing now, and what will continue to change over the next decade, is what kind of image professional women want their clothes to project.

"The symptoms are changing, but the basic condition has not changed," says Dr. Michael Solomon. "There's still a lot of importance attached to appropriateness of an image but what defines appropriateness changes, just as fashion changes."

Perhaps the key change in image is that professional women now want to dress like women. As noted in the section "Style and the Corporate Woman," this turnabout is due to the enormous increase of women in the business world in general, and in positions of power in particular. Professional women are no longer "deviants" who must overcorrect for their different gender. Dresses are now as appropriate as suits in most corporations; suits are often made in more fluid, more feminine fabrics; jackets are shaped or detailed—still formal but distinctly not like a man's; jewelry is larger, more distinctive; colors are brighter or softer, not necessarily neutral.

Susan Kaiser says, "I look at it from a feminist theory perspective. Clothes and expressiveness through clothing have always been part of the female culture, and now women are feeling, Why give that up? For a while we were throwing out the baby with the bathwater, and now we're realizing that's not absolutely necessary."

"It's [this new, more feminine way of dressing] symbolic of the ways in which women are expressing themselves at work, with motherhood coming out of the closet, women asking for additional leave time," says Conference Board research analyst Dana Friedman. "Clothing is very much reflective of women's newfound acceptance in the corporation."

And, according to Friedman, this acceptance isn't likely to wane. "Demographics are on the side of women," Friedman says. "By the year 2000 only 17 percent of new entrants into the work force will be white males, and the rest will be immigrants and minorities and women. The choice to discriminate doesn't exist anymore."

Demographics may be influencing not only the choice, but the desire to discriminate against women. "A lot of older, traditional, powerful men who used to discriminate against women now have daughters graduating from college and not getting hired, or being offered lower salaries," says New York University professor Patricia Mulready. "It's like looking in a reverse mirror. These fathers see that their daughters are perfectly capable young women and then they go out in the world and some asshole is not hiring them."

The fact that older, powerful men are becoming more liberal through this firsthand experience with discrimination, that many women are now in positions of power, and that new entrants into the work force are a more eclectic group than ever is forcing a change in the nature of the corporate world itself. "All of this new diversity in the workplace," says Dana Friedman, "is wreaking havoc with standard practices and corporate cultures."

In fact, diversity is another key to how professional image is being redefined, and why. Women are increasingly looking for clothes that suit, as it were, their personalities, reflecting a social as well as a corporate trend toward individuality and away from conformity.

"There's an idea, as evidenced in *In Search of Excellence* by Tom Peters, that conformity in the workplace isn't always good for companies, that you need people with diverse opinions," says Patricia Mulready. "Any time you have variety in people's thought patterns, you also have variety in dress."

A reappreciation of the sixties, a deepening social conscience, a new emphasis by leading universities such as Harvard and Yale on liberal arts education, and the stock market crash of 1987 and the subsequent corporate recession are all combining to promote this idea of individuality, says Mulready. "The whole idea of conforming and trying to fit in doesn't look quite as good anymore," Mulready says. "In the movies you've got Bette Midler, Cher—there's a woman who's been made fun of for twenty years because she looked weird. But they've stayed themselves and it's taken them over the long haul. There's a new awareness that people who are different have a lot to contribute, which works in with the corporate celebration of individuality."

And it may simply be time for the fashion and image pendulum to swing the other way. "Even though I study the psychology of dress, and I know that people put great stock in the right clothes, I think we've gone overboard," says Mulready. "How you look has become a critical factor in whether or not you're an acceptable person."

Whatever becomes defined as the new "right" professional image depends in large part on the whims of the baby boom, which, after all, created such social (and fashion) trends as the hippie culture, feminism, and yuppiedom. What's next? According to some trend-watchers, it may be a sort of Anti-Image. The signs: a disenchantment with the eighties notion that money can buy happiness, a turn to more spiritual and ecological concerns, the popularity of such irreverent-about-everything magazines as *Spy*, and the mass aging of all those perennial kids into their forties.

"Gail Sheehy writes about the forties as being a time of calming down, of realizing you're not queen of the empire and coming to terms with that," says Patricia Mulready. "Women who've stayed at home reenter the workplace, women who've been working stand back and regroup, men who aren't on the fast track pay more attention to their feminine side, and men who are on the fast track stand back from it."

The result of the baby boomers' collective aging and slowing down, Mulready believes, may be a rediscovery of the ideals they held so fervently back when they were just becoming adults. "In the sixties and seventies it was do your own thing, dress didn't matter, dressing down; somewhere among much of the baby boom generation that's percolating in the back of their minds."

In fact, some image consultants have begun saying some very anti-image things.

"I'm such a feminist, and I'm dying to see women succeed in a man's empire, and I love beautiful clothes and I was a rebel before other women were, but in reality you have to look at what we're really dealing with," says Vicki French Morris, owner of French-Haines fashion consulting in Chappaqua, New York. "Some of the most successful women are really terrible dressers, and that may enhance their success."

"I've seen women who dress atrociously who have high positions," agrees Impression Management's Joyce Grillo. "I don't know of any absolute rules anymore, other than the real obvious ones. I think I'm getting more conservative, and my clients are getting less, and it's flipping. My style has changed since I started my business. At first I was really trying to make a statement that I was creative and stylish, and now I feel I don't need to make that statement with my clothes anymore."

Grillo's feeling—basically, that clothes aren't everything and that what you do may, ultimately, be more important than how you look—is one that's beginning to be shared by many women. People have learned that looking powerful does not mean that you are powerful; dressing creatively does not invest you with creativity; dynamic clothes do not a dynamo make.

"That you have to dress a certain way in order to be effective on your job—I truly don't believe that," says Patricia Mulready. Mulready says that, from her experience in management, wearing traditional business clothes may actually hamper productivity. "The sloppier people were working their rear ends off and the ones who looked nice were just sitting there, getting raises and promotions."

Ah, there's the rub. While the proper clothes may not make a fig of difference in how productive or hardworking you are, those qualities may not, after all, be the tickets to success, especially not for women. In a 1985 study on why people fail, the Center for Creative Leadership found that poor image was one of the ten most important reasons some women fall off the fast track, while image was not cited as a reason for men's failure in the corporate world.

"A lot of women think that if they look like a wreck that people will really think they're working hard," says Sheryl Spanier, vice president of Fuchs, Cuthrell, a New York management consulting and corporate outplacement firm, "when all that's required to be successful is not working hard at the job, but rather learning how to affiliate and associate and identify with things outside yourself."

For this reason, according to Dr. Michael Solomon, however much the concept of professional image changes, it's unlikely to die entirely. "As a psychologist I know that if there's such a thing as a ubiquitous phenomenon, it's that people always care what other people think," Dr. Solomon says. "While there's a broader range of legitimate options now for how to live and how to look, which makes it possible to pick and choose a little more which set you're going to conform to, people will still conform. Anti-conformists are conformists, because in order to rebel you have to be conscious of what you're rebelling against. If you're anti-chic, that implies you know what's chic and that you're going the other way. I don't agree that people will get totally fed up and just be themselves, because part of being themselves is being social animals."

In ten years, says Dr. Solomon, "I predict the demise of the image consulting industry." But not, he hastens to add, the demise of image itself, or advice on how to achieve the "right" one. "Corporate image consultants may die out," he says, "only to be replaced by a spate of articles and a legion of advisers telling people how best to use clothes to express their personalities."

• *Style Analysis* •

CATHERINE CRIER *the anchorperson for Cable News Network, is a former state district court judge from Dallas. For her photograph, Crier wore a black-and-white Ungaro suit that she bought a year ago at Saks. The price? Crier is reluctant to say, but admits "it was frankly one of my more expensive purchases." She is happy to disclose, however, that her earrings are costume pearls, enamel, and rhinestones, and cost under $100.*

WHERE DID YOU GROW UP? HOW DID YOUR STYLE EVOLVE THROUGH YOUR EARLY YEARS?

I grew up in Dallas proper but we began raising horses when I was about eight or nine so I spent most of my time after school on the back of a horse, and clothed accordingly—blue jeans, T-shirts, bare feet. It really wasn't until I got out of law school and began acquiring suits for job interviews that I began worrying too much about my attire.

However, I've always had an understanding that appearances are very, very important in terms of that proverbial first impression. Before a person has an opportunity to get to know you they observe and perceive, and you have to then work to alter that impression if you give them input that's not correct. When I went out and began acquiring interview suits and started to work, I realized that what you need to project is competence, efficiency, knowledge, all those characteristics of the budding young lawyer.

THAT SOUNDS LIKE STANDARD DRESS FOR SUCCESS WISDOM. WOULD YOU SAY WHAT YOU WORE AT THAT POINT WERE STANDARD DRESS FOR SUCCESS CLOTHES? WHAT HAPPENED BETWEEN THEN AND NOW?

I woke up. It has a lot to do with a person's evolution in the business world. From a visual perspective you can really track my evolution. When I was in the district attorney's office

that was a very conservative position—trying cases for the state—and the image I portrayed was basically the old Dress for Success: the paisley tie, the oxford shirt, the pin-striped suit. As I moved up the ladder, even within the district attorney's office, that began to loosen up a little bit. More authority, more responsibility, permits more individuality.

Once I left the district attorney's office I went into private practice and that freed things up quite a bit. You're outside that government regimentation and I had a lot more latitude, certainly spending a lot of time in the office as opposed to just the courtroom.

DO YOU PAY FULL PRICE FOR YOUR CLOTHES?

Unfortunately, yes. My problem with sales and discount shopping is that I have little patience for shopping. I don't particularly like to shop and I don't have the time for it. I shop early in the season because the things I look for, particularly nowadays, will be gone. In fact, I mostly shop trunk shows—which are showings of designer's lines before the season—now and rarely even go into the store.

YOU SAID YOU'VE ALWAYS BOUGHT QUALITY BUT WOULD YOU SAY YOU'VE MOVED CONSIDERABLY UPSCALE?

Yes, unfortunately, no question about it. As my income went up, so did what I would pay. I have always been, since after law school, this horrible clotheshorse and I really enjoy clothes; therefore I tend to buy the most I can afford in terms of quality and style. I'm attracted to couture clothing, to high-fashion clothing, and to quality fabrics and design, and so I end up paying more for them.

IS THERE ANYTHING YOU SCRIMP ON?

I always use the L'eggs catalog and send in for the irregulars. I have never once bought a pair of irregulars that I can see what's wrong with them. They're $1.69 or something instead of $3.50. It makes absolutely no sense: I pay $1.50 for my pantyhose and then go out and spend $600 for a suit.

DO YOU HAVE ANY IDEA HOW MUCH YOU SPEND IN A YEAR ON CLOTHES?

No, because it varies. I really do try every year to look and see what I've got and not duplicate, not buy because styles have changed. You can go into the closet and see you can change those hemlines. I might add a suit or two each spring or fall. When I was a judge,

I had to put on a black polyester robe each day. I might spend more time and certainly a lot less money going to find fun clothes, shorts and resort wear and something I'd wear away from the office. I don't want to imply that I stay out of the stores, because I don't, but I really try to be more selective and just buy a few things from the designers I like.

WHICH DESIGNERS DO YOU LIKE?

I like a lot of the younger, more adventurous designers: Byblos and Jennifer George and Michael Kors and Jimmy Gamba and Donna Karan. I consider those nontraditional traditional, with clothing that's certainly appropriate in any business setting, but with a little flair to it. Something like Ralph Lauren is pretty, but is a little too staid, a little too sweet, too preppy. Calvin Klein does things that are traditional but pretty, and I'll find pieces there to fill in, but what I'm really intrigued with is moving a little more to the extremes.

YOU SEEM TO LIKE BRIGHT COLORS.

I used to be beige, black, and navy blue, and that's changed quite a bit. After the election in '84 was about the time I felt comfortable coming out of that. Through the election process I felt going out and meeting the voters, they only had five minutes to get to know me and I didn't want them to worry about whether that woman in the bright red suit was competent. After the fact I began to feel comfortable with expressing freedom in my choice of clothing.

WHAT ABOUT SHOES AND ACCESSORIES?

I probably have more pairs of closed-toed, three-and-a-half-inch-heeled pumps in my closet than anybody you know. I wear the same shoe with just about everything. I'm a big girl and I have big feet, and to me they look better in high heels.

Accessories are one area I would like to be a lot more playful. I like belts. Earrings are hard at work because I don't like anything that's going to be distracting, so work earrings are pretty basic. I don't wear a lot of bangle-type things; I don't want to be clanking. You can be more adventuresome, even with a traditional business suit, with an interesting pin than you can with earrings. I've got some interesting Santa Fe pins, some of the Donna Karan free-form matte gold things. I've got some pins that I've found at flea markets, old antique things that are fun.

WHAT KIND OF REACTION DID YOUR CLOTHES GET IN THE BUSINESS COMMUNITY IN DALLAS?

*W*ell, they came to me as often to do articles on women and fashion as they did to talk about the law. The reaction was very positive. I think I made a bit of a statement that it's okay to be feminine and assertive, to dress in a feminine style. None of that takes away from doing a good job.

SOME WOMEN SAY THEY FEEL THEY GET BETTER RESPONSE FROM FELLOW BUSINESSPEOPLE WHEN THEY DRESS MORE ADVENTUROUSLY THAN WHEN THEY TRIED TO DO EVERYTHING "RIGHT."

*B*oy, I agree with that 100 percent. It all goes hand and hand. When a woman moves up the ladder and feels that freedom in her choice of clothes, it can make a difference in her personality and the work she does and the way she responds to other people. If you get up in the morning and you're feeling kind of crummy and you pull out that black dress and the frown that goes with it, it's a lot different than when you feel great and you feel like you look good and you're out there ready to take on the world.

WHAT KINDS OF THINGS WOULD YOU NEVER WEAR? WHAT DON'T YOU LIKE?

I don't like preppy types of clothing. I don't find even in my fun clothing what you would consider funky things. I don't like real baggy things. When I'm playing I've got my long denim skirt or my big sweater, but for the most part my clothes are tailored.

HOW WOULD YOU DESCRIBE THE DALLAS STYLE AND HOW DOES YOUR OWN STYLE FIT INTO THAT?

*T*he Dallas style and the Dallas image are two different things. The Dallas image from the television show may be a bit glitzy; the bleached blonde with leather and sequins and sparkles wearing her money, so to speak. You do see that in Dallas, you see it in southern California, you see it in Miami. But for the most part that's not the Dallas style. Dallas is a city of entrepreneurial businesswomen. In a lot of the organizations that I belonged to, such as the Executive Women of Dallas which is an offshoot of the Chamber of Commerce, the style I'm talking about for me is the style that you see represented: definitely business but an individual personal statement.

WHEN YOU WERE A JUDGE, DID YOU SEE WOMEN LAWYERS DRESSED INAPPROPRIATELY, IN A WAY THAT PUT YOU OFF?

I don't recommend that a woman come to court dressed in pants. She's free to do so, but I really don't think that's the time or place.

What doesn't work is anything that is distracting as opposed to accentuating. If a woman is heavily made-up, where all you can see is the two red cheeks and the purple eyeshadow, it's hard to look at her and hear what she's saying without thinking about that. Or if she's got a gauzy blouse on or things that are not taken care of—the shirts are wrinkled.

I enjoyed seeing women come in the courtroom and expressing their own style. In any business environment we're saying to the world we have specialized knowledge, information, and abilities that they should come to us for. I like to see women express that in their attire. Interior decorators can wear things that a judge or a lawyer can't wear, but within that sphere, men and women should express their individuality. It's a little area where we can play in an often much-too-staid world.

First Impressions

You walk into a job interview. You meet an important client for the first time. You are introduced to someone at a sales conference. You smile. Your handshake is firm. You're smart and friendly and articulate. This may not matter a lot. What may really matter is what you're wearing.

"Clothes are critical in first impressions," says Lisa Lang, a Rhode Island headhunter. "In my business, we say that a person can be selected for a position in the first three minutes of an interview, based on eye contact, body language, and clothing."

Some experts put the decisive point in making a first impression at something less than three minutes: "It can take as little as five seconds for people to look at you and make a conclusion," says Susan St. Charles, an Atlanta image consultant. "The eye is a camera, and makes a snapshot, and what the person sees the very first time will be in his or her mind forever."

Forever? While it can be frightening to realize that clothes have so much power in determining how others perceive you at first meeting, it can be even scarier to think that those first impressions linger indefinitely, setting the tone for every interaction that follows. However, say experts, that's exactly what often happens.

"When you meet someone for the first time, what you wear is a statement of what you want the other person to know about your status, education, and taste," says Arlene Kagle, Ph.D., a New York psychotherapist. "First impressions are emblazoned in our mem-

ories, particularly when the people are important to us. On my first job interview, in 1965, I wore white gloves. I worked for that boss for eleven years and he never let me live it down."

Confirms personnel director Ron Rau, "When I see someone for the first time, I always remember my impression, good or bad. The first impression, you can never get away from that, fair or unfair."

When we meet someone new, according to Michael Solomon, Ph.D., a psychologist and head of the marketing department at Rutgers, we immediately try to place that person in a category based on what she's wearing, and then look for behavior that's consistent with that category.

"We have certain expectations of how people in each category are supposed to behave," says Dr. Solomon, "and we evaluate each person's behavior in light of those expectations. We look for things that will confirm what we already believe."

In other words, if we think someone looks confident and sophisticated and well educated, we'll work to find everything in her words and actions that's evidence of confidence and sophistication and a good education. Conversely, if someone's clothes make her look awkward or unimaginative or rebellious, we're likely to pick up on everything in her behavior that signals rebellion or awkwardness or a poor imagination.

Often, says Solomon, we put a different gloss on the same behavior to make it confirm our expectations. If a confident-looking job candidate accidentally knocks over a vase on the desk, for instance, we may attribute it to her energy and enthusiasm. If an awkwardly dressed job candidate makes the same blunder, we may interpret it as further evidence of her clumsiness.

Even if, over time, the person's behavior proves to be completely out of line with that first impression—an impeccably dressed person who's always late and whose desk is a mess, for example—we may still cling to our initial reading. For one thing, we continue, long after the first meeting, to notice everything that confirms our first impressions, ignore or re-interpret everything that denies them. And, says Solomon, "Part of yourself is invested in that person proving to be what you thought she was because you made the decision to hire. To do otherwise would be to admit that you made a mistake."

It's only when someone's actions differ radically from her visual presentation that we allow ourselves to switch her from the original to a new category. The trouble is that the new category we choose is usually "Impostor." If a woman walks into a meeting, for instance, wearing a demure pink-flowered dress best suited to a shy twelve-year-old, and then proceeds to dominate the meeting, we tend to think she's a fake. Whether we see our initial "Powerless and Subservient" category as the false one or the later "Sharp and Aggressive" category as the one that doesn't jibe is really beside the point: we feel that, one way or another, she's pretending to be something she's not, and we don't like it.

In fact, what experts counsel clients to wear to job interviews or other important first meetings, and what employers look for, are clothes that suit both your own personality and the personality of the people or company you're trying to impress.

"My job is to let people know as much as possible about the environment of the company, what to expect," says Lisa Lang. "If they're comfortable with that they'll probably go in dressed appropriately anyway."

The point: beware of any job interview that requires an entirely new and different set of clothes. "If the company is not exactly your personality, you'll spend a fortune on an outfit and will just have to throw it out afterwards," says Los Angeles image consultant Andrea Sells. "There's a compromise between what is you and what the company stands for. But don't give up yourself completely just to get a job, because you won't be happy then anyway."

Nor would an employer want to see you give up your own identity. Clothes that somehow "fit" you are one thing prospective bosses say they look for. "I would not want to see someone dressed in something in which they were obviously uncomfortable," says Peter Poser, president of Premier Business Services in New York. "When you're not comfortable that comes across in an interview—people tend to be very fidgety. My first criteria for what I want to see is something that's comfortable and fits your image and looks good. Wearing a style that doesn't suit your body shows poor judgment."

And while employers may expect to see you at your best during an interview, what they want to see is the best of your own style. "When you're interviewing you're selling and you should do your damnedest to look your best; take out your best dress or best suit," says Poser. "But I'd be surprised to see someone in a Brooks

Brothers suit for an interview and then a plaid suit and white socks at work, because then they were obviously lying, and if they're lying about their dress it's possible they weren't completely truthful about themselves."

While making a good first impression is essential to initial acceptance, and while it may color what happens next, that's not to say that it can't be dominated, over time, by other more essential qualities, according to psychiatrist Ellen Berman. "Clothes are all about getting your foot in the door," says Dr. Berman. "But when you really get to know someone, a different set of needs comes into view. In a setting where you do get to know somebody, the clothes don't matter. But to really get to know someone can take months, sometimes even years."

Nine Things Never to Wear on a Job Interview

The old rule of what to wear to a job interview—a navy or gray suit, white shirt, and bow tie—no longer applies, even at the most conservative of companies. Today, an unmatched suit or a dress may be just as appropriate. The only rules that remain in effect are those of what not to wear, no matter what kind of job you're interviewing for:

1. **PANTS**—While pants may be appropriate for work at many companies, they're still too risky for interview wear. Some interviewers may see pants, even dressy ones, as overly casual, others may view them as sexy, still others may see them as masculine or rebellious—in any case, not the image you want to present straight off.

2. **A LITTLE BOW TIE**—What was once an essential component of the interview uniform has become a symbol of naïveté, stodginess, and lack of imagination. The concept behind wearing a stock tie—formality, drawing attention to the face—may have been a good one, but there are better ways now to achieve the same effect: with a scarf or a pin or an interesting high collar.

3. **AN OXFORD SHIRT**—The cotton oxford shirt has met the same fate as the bow tie: it's now seen as something only entry-level women, coached by college placement counselors, would think of wearing. While some image consultants say any cotton shirt is wrong for an interview, this seems too narrow a view: some fine cottons, or cotton and wool or silk blends, may be more professional and formal than silks.

4. **A SKIRT THAT HIKES ABOVE YOUR KNEES WHEN YOU SIT**—When you choose a skirt for an interview, test it sitting down as well as standing up. It's not good to sit there with four inches of thigh showing; equally uncomfortable to tug at your hem while trying to enumerate your qualifications.

5. **ELABORATE SHOES AND/OR STOCKINGS**—The theory is that, in an interview, you want the interviewer to focus on your head (brains); patterned or colorful stockings and/or shoes draw attention to the opposite end of your body. This is not to say that you must wear standard-issue pumps and clear stockings to every job interview—just be sure your legs and feet are not distracting.

6. **ANYTHING BRAND-NEW**—By brand-new I mean something you actually wear for the first time for more than ten minutes on the morning of your interview. Yes, interviews sometimes demand new clothes, but if you've bought something new, try to wear it for at least an hour—even around the house—before the big day. Why? Because in an interview, you don't want to be aware of your clothes at all, and you certainly don't want to find out too late that the buttons tend to pop or the waistband itches or that the back of the skirt has a tendency to slip around to the front. The best interview clothes are those you've worn before, things proven to make you feel terrific.

7. **ANYTHING SLOPPY**—Does this still have to be stated? While no intelligent woman would show up for a job interview with a run in her stockings or a button missing from her jacket, it's worth pointing out less obvious errors: a shirt with worn cuffs, scuffed shoes, shoulder pads that slide toward the back and make you look like the Hunchback of Notre Dame. Also, don't carry both a purse and a briefcase: consolidate everything, any way you can, into one bag.

8. **ANYTHING SEXY**—Again, almost no one needs to be told not to show up at an interview in a plunging neckline, skirt slit up the thigh, and fishnet hose. What's sexy in a more subtle way is, of course, subjective. It's safest to play to the most conservative opinion: a high-necked blouse is better than one unbuttoned even one button; a neutral color is better than, say, pink; long sleeves are better than short; a skirt with no slit is better than one with even an inch of an opening. On the other hand, you don't have to show up dressed like Mother Superior. Just be aware that some men—and this is particularly an issue if the interviewer is a man—can see the edge of a collarbone and judge it sexy.

9. **DANGEROUS COLORS**—According to Atlanta image consultant Susan St. Charles, there are some colors that are just too dangerous to risk wearing to a job interview. Pastel pink, says St. Charles, may elicit a sympathetic response from a female interviewer but may make a male "beat up on you"; magenta may be too sexually exciting, in an atavistic way; and yellow and black, worn together, are the standard colors of danger—think of bumblebees, warning signs. Is all this true? Hard to say. But after hearing it, I'll never again be able to wear those colors to an important meeting with impunity.

EMOTIONAL ISSUE:
HIGH-PRESSURE DRESSING

It's the morning of the big meeting. Your boss will be there, and her boss, and your company's five top clients, all waiting to hear the results of the project you've been slaving over for the past six months.

How you handle dressing for a high-pressure situation—from a big meeting to a job interview to an important dinner—has a lot to do with how you handle pressure itself. Women who thrive on pressure, who pursue careers in which they're constantly on the spot, tend to dress for high-pressure situations as they would for any other day. Women who are less experienced in their jobs, less confident, and less accustomed to being in the spotlight tend to invest more thought and energy in what they wear in high-pressure situations. And women in low-profile careers—those who work alone or those who work in creative fields where anything goes—often approach high-pressure dressing with high anxiety.

"For a high-pressure situation I absolutely agonize about what I'm going to wear," says Susan Pomerantz, who organizes parties for a caterer, does the bulk of her work in jeans. "When I had to meet with executives from a department store, I was sure all these women would be dressed to the teeth and changed my clothes about twenty times in the morning."

"I always buy new clothes when I have a high-pressure meeting," says a free-lance writer. "I start thinking about it a week before. If I don't buy a whole new outfit, I buy either new shoes or earrings or at the very least, tights.

My aim? To look chic, confident, together, thinner, younger, and more attractive."

One reason women who work alone or in creative jobs say they agonize over high-pressure situations is that they don't have complete, up-to-date wardrobes appropriate for any business situation. Another reason is that their brand of high-pressure situation is often actually more high-pressured: on completely unfamiliar territory, with completely unfamiliar people, with unknown criteria for what's powerful, what's attractive, what's congenial.

"I'm in these situations maybe only once every two or three months," says the writer, "and I'm always there to sell something. It's not the selling itself that makes me nervous, but trying to psych out the style of the place. I know I feel most comfortable if what I wear is consistent with what the other people are wearing, but some publishers are very informal—jeans and sweaters—and some are sort of academic and tweedy and some are very glossy. I go crazy trying to imitate some look while having no idea what the look is."

The more familiar the setting and the participants in a high-pressure meeting, the less pressured the dressing. "I don't really feel nervous about dressing for presentations to art directors or fashion editors anymore," says Linda Nicholas, a New York makeup artist who works frequently for magazines. "The more I work with the same kind of people, the more comfortable I feel with myself and I don't need clothing to say or do that much more for me. When I first started working in this business I was not so confident; I didn't know what it was all about. Now, I don't agonize; I just get up and put on something that's comfortable and makes me feel good."

Wearing clothes that make you feel good can help balance the inner pressure wrought by a big meeting, say other women. "If I have an important meeting and I know I may be called on, I always dress up, I always pick something I feel good wearing," says Teresa Sokol, who does public relations for the graduate school of business at Carnegie-Mellon in Pittsburgh. "Even if I feel less than confident, even if I don't necessarily want to be at the meeting, I know I look better than I feel and that gives me a boost."

Women who are constantly in high-pressure situations at work have their dressing techniques, and their feelings about what they're going to wear, most in control.

Carol Sholler, a fund-raiser for nonprofit corporations, says that while she never buys anything new for presentations, she always thinks about what she's going to wear ahead of time. "I have a few suits I might pull out, and I make more of an effort with accessories. I make sure whatever I'm going to wear is very comfortable, especially if I'm going to be moving around or pointing to a board."

Judy Patrick, an executive for a corporate relocation firm, who is continually on center stage at meetings, defines a high-pressure situation as making a first sales call on a large corporation for whose business she's competing with several other companies. "That first call makes all the difference on whether I even stand a chance," says Patrick. "These people only see me, they don't see the rest of the company, so how I look in clothes gives them an impression of my entire company."

Patrick's strategy is to look professional but not overdressed, and she often relies on something red. "I somehow feel the need to have something red on; not always, but if I'm really nervous I sometimes wear red to counteract that, because I think it gets a favorable response."

Dale Venturini, general manager of a manufacturing firm branch office, says the only time she varies her clothes is when she's making a presentation to a large and unfamiliar audience. "Usually if I've got a pin on it might be three inches across, but I might not do that in front of a large audience. I wouldn't wear as much jewelry or anything distracting."

Usually, though, says Venturini, echoing the sentiments of other women whose entire careers revolve around high-pressure situations, "I make an extra effort every day."

WORK

•3•

Style and the Non-Corporate Woman

•

t is your first day at work. Not in the office—that was your old life—but at home or in the studio or in your own business. The only rules governing what you wear are the ones you make yourself. No one will be seeing you, and if someone does, it won't be someone who's judging your clothes by what's proper or powerful in the corporate culture.

The only problem is: what do you wear?

For non-corporate women, style becomes more of an emotional than a practical issue. The criteria for work clothes is often what feels good above what looks good, what's comfortable above what's appropriate, what sparks that inner drive rather than what conforms to the outer world. While many non-corporate women say they spend less money and effort on their clothes than do women who work in the corporate world, they also say they have a closer, almost symbiotic relationship with their work clothes. What they wear, they say, is central to how they feel about their work, and how they feel about their work has a lot to do with their clothes.

"One of the reasons I've chosen not to work in a large corporation has to do with dressing," says Lisa Amos, owner of a management consulting firm in New Orleans. "I don't want anybody to tell me how to dress, and I don't like to dress like other people unless I want to."

Amos says that, when she first started her own business, she conformed more to corporate standards, wearing suits much of the time. Now, she says, "I don't always wear suits. I have a few linen-y jackets I usually put on when I'm with clients, and I often wear dresses that are not particularly stylish but that are comfortable and good-looking."

How do Amos's corporate clients respond to her nonconformist clothes?

"I have and sometimes do pay a price for my choices," says Amos. "It's sometimes judged that if I don't wear a suit I'm not credible, and I lose an ear there. But over the years I figure it's a cost-benefit analysis. Also I've consciously added a lot more different kinds of clients, more small businesses and not-for-profit work, and part of the reason for that is not wanting to work in corporations where there are so few women and where there are rigid rules."

"When I worked for a corporation I looked like a little man," says Jody L. Serkes, St. Louis-based co-owner of a voice-mail company headquartered in Chicago. "What's changed mostly is that I feel more comfortable with my sense of style. Before, I wanted to blend in and look like everyone else; now I need to leave an impression."

Serkes's main role in her company—selling to corporate clients—means that she tries to balance her own sense of style with such considerations as looking competent, professional, and serious. "I generally try to find good-looking nonmasculine business suits that have some style and that aren't pink or square," explains Serkes. "I work with Fortune 100 companies, and they have to perceive me as representing a corporate image that they feel comfortable buying, but what I wear has to have style because that makes me feel good."

Serkes likes neutrals and red, textured fabrics, long jackets, and to-the-knee skirts, and, above all, "nothing boring." "I have about ten minutes where they're going to decide whether to see me again, and a lot of it has to do with what I look like," she says. "Sometimes I'll write down what I wore so the next time I visit I can vary it."

When she wants to sign a deal, Serkes wears what she calls a "closing outfit." "It's a black skirt and black and beige and fatigue green tweed jacket and a silk blouse that gives this warm, dark, authoritative serious look. If I walked in wearing something open and airy and fun, they'd want to play. The very powerful colors and lines say I'm not there to do anything but sign a contract and get a check."

Some women who've traded corporate for non-corporate jobs say they've discovered that they can play by their own rules, and still win the game. "I increasingly wear what I want to wear, and I feel as if it works anyway," says Paula Golden, the executive director of the Massachusetts Seatbelt Coalition. A lawyer by training, Golden once worked for a larger state agency and followed more conventional dressing rules. "I went to law school in the seventies, when women were just beginning to infiltrate the men's world, and we were told to dress like them and we'd get in the door. I think this is a big lie," says Golden. "Men aren't going to let you in the club anyway, so why not use your own powers?" Now, Golden wears colors rather than neutrals, dresses rather than suits, and loves scarves and costume jewelry.

For some non-corporate women, bucking the rules may in fact mean dressing more conservatively than their colleagues do. "I could wear sweats or jeans and high tops to work but I don't feel comfortable doing that," says Carolyn Gutjahr, a planner for an architectural firm in St. Louis. Gutjahr says she favors more formal clothes—she usually wears separates by Perry Ellis or from Ann Taylor, often with a jacket or a cardigan—not because they make her feel more professional about her work but because they give her "a feeling of comfort and happiness with the way I look."

In fact, not being governed by corporate rules often frees women to pay closer attention to the flattery and comfort potential of whatever style clothing they choose to wear.

Susan Pomerantz, who organizes parties for a New York caterer and is also launching a career as a kitchen design consultant, says, "I don't feel I have to follow any corporate rules but I can't wear something I don't feel good about or that doesn't have a certain amount of style."

Once upon a time, says Pomerantz, she insisted on wearing only jeans, and whoever didn't like it could be damned. Now, however, "I've found that people in catering are more comfortable if I present a well-groomed, not very far-out image. I don't have to be Brooks Brothers; I don't feel I have to mirror my corporate clients, but I've taken what I feel is me and gone somewhat conservative."

Other women find their comfort level is clothes that are increasingly casual and practical. "I just started wearing jeans once in a while for locations in the city," says Linda Nicholas, a hairdresser and makeup artist who works mainly on photographic assignments. "I bought a pair that were three sizes too big that are so comfortable, and that I don't mind getting makeup on."

For Nicholas, practicality is a top consideration. "Because I'm working with makeup and constantly doing things like sticking my elbow in the eye shadow, I want things that are easily washable and so I love cottons. On outside locations, I usually wear layers, because we start early in the morning when it's cool and then later we're out in the sun. I always go to a studio assignment in a jacket because sometimes it's very cold in the studio. I like to wear things with pockets because I constantly need to carry a brush or powder in them."

Women who work alone feel the greatest freedom about their clothes—and the greatest ambivalence. "Sometimes I drop my husband off at the train station and find myself feeling very envious of the women dressed up with the little briefcases," says Kate Broughton, who runs her own advertising and public relations business from her Boston home. "It's nice to be out of the rat race and not be so concerned about the latest accessories and trends. I feel freer to carve out my own style, but I also feel something's missing; I don't feel quite as exciting or colorful."

Broughton, a former editor of *Boston* magazine, says she has a newfound relish of dressing up when a meeting takes her to town. "I like to dress up now that I don't have to do it every day," she says. "It reminds me that I am a professional. Otherwise I spend a lot of time at home in tennis shoes and sloppy pants and somewhere along the line I lose track of myself as someone of accomplishment."

Broughton says she feels this negative side of anything-goes work dressing most keenly when she leaves her typewriter to run an errand. "I get so embarrassed to say this or even admit it to myself, but I find myself needing to have that external proof to neighbors and the community that I am not Susie Homemaker. When I go to the supermarket I almost want to tell someone at the cash register: 'I work at home, I'm a writer.'"

Dressing only to please yourself has its advantages, however. Last summer, when she was eight months pregnant, Broughton was able to indulge the ultimate work-dressing freedom: on hot afternoons, she'd run a cool bath, turn on her cordless phone, and make her business calls from the tub . . . nude.

• *Style Analysis* •

PATRICIA CAREY *is assistant dean for student affairs at New York University in the School of Education, Health, Nursing, and Arts Professions. In her photograph, Carey is wearing a silk Oleg Cassini blouse bought on sale in Bloomingdale's two years ago for $50; a wool Regina Porter Signature Collection skirt (sans its matching jacket) also bought on sale in Bloomingdale's for about $70; Italian leather boots bought at a half-price sale while on a business trip to Texas ("People in Texas do not wear Italian boots a lot") for $100; a Ralph Lauren silk scarf that was a gift from her sister, and gold earrings that were a gift from her husband.*

JUST IN THE PAST FEW YEARS, THINGS HAVE REALLY CHANGED IN TERMS OF WHAT WOMEN WEAR TO WORK. WOMEN ARE A LOT MORE CONFIDENT ABOUT WEARING MORE RELAXED THINGS, WEARING PANTS, WEARING KNITS . . .

I think what's happening is that we are no longer so afraid to make our own statements, and that goes from statements about our workplace or what we have chosen to do to statements about how we want to look. That's tempered in terms of the particular environment in which one is working. There are ground rules, certainly, but there is some room.

WHAT KIND OF RULES DO YOU HAVE WORKING HERE?

This is academe, and academe is a little more relaxed than, say, the business world. On the other hand, one needs to look like one is in charge as opposed to looking like a student, so in my position I would not wear jeans and a T-shirt. That would not be appropriate. In academe we act as role models so we have to look like we are indeed in charge, we are professional.

When I was director of the counseling service at NYU, my dress was a little more relaxed; I wore pants more often. As dean, I have assumed a much more public role. It's working with students, with faculty, administration, and also representing the university outside of this community. While my style has remained the same, my choice of how I interpret that style has changed. I wear suits. If I wear dresses, I usually wear a two-piece dress with a jacket, and I like loose-fitting clothes. I have a few little pudges here and there, which would not make a big difference, but I choose to wear loose clothes. I wear belts sometimes, but you rarely see me in a dress with a belt. That's just not me.

I like wearing jackets, which has to do with my casualness. Even in being dressed up, a jacket makes me feel relaxed. I can move about without having to worry about holding my stomach in. A jacket helps to not only keep me relaxed but to look like I am together, and it also tops off whatever I'm wearing. It makes me look like I am a complete person, clotheswise.

HOW HAS YOUR STYLE EVOLVED OVER THE YEARS?

I grew up in Chicago, and my father was a minister, which meant that every Sunday we went to church, and we were dressed up. We wore these nice, cute little dresses and shoes and socks, and things matched, and on special holidays we wore special things. At Christmas or Easter, there was always a new outfit. My father was not big on our wearing pants, so we did not wear a lot of pants. I remember wearing a lot of skirts and dresses.

When I moved away to college (to Michigan State), while dress was casual—slacks and a big sweater—those things were clean, and they looked clean. We did not wear Levi's with holes in the knees or dirty T-shirts.

Then I came to New York twenty-three years ago and adopted a little bit of this or that from a lot of different sources to come up with my own style. When I go to other places around the country I'm told that I look like I'm from New York, so I must have the New York style, but the New York style is so broad, and you can wear anything you want to wear and still look New York. Rather than sequins we might use simply silk and make the same statement, and so it becomes more subtle, quietly elegant.

WHAT THINGS DO YOU HAVE A PASSION FOR?

I like boots. Boots fit into my need for comfort and for being able to move. I walk fast and I move fast. While I like shoes, when I put on shoes my feet don't look like I want them to. If I were to define my style I would say the kinds of clothes I choose are those that can be dressed up or dressed down. If I buy a suit and I want to wear it to a meeting and then to a dinner, I should be able to do that with a little scarf or jewelry, as opposed to having to buy two different suits for two different occasions.

HOW DO YOU SHOP?

I really do not go shopping. When I go shopping I do not find what I'm looking for. I bump into things, and I try to drop into stores so I can indeed bump into things. If I see something I like it's better that I get that right then and there rather than waiting. Early in my life I used to vacillate—should I buy it, shouldn't I—but I don't do that anymore. I think what changed is that I realized when I go looking for something I can't find it, but when I see something I like I should get it, within reason, because I will use it.

AS A PSYCHOLOGIST, DO YOU TEND TO PICK UP ON WHAT PEOPLE ARE WEARING AS CLUES TO HOW THEY'RE FEELING, AND ARE YOU SENSITIVE TO THAT IN YOURSELF?

Yes, I'm sensitive to that, although it's not always uppermost in my mind. If I'm working with a student, for example, I notice what the student is wearing. If the student is depressed and wearing very dark clothes or just looks unkempt, that gives me a clue to what's going on with that person.

I used to wear clothes that reflected a depressed or an unhappy person. It wasn't that I was abnormally unhappy—I was going through my stages of transition like everybody else—but I became aware of that and what statement I was making. I like black and I like blue and there's a dark brown that looks good on me, as a brown person, but I brightened those things up with a splash, so the statement is, "She is not depressed. She likes these colors but there's a happy exclamation point behind the statement."

WAS THERE ANY TIME IN YOUR ADULT LIFE WHEN YOU DRESSED VERY DIFFERENTLY FROM HOW YOU DO NOW?

I don't think so. While it's been an evolving style, I think I've always been in this mode. I hardly ever wore pink. I do own a pink linen skirt that I bought on sale, and it's lovely, but it's not hot pink, it's almost white. I've always tended to wear blues and blacks and maybe checks but not ostentatious checks or prints.

One change is the introduction of red into my wardrobe. I have a red suit. I didn't know that I would look good in red. I think we're socialized to believe certain colors look good on us. Red was not a color I wore a lot as a child, although I did wear pink and baby blues. I don't know whether that had to do with what red has been associated with—loose women—and I think that must be part of it. I'm sure it goes back to my childhood; I didn't wear lipstick because it was a sin in our church, and I still don't wear lipstick. Darker people have been taught to wear dark colors and not loud, loud, like red, colors. It's part of our culture.

DO YOU ALWAYS WEAR GOLD JEWELRY? DOES THE JEWELRY ITSELF HAVE SIGNIFICANCE?

I wear gold jewelry a lot. These are things that friends have given me, so I don't necessarily go out and buy jewelry. I wear my sentimental things—I got this bracelet when I was in Africa, and this was my first wedding ring, and this was my engagement ring [a gold signet ring] that my husband's grandfather gave him when he was eight years old. Under my clothes I wear a Taurus necklace a friend gave me—I don't wear it out, but I wear it all the time. If I don't have these things on I miss them. I tend to wear them over and over again, the same things, every day.

ANY PEOPLE WHO'VE HAD AN INFLUENCE ON YOUR STYLE?

Well, I'm sure my sister who is in California has helped with some things. She's a supervisor in the airline business. She loves clothes—she's a real clotheshorse. I have some other friends who are much more clothes-conscious than I am. I look at their clothes and choose different things from each one of them.

I was in an all-black women's group, and the women in my group were so well dressed, and I was very informal or casual, but I decided that maybe I did need to look a little more dressed-up or a little more grown-up, especially when I became a dean.

DID YOU TALK ABOUT CLOTHES IN THE WOMEN'S GROUP?

We talked about clothes in terms of a statement clothes make, or the clothes we choose because we try to cover up our shape. It was more in terms of getting in touch with ourselves. It was a feminist group.

FOR A WHILE CLOTHES WERE SEEN AS ANTI-FEMINIST, AND NOW FEMINIST SCHOLARS ARE SAYING CLOTHES ARE ACTUALLY A FEMINIST THING BECAUSE THEY'RE TRADITIONALLY FEMININE.

Yes, yes, and we don't have to deny that part of us, we don't have to want it to go away. As we get more accepted and more powerful in the workplace we can make our own personal statement more dramatically.

Sometimes when I look at a student with purple hair, I say, "Where can that person work?" That's a caricature of the point that if you're going to join an organization you do have to look like you belong there, and then as you become more a part of that, you can digress a little bit. You can say, "I belong here, but this is me." I bring some differences to this organization through my clothing—this is my choice.

How you look is a really critical issue. We might say that it doesn't matter, but it does matter because we react to people based on our expectations of what that person is supposed to look like.

WHAT WOULD YOU LIKE PEOPLE TO THINK ABOUT YOU, BASED ON YOUR CLOTHES?

I want to get immediate respect from the person who's seeing me, because when you have respect for someone it means you think they have something to say even though they have said nothing. You will take the time to listen; they are worth listening to. And then you can find out they have a sense of humor or that they like to relax. I tend to be a little more formal than not; that's just the way I am. I want my clothes to make a statement about who I am, some of the values I stand for, and that's a huge statement—paragraphs, semicolons, compound sentences. It's very complex.

EMOTIONAL ISSUE:
CAN CLOTHES MAKE YOU FEEL MORE SUCCESSFUL, EVEN WHEN NO ONE'S LOOKING?

You work at home, alone. Theoretically you could get up, have your coffee, and then pad into your office and work all day in your pajamas. Or you could pull on the clothes you left in a heap after the touch football game last night. Or you could go halfway—wear "nice" casual clothes, a little makeup, perhaps some earrings. Or you could get dressed as if you were going to any office, except that yours just happens to be down the hall from your bedroom. The question is, Since you're not leaving the house, since you don't have to see anyone, does it make any difference at all what you wear?

Well, yes, it makes a difference, but only to the extent that your clothes can affect how you feel about yourself, which can affect how you feel about your work. And the clothes that make women feel more successful, or more creative or more motivated, when no one's watching are determined by personal idiosyncracies rather than standard business-dressing rules. At home alone, a feeling of success is as likely to emanate from wearing lipstick or a favorite T-shirt as it is from wearing a business suit.

That's not to say that dressing up in conventional office gear isn't what it takes for some women to draw the line between home and work. Carol Sholler, who runs a fundraising and marketing company out of her Rhode Island home, says, "I find I work more efficiently if I'm dressed up, complete with stockings and shoes."

While Sholler says some of the clothes she wears in her home office may be "more comfortable and less formal" than those she'd wear to, for instance, a meeting with a client, she never relaxes completely into jeans or sweats. "I tried that for a few days and I found I got more distracted," she says.

Kate Broughton, who does public relations and advertising writing out of her Massachusetts home, doesn't dress up as much as Sholler does, but does make more of an effort to pull herself together than she would on, say, a nonworking Sunday morning. "Because this line of work is loaded with paper and files, it's easy to feel cluttered, so if I feel I'm cluttered in the way I look—if I'm wearing some big sloppy thing with sleeves I have to keep pushing up—somehow subliminally that makes me feel disorganized or disheveled," Broughton says.

For working at home, Broughton favors oversized sweaters, comfortable but pretty rayon challis pants, and flat shoes: "prettied up but not like an office." But the real mood-changer for Broughton is the details: "The point where I feel really ready to work is when I put on lipstick and earrings."

Another writer feels most productive in whatever's most comfortable: "Pants and a T-shirt and slippers; and in winter, pants and a sweatshirt and slippers. Sometimes I wear my husband's or my daughter's T-shirts—whoever has the best one around."

When this writer needs the psychological edge more dressed-up clothes provide is when she's making phone calls. "I have to be dressed a little better and have makeup on and I definitely have to have my contact lenses in or I'm not fully functioning," she says. "Those things give me more confidence because I have a better self-image."

Of course, self-image is the bottom line since, when you work alone, that's the only image that counts. Susan Pomerantz, a former caterer, says, "When I was working alone I would get very gross, wearing sweats that were four years old with food dripping down me.

After three or four days I'd start to feel really badly about myself, real androgynous, like this nonentity—not about my work, but about myself."

Now, Pomerantz plans parties for another caterer, designs kitchens for corporations. "Now I have to get it together to some extent every day," she says, "and I feel better about how I look. I realize I need to pay a little attention to that."

Tie a Yellow Ribbon 'Round That Empty Head

Do you have trouble concentrating? Find yourself picking up the phone only to forget who you were going to call? You may be able to solve your problems by wearing a yellow turban, or even tying a yellow rag around your head.

Susan St. Charles, an Atlanta image consultant, says that if you work alone you should wear "whatever will support your creativity." And what's most powerful psychologically, says St. Charles, is color.

"You should wear colors that you love so much you could eat them," says St. Charles. "The indicator of what colors are best for you is not a color chart but what you're highly attracted to."

Gray tends to be a draining color, says St. Charles, while reds, yellows, and oranges spark high productivity.

"Orange is very good when you have to get physically involved with your work because it's the color of action," she says, "and if you wear a yellow turban, your memory will increase."

Will it really help? I have my daughter's bright yellow T-shirt tied around my head at this very moment, and the most I can say is it doesn't seem to hurt.

The Best: Trousers

Extended Waistband—For smooth fit at waist.

Hidden Button at Top of Zipper.

Piping Along Inside Edge of Waistband—Neat edging; helps waistband lie flat.

Pleats Stitched Down One Inch—Makes tummy look flatter; helps keep pleats from gapping.

Slash Pockets—Set into side seam or angled from waistband to side; must lie smooth and closed!

Generous-sized Pockets—Let your hands be the judge.

French-seamed Pocket Lining—Sturdiest, neatest.

Back Darts from Waistband—For shape, good fit.

Full Lining—Not essential for looks or quality, but can be more comfortable.

Perfect Fit at Crotch—Not tight (no horizontal pulling), not saggy; good fit here a must for looks and comfort.

Double-stitched Crotch Seam—For strength.

Finished Seam Edges.

Generous Seam Margins at Inseam—In case you ever need pants let out.

Deep Hem—In case you ever need pants let down.

Wool Gabardine—Though you'll find perfectly wonderful trousers in other fabrics, from flannel to linen, wool gabardine is the best for comfort, versatility, neatness, and is often the most flattering.

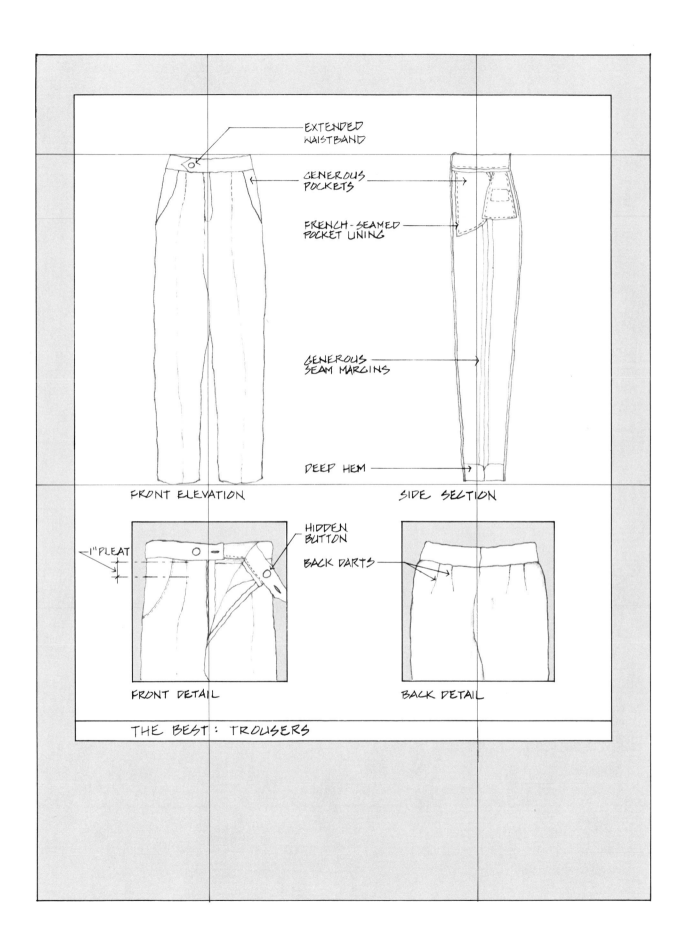

EXTENDED
WAISTBAND

GENEROUS
POCKETS

FRENCH-SEAMED
POCKET LINING

GENEROUS
SEAM MARGINS

DEEP HEM

FRONT ELEVATION

SIDE SECTION

1" PLEAT

HIDDEN
BUTTON

BACK DARTS

FRONT DETAIL

BACK DETAIL

THE BEST: TROUSERS

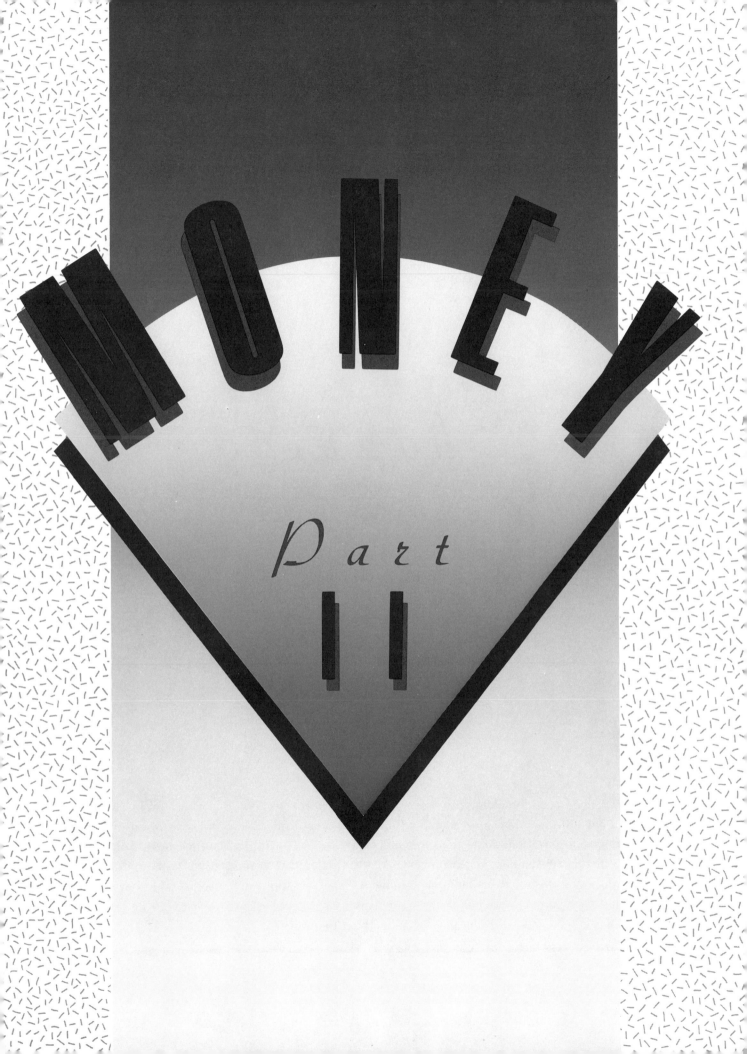

MONEY

·4·

Shopping

·

You need some new clothes, which means you need to shop. But where to go? Do you want to brave Macy's or Sears or limit yourself to Ann Taylor? Pay the prices at Saks or try to ferret out some treasures at Loehmann's? That little boutique next to the post office is convenient, and even easier is the catalog that is right at your elbow. Not only do you have an overwhelming number of choices, but each has its advantages and disadvantages, different draws and different demands. The question has become not simply where to shop, but how to cope with the place once you get there.

Shopping for clothes has become a sophisticated venture. The prime reason: the nature of retailing has changed dramatically. Consider that in the 1960s certain things we now take for granted were in their infancy: malls, for example, and boutiques—the kind with personality. Consider that such things as Calvin Klein and Liz Claiborne outlets were nonexistent. Consider that Calvin Klein and Liz Claiborne—designers for the middle-class working woman as opposed to couturiers or "better manufacturers"—were nonexistent. Consider that middle-class working women as a force on how clothes are made and sold were themselves nonexistent.

Now, there are a lot more places to shop than the big department store and Zelda's Dress Shop downtown. More stores means more competition between stores and more competition means more sophisticated selling techniques. The rise of boutiques and of outlets has forced department stores to liven up their acts and become more aggressive with markdowns and service. Specialty stores and designer shops sell not only clothes but a complete image.

What does this have to do with you? Everything, if you're going to shop with the most savvy and the least stress in minimal time making the most of your money. If stores have become ultrasophisticated in how they sell, it behooves you to become just as sophisticated in how and where and what you buy. To find out how stores are set up, how they get you to buy, and how you can best shop them, I talked to all types of retail insiders: department store executives, boutique owners, salespeople, marketing experts, manufacturers, and shopping consultants who agreed to share their secrets, most of them in exchange for anonymity.

Here, divided into three sections—Big Stores (department and large specialty stores); Small Stores (from the corner boutique to the sportswear shop at the local mall); and Cheap Stores (from designer outlets to discounters selling everything from dishpans to dresses)—is the inside story on how stores sell, how you can best buy.

Big Stores

Their Selling Strategy

Big retailers are big businesses, which means they devote tremendous resources to designing stores that maximize both the time and money you spend there. It's no accident, for instance, that you-deserve-a-treat-today items like cosmetics, jewelry, and hosiery are usually found on the first floor or that the more expensive clothes are often on a lower floor than cheaper ones: the point is to tempt your impulses before your sensibilities, to force you to pass the $500 dresses before the $100 ones. Ever wonder why it can be so much easier to find the "Up" escalators than the "Down" ones in a large store? Or why the elevators are hidden away in the back of the store? Because the store wants it to be easier for you to get in than out, to pass through every department on the way to the ninth floor rather than to shoot straight there.

Let's say you go into a large store in search of a black turtleneck. Where, you ask at the information desk, is the black turtleneck department?

Ha! comes the answer. There are black turtlenecks on floors one, two, three, four, five seven, nine, and ten. There are black turtlenecks in the junior department, the better missy sportswear department, the designer department, the men's department, the sweater department, and on the Avenue de Shoppes. What sort of turtleneck are you looking for? Oversized or fitted? Sweater or shirt? Italian or Taiwanese? There are, you see, lots of black turtlenecks in this store. Black turtlenecks virtually everywhere.

Well, you say, you'd like to see a range. Isn't there one place where there are more turtlenecks than any other?

Sorry. There are turtlenecks everywhere. The entire store is turtleneck territory.

If at this point you walk away shaking your head, wondering why the store is so stupid as to not have a turtleneck department, you should know that the store does not want to have a turtleneck department. That the store in fact has given it considerable thought and has decided it is much smarter to have turtlenecks in twenty places, and white blouses on every floor, and brown pumps on two, four, and seven. The store has decided this because the more places you have to go, the more things you are likely to buy.

"Department stores don't want everything in one place," says Michael Solomon, Ph.D., a consumer psychologist and head of the marketing department at Rutgers. "They want to maximize the amount of square footage people cover in an average trip, which maximizes impulse purchasing."

Don't large stores want to make it easy for you to shop? Well, yes and no. Basically, they want to make it easy for you to stay and harder to leave, because the more time you spend in the store, the more likely it is you will buy, out of either a sense of security or desperation.

"The more time you spend in the store the more you need to justify why you're there," says Solomon. "The pressure builds for some kind of closure."

The store also makes it easier to buy expensive things and impulse items than cheap ones or sensible ones. On the designer floor, each tiny boutique has its own saleswoman and its own dressing room. Why not try it on since the dressing room is right there? Why not buy it when there's no line? The headband counter has its own checkout person—might as well! Raincoats may have only one salesperson for the entire department—but you need it anyway.

As you already know, expensive and impulse items are usually placed in the path of most exposure. Sometimes, though, designer clothes are on a higher floor than junior items, so that on the way upstairs to buy your interview suit you're attracted by the flashing lights and music in the "fun" department (hey, you're not old! you work hard and you deserve to play!) and on the way downstairs—depressed that all the Calvins now cost a month's rent—you can cheer yourself up with a little T-shirt that at least you can afford.

This catch-your-eye philosophy is also reflected in the placement of particular items within a department—the jacket or the blouse you can't miss when you first walk in. The store figures you'll figure that it's what's up front that counts: the best styles, the newest look, the clothes the store really believes in. In truth, these featured pieces may be a bit more expensive—and not incidentally, a bit harder to sell—than those you have to work to find.

"If you see something all over the place, that doesn't mean it's the hottest fashion," says a retailing Deep Throat. "If it's really hot or it's really a great buy, it sells out in a day."

Other "we know best" selling techniques include clothes grouped in outfits: the skirt you want next to the blouse and the jacket and not incidentally the shoes and the necklace and the scarf and the hat that go with it. While such groupings can give you potentially useful style ideas, they can also make you feel that as long as you're buying the skirt, you "should" buy all the extras, too.

Your Shopping Strategy

Which strategy you employ to shop a large store depends on your goal: to look at what's there, perchance to buy, or to get a specific item and get out.

If you're just looking, the best tack is to choose one store and explore it in depth. Why you're looking has something to do with which store you choose: if you need a dress for a special dinner a few weeks down the road (supposing a certain amount of leisure), you'd do best to look in a department store you know, where you can focus on the floors or departments that may have what you need; if you're looking just to look, you might want to choose a store you'd like to know better, and use your trip as an opportunity to case the joint for future buying trips.

The first step of your looking trip should be to survey all the windows to get an idea of what the store is promoting and where those things are (there's often a placard telling you). If you fall in love with something in the window, head directly to that department. If not, head directly to the escalator (or the store directory, if you can find it) and aim yourself toward the department most likely to interest you. To look constructively, it makes sense to start with what you're most interested in, not to arrive there when your attention and stamina have been dissipated by the belts and bras.

Once you arrive on your designated floor, make a quick circle (remember, you've still got a lot of energy) of the whole floor, pinpointing the areas of highest interest, advises Joyce Grillo, president of Impression Management in New York, who shops for a living.

After circling, you're free to stop and focus on specific items and specific departments. Read labels before you try on—no sense finding out that blouse is hand-washable only after you already love it. Reasons to try on: you see something that might be perfect, or you want to experiment with styles or colors. A note on experimenting from Grillo: you don't need to try on six miniskirts to see whether they look good on you when one will tell you.

If you find something that might be right (but you're not sure), make a note of exactly where, what, and when—you'll forget by the time you wend your way back to the first floor. In the case of perfection, you have to buy right away or risk its not being there when you get around to returning to the store. One advantage of shopping at a department store is that almost everything is refundable, if you find later you've made a mistake.

Continue this pattern through the store's other departments, in the order of their interest to you. If what's there hasn't appealed to you, don't fall into the trap of buying to "justify" your trip. Your justification will be that you came, you saw, you didn't like, and now you never have to go back.

If you're going to a large store to buy something specific, you should definitely choose a store you know and like. Head directly, and I mean directly, to the department most likely to have what you need, and if you find it, buy it immediately. Your buying juices sated, your mission accomplished, you are now free to look around in a healthy and productive state of mind. What if the store doesn't have what you need? Don't drain energy by wandering around, going up to the junior department you've never liked with the thought that by some miracle you'll find something there. Just get out and go somewhere else.

Small Stores

Their Selling Strategy

Small stores, by their nature, cater to very specific customers, tastes, or needs. Many are individually owned, and so reflect the style sensibilities of their owners: good, bad, staid, or eccentric. A recent trend has been toward the super-specialization of boutiques: one that sells only cashmere, for instance, or just small-sized shoes. There are also chain boutiques that sell swimwear or bright cotton knits or jeans. And then there are small shops that are outlets for particular designers' clothes.

Obviously, boutiques range from the most sophisticated of stores to the least sophisticated. There's an enormous difference between Kenzo on Madison Avenue or Scruples on Rodeo Drive and the Mom 'n' Pop Dress Shop down on Main Street. So too are there enormous differences in their design and marketing techniques— from highly developed "buy me" atmospheres to haphazard arrangements that can turn off all but the most desperate or the most adventurous of shoppers. What it all boils down to is personality and image: that's what most small shops are selling and what you, to a large extent, are buying when you shop at a boutique.

Prices at most small stores are usually as high or higher than at department stores. Besides image, what you're paying for is usually convenience and service.

The omnipresence of sales help at a small store is a double-edged sword. The service can be better at a boutique than at any other kind of store—some boutiques keep index cards on customers with notes of what they've bought, pulling pieces each season to add to their wardrobes, even sending items to the client's home or office to be tried on and either bought or sent back without ever having to set foot in the store. This is what keeps many women coming back again and again: for better or for worse.

In sophisticated boutiques, salespeople are an important part of the store's image. Their ages, their looks, their personalities, and of course their clothes play a large role in convincing you to shop and buy at the boutique. Some boutique salespeople purposefully play it cool, if cool is a prime element of the store's personality. In general, the hard sell is out,

but friendliness—friendliness that builds trust and, not incidentally, sales—is in.

Savvy saleswomen confess to casing a potential customer's ring finger and figure for evidence of a husband and/or kids—prime ground for casual and comfortable conversation. Weather conditions—"How are the roads?"— is another favored topic. The point is to ask a question or make a statement that demands more than a yes or no response, something off the subject of why both you and she are there.

Why are you there? That question may come later. Are you going to a big party? Heading off on a business trip? Gee, that sounds exciting, and have you seen these new briefcases that double as overnight bags?

It's not that most salespeople don't genuinely want to help—they do—or that they want you to be unhappy when you leave the store—they don't. But they'd ideally like to achieve these goals and sell you as much as possible at the same time. And the more a salesperson comes to seem like a friend, say experts, the more likely you'll buy something to please her.

Because image is so important at boutiques, the atmosphere of the store is another well-thought-out component of selling strategy. "Retailers are putting a lot of emphasis on atmospherics, on the feeling in a store," says Michael Solomon. "They work at getting people in the mood to buy; it's well known that mood influences behavior."

Consider the basic element of space: "The more space there is in relation to the clothes, the more upscale the store," says Michael Solomon. "The really swanky stores don't have any stuff at all; the ultimate is that they bring it to you from some hidden place. The store is saying, 'Our stuff is so exclusive we can afford to spend all this money on rent and not fill the place up.' "

Lighting is another important factor in determining a small store's atmosphere . . . and your buying mood. "We associate dim lighting with higher status," says Solomon. "A really well-lit store has a different feeling—it's more vibrant, younger." What a store may be trying to do is heighten the part of you that's right for their clothes, to make you feel a little richer, or a little younger, or a little more energetic than you may have felt before you walked in the door.

Your Shopping Strategy

Shopping at small stores is an entirely different venture than shopping at department stores or large specialty stores, and should be done on a different trip—in a mall, for instance, visit the small stores on one day; tackle the big ones another time.

You can (and should) visit several boutiques per shopping outing. Choose one city block, say, or one "arm" of a mall, and make a quick circle of the entire thing before going into any one store. Because boutiques are so small and distinct, most times you'll be able to tell from the window display and from peering inside at the salespeople, other shoppers, and merchandise whether it might be right for you.

When you've completed your circle, step inside each store that holds promise. Once inside, pause for a moment and take in the atmosphere. "You should be able to tell in thirty seconds if a boutique is right for you," says one expert. "If not, leave."

If you decide to stay, take advantage of the sales help, keeping in mind what you learned about selling strategies. The more clear and specific you can be about what you want and need—"I'm looking for a white or gray blouse to wear under a suit, I hate polyester, and I don't want to spend more than $100"—the better able the salesperson will be to help you. If you need something for a specific occasion—a drop-dead outfit for your boss's daughter's wedding—you can also say just that, and let the salesperson do the work of gathering the best the store has to offer.

Don't be shy about asking the boutique owner or salesperson to help you find sizes or carry pieces to the dressing room. On the other hand, if you want to look around for a few minutes, say that, too. Instead of saying, "Just looking,"—and begging the question, "What are you looking for?"—you might try something like, "I always need a few moments of silence to shop by myself before I can think."

If you like the boutique and the salesperson but don't want to buy anything, ask for the store's card and the person's name. Next time you're shopping for something specific—a silver beaded top, or a certain skirt in a size the department store's out of—you can call your new contact.

And if you do want to buy, ask about special services: alterations, for example, or same-day delivery or mailing lists for sales. Since you may be paying more at a small store, you should take advantage of all the perks one has to offer.

Cheap Stores

Their Selling Strategy

There are really three distinct kinds of stores where you can buy clothes at low or cut-rate prices: discount stores (such as K mart), outlets (Loehmann's, for example, or a Ralph Lauren outlet), and off-price stores (such as Labels for Less and Hit or Miss). What they all have in common is that their main selling point is price.

Discount stores are organized to look disorganized. They don't want you to be able to find the $12.99 skirts quickly and easily: they want you to have to pass the $1 earrings ("A dollar is nothing") and the dish drainers ("Gee, mine is getting kind of scummy") and the kids' toys ("That's right—Jeremy's birthday is coming up") on the way.

The bright lights and the upbeat music and the jumble of items and colors say "Save!" which at the cash register may add up to "Spend!" All those little things can mean a big bottom line—which is exactly what the store is counting on.

Outlets are basically stores that sell at discount what manufacturers and designers can't sell to mainstream retailers. Fast gaining in popularity and sophistication, outlets include stores such as Loehmann's and Annie Sez that sell many different brands of clothing, as well as outlets owned by individual designers (Calvin Klein, Ralph Lauren, Liz Claiborne) and selling only that designer's clothes.

How do clothes end up at outlets? Some are admittedly leftovers that stores can't sell at end-of-season sales, and some are irregulars or seconds. But today, many of the clothes found at outlets are overruns—when more is produced than is sold to retail stores—or late shipments refused by retailers. Clothes usually arrive at outlets about a month after they do at department stores: fall clothes are delivered in late August instead of July, for instance, still in plenty of time for the start of the season. Conversely, sales usually take place earlier in the season at outlets than at department stores.

Most outlets don't want to rile department stores (which are the designers' bread and butter), so they're usually located where they won't compete head-on with big retailers, and either don't advertise at all or, if they do advertise, are not explicit about the store's location or which designers' clothes they sell.

On the other hand, to attract the sophisticated shopper who visits Bloomingdale's one day, Daffy's the next, many outlets have upgraded their store setups and services: grouping clothes by style and color, installing carpeting and attractive lighting, accepting credit cards. Even Loehmann's—which still has a warehouse look, and not incidentally, the best true bargains—has relaxed its cash-only policy.

But because the main selling point of outlets is price, many also use techniques designed to feed shoppers' discount frenzy: bright lights, sale items crowded and jumbled together, a sense of both confusion and excitement. The reason many outlets have installed carpeting, instituted special displays, and started taking credit cards while still leaving the dressing rooms open isn't because dressing room curtains are prohibitively expensive, but because open dressing rooms encourage eavesdropping, conversation, and admiration. You see other people's finds, you see them looking good, you see them deciding to buy, and you want to do the same.

Also, price tags in outlets almost always include not only the current selling price but also the full retail price, to emphasize not how much you're spending for the item but how much you're saving. Of course, that full retail price may only be theoretical: if the garment had been manufactured, and if any store had agreed to buy it, that is what it might sell for.

It's a mistake to take outlet or off-price stores at face value, assuming that everything inside is a great bargain. Sometimes clothes at outlet or off-price stores are not well made to begin with, sometimes the "discounted" price is not any less than what you'd pay for a comparable item from a conventional retailer, and sometimes the clothes in outlets are so ill-fitting or unflattering or poorly constructed that no self-respecting retailer would offer them for sale in the first place.

The main difference between outlets and off-price stores such as Hit or Miss and Labels for Less is that off-price stores are usually found in malls or downtown areas alongside conventional retailers and are set up just like regular stores. However, this is a bigger difference than it seems, signaling that many off-price stores are not competing for the same brands and quality of clothing as are found in department stores. Sometimes, what's in off-price stores is not truly discounted designer clothes, but second-rate items manufactured specifically to be sold at lower prices. In an off-price store, you may in fact get exactly what you pay for.

Your Shopping Strategy

To shop successfully at any kind of bargain store, you've got to first give yourself a complete fashion education. Before you go, page through fashion magazines, look through more expensive stores, pay attention to well-dressed women on the street. You want to become as thoroughly versed as possible in style, quality, and accessories before you go hunting for bargains.

In a discount store such as K mart, put aside your preconceptions of what you're going to find, and where. It's worth riffling through a wall of horrendous handbags on the chance of finding a great one, or wading through the nylon nighties in search of a classic terry robe. Always look in the men's department, where classic styling often means better quality for the price. If you dress adventurously, you may also want to look at certain items in new ways: a pair of men's slippers may make great loafers; fishing lures can double as earrings.

In general, discount stores are good sources for items at both ends of the fashion spectrum: basics and fads. With basics, you wear them so often they tend to get dog-eared after a season whether you pay $15 or $150 for them; fad items will go out of style before even the cheapest versions wear out. Buying a fad item at a discount store can also be a low-cost way to experiment with a new color or style—if you discover you hate lime green or feel fat in leggings after all, you're out only a few dollars.

To get the best-looking, best-quality clothes

at discount stores, opt for simple pieces over detailed ones, dark colors over lights, and solids over prints. Go up a size from your normal one (cheap clothes tend to be cut skimpily), and look through several variations of the same item for the one with the best color, sewing, matching of stripes or plaids.

If you're shopping at an outlet store, don't go with just a vague notion of buying something beautiful and cheap: outlets can be exhausting and overwhelming, and it can be too tempting to buy what you don't need. Better to venture out with a few specific items in mind: a spring jacket you can wear with both your black and your beige skirts, for example, plus a white or cream blouse to wear under it.

A note here on deciding which outlet to visit and how to find it: because there's little advertising, you often have to rely on a friend or a friend-of-a-friend for even general locations of stores. If you don't know anybody who knows anything, consult one of the excellent guide-books available on off-price or outlet shopping. Outlet centers or towns often have consumer-relations departments that can give you directions, information on hours and policies, and even maps and pamphlets on the outlets in their area.

If you're heading to one of these outlet centers or towns, start with the store most likely to have what you most need, and once in the store, head directly for that item. At Loehmann's, for example, the blouses are all hung together, as are the evening dresses, the coats, and so on. Other stores have other arrangements—clothes grouped by color, or by season, or by fabric—that are not difficult to figure out. And even the largest outlet stores are usually compact enough that you can take in the entire layout from the entrance.

At an outlet store, you should look more carefully through each rack than you would at a regular retail store. Usually, the cashmere sweaters and silk shirts are not pulled out and highlighted for you; they're wedged in between the tacky acrylics and the bottom-of-the-barrel polyesters. If brand labels are cut out, examine fabric labels and details such as buttons and seams to get an idea of quality. Grab whatever looks good (it helps to have strong arms) and head to the dressing room when you can't hold any more. Most outlets allow more garments in the dressing room per trip than regular retailers do.

You can't be shy in the dressing room. Because some of the clothing will be irregular—with crooked seams or missing buttons—it behooves you to try each piece on carefully, which means removing all your clothes. If you find something you want, it can often be held at the front desk while you continue to shop.

Since it's worthwhile to comb outlet stores carefully for the real finds, concentrate on one store in depth rather than trying to cover a lot of territory. If you're shopping with a friend, the best tack may be to split up either within one store or in two separate outlets rather than to cover the same territory. You can meet, swap information, and perhaps save each other time and mileage.

The most important component of successful shopping in outlets is to keep your eye on the bottom line: try, if you can, to ignore the depth of the discount and concentrate instead on what you're really spending. Try to forget the prestige of the label or the quality of the garment and decide whether it really looks good on you and works for your life and with your wardrobe. And don't buy single pieces, no matter how good the buy, that don't go with anything at all that you own: you may end up spending hundreds of dollars to make an outfit of that $12.99 skirt.

At an off-price store, your primary task is to forget your preconception that everything inside is a bargain just because the sign in the window says so. Forget the "savings" noted on price tags, the signs trumpeting "designer" bargains, and focus on the quality of the piece. If the bottom-line price seems suspiciously high for the quality of the item, don't assume you're overlooking something: you're probably right.

• *Style Analysis* •

DEANIE SHARPE *works part-time with her husband, a photographer in Alexandria, Virginia. Her cotton moon-and-star-embroidered shirt is from Nordstrom's, $20; her cotton knit cardigan, $15, and pants, $25, are from the Fenn, Wright and Manson outlet. Deanie bought her suede shoes at Nordstrom's ("For me those were expensive shoes—$50"); her bat pin was a gift from Urban Outfitters ("I know it cost $10"); her sterling moon-and-star earrings were a present from a friend met in the labor room; her silver bracelet was made by her father; the other bangles were bought at Virginia Beach and Objects by Design, all for about $32 ("When I bought them I thought they were painted wood, but they're plastic").*

WHAT WAS IT LIKE GOING SHOPPING WITH YOUR MOTHER WHEN YOU WERE A KID?

Where I grew up, in Williamsburg, Virginia, there weren't that many places to shop. My mother isn't a cheap person, but what she taught me was that you could get good quality stuff that wasn't necessarily in a department store. Sometimes we would get shirts that looked like Villager shirts, but they weren't. They were just as good, but they were a little bit different. She taught me to go for quality and not just a name.

HOW DOES THAT WORK FOR YOU NOW?

I shop a lot; to get bargains you have to shop a lot. I go to the discount store and the thrift store and I do it often. It's not that I never buy anything in a department store—I sometimes do—but I like to get it on sale.

DO YOU SHOP OFTEN BECAUSE YOU HAVE MORE TIME OR BECAUSE YOU LIKE TO SHOP?

It's a form of exercise. I do have more time, I think that's part of it, and I like comparison shopping, and I like nothing better than to get a really good price.

WHAT ARE SOME OF YOUR FAVORITE PLACES TO SHOP?

I like going to the thrift store. We think there's someone there who just funnels things to me. I've gotten really great things for $1.45. It's like Salvation Army, but it's privately owned and the money isn't going to any good cause. I like going to a discount mall here that's really trashy. Most of the places are really awful but they have a couple of stores that carry high-quality stuff, brands I would buy in a normal store. There's a shop that sells Fenn, Wright and Manson; there's a Calvin Klein outlet; there's a Laura Ashley outlet. At Marshall's, you can pick up Liz Claiborne things. And sometimes I buy real trash if it costs $10.

I buy cheap clothes; I don't buy expensive clothes. I don't usually spend a whole lot on one piece of clothing; I just happen to have bunches of it. In my intellect I know that this is not the right thing to do, that it would make more sense economically to buy classic pieces, but I'm not into classics.

TELL ME ABOUT SOME OF YOUR FAVORITE STUFF, WHERE YOU GOT IT, HOW MUCH IT COSTS, AND WHY YOU LIKE IT.

I have a turquoise jacket that costs $8 and it's 100 percent linen. I got it at the Fenn, Wright and Manson store; it was one of their other labels. The woman in the store, who knows me, said she thought it was a buyers' sample, because they only had one of them. I love that jacket; I don't wear it often because it's a brilliant color, but for $8 it was really wonderful.

I especially like my shoes, my belts, and my jewelry, more than pieces of clothing. It's hard to pick favorites, because I have so many. Nordstrom's opened up here, and it's shoe heaven, shoes on every floor. One week I bought three pairs of shoes, and three weeks later I bought three more pairs of shoes. I got little plaid shoes with great big black bows and I got beautiful dark green suede flats—I only wear flats—with three little black satin rosettes. I got a pair of black shoes that lace up with black grosgrain ribbons; I call them my nun shoes.

I have a whole bunch of jewelry; none of it fine jewelry. We're not into that, although I wanted a tennis bracelet, which everybody said was totally not me, but I wanted the diamonds. I have a number of silver cuff bracelets that my father made for me that I wear a lot—my father was a master silversmith. I have a lot of pins, most of them that my husband got me, and they have no common thread except that they're whimsical. Most of them are things people have made as opposed to things you could buy in a department store. I also like to make my own pins—I made some from precut mirrors from the dime store with glitter on them and then I make some from ceramics.

AT WHAT POINT DID YOUR STYLE BECOME WHAT IT IS NOW?

Not until after my son was born, which was ten years ago. Before that, I didn't spend money on clothes because we didn't have it. And before that, I was a hippie. There are a lot of things in my personality I don't like to admit, because intellectually I don't want to be that way, but I do sort of follow fads. It's not like I see something in a magazine, go out and replicate that outfit: I think that's really awful. But if they say it's short skirts, I'm going to wear a short skirt.

About five years ago I really started honing down the style that I have now. If there was one word that I would use to describe my feeling about dressing it would be "whimsical." To me, dressing is not a serious thing. I don't take it seriously, like people who are really into fashion. I'm into stuff.

HOW MUCH STUFF DO YOU HAVE THAT YOU WEAR WITH REGULARITY?

Lots, because my mood changes and I change my clothes at least once a day. I buy a lot of stuff and there will be things there that I won't wear for a year and then I'll start wearing them, but I'll buy them just because I like them. I buy when the impulse hits and figure that if I like it I'll end up wearing it eventually.

HOW DO YOUR CLOTHES COMPARE TO THOSE OF THE OTHER WOMEN IN ALEXANDRIA, VIRGINIA?

They think I'm weird. I don't dress like anybody I see here. I don't want to look like I'm wearing a costume, which I have been accused of by some really buttoned-down people, but I don't want to go to Talbot's and buy my clothes just so I'll look like everybody else in Old Town.

I try to fit in with the people we work with, not the people around me. We have lots of friends who are artists and musicians, and the way I dress is much more the way they dress. But if I'm taking my son Oliver to a soccer game or going to the grocery store or going to school on Back to School Night, I always stand out.

DO YOU HAVE ANY PERSONAL RULES FOR DRESSING?

Lots of them. I'm a very dogmatic person and I have very strict rules that other people don't know exist. My biggest thing is I can't handle white shoes. When there's a warm snap in February and people pull out their white shoes, that just makes me crazy. After Labor Day, you don't wear them, that's it. Another rule is, When in doubt, wear black pants. There's no place you can't wear black pants: you can wear them to a wedding or a funeral or to work or to a dinner dance.

WHERE DO YOU KEEP ALL YOUR CLOTHES?

We have a big walk-in closet where I keep seasonal things. When it's not the season, Oliver has two closets in his room and I have trunks in the storeroom. I go through those trunks regularly. There's always a kind of shifting. When I go to the thrift store, I donate a box of clothes and I buy a box, so there's always this ebbing and flowing.

HOW DO YOU DECIDE WHEN IT'S TIME TO RECYCLE SOMETHING?

I've heard that if you haven't worn something in three years you should give it away, but I just pulled out a jacket that I bought nine years ago and never wore, but I know I'll wear it this winter. I kept it, because I liked it. It really depends on when I stop liking it.

IS THERE ANYTHING ABOUT YOUR FIGURE YOU WORK AROUND?

I am five feet four inches tall and I have big thighs. I tend to buy things that are too big for me, and to dress like I'm pregnant a lot to hide my thighs. I'm very, very self-conscious about that, even though I've been told—especially by my husband for eighteen years—that it's all in my head. I go into a store and ask for a large and they say, "You don't need a large." Also, I have a large bust. I'd do anything, I'd even keep the thighs, if I could get rid of the bust. It gets in the way when you're dressing. It tends to make you look dumpy.

ARE YOU CONSCIOUS WHEN YOU TRY SOMETHING ON OF WHETHER IT MAKES YOUR THIGHS LOOK THINNER, YOUR BUST SMALLER?

It's not whether something makes the thighs look thinner as if you can't see the rolls. It's a more pessimistic view. I won't wear something that's tight. The idea of these women who wear tight tight tight blue jeans, that's just unnatural. I like to be comfortable.

The first most important thing to me when I shop is color; the second most important thing is comfort. My best color is blue, because I have blue eyes. My other best color is pink, so you look in my closet and everything is black, gray, white, blue, and pink. I can remember all the way back to high school knowing that when I wore these colors I felt good and I looked good. Every once in a while I will be the obvious fashion victim and buy something in a fashionable color, but I don't end up wearing it as much.

DO YOU HAVE ANY IDEA HOW MUCH YOU SPEND IN A YEAR ON CLOTHES?

A lot, and I know that sounds like a contradiction. We're talkin' a few hundred dollars a month. I bought a black leather jacket the other day and I broke out in a cold sweat. It was the most expensive thing I've ever bought: $325.

WHAT'S YOUR HOUSE LIKE?

My house is just like everything else: it's real eclectic. We have antiques and we have modern. I'm into fish right now. I've got fish plates coming out the wazoo. At Halloween I bought a fish mask. But fish are getting chic now so I'm afraid I'll have to give them up.

Vintage Clothing/Thrift Stores

How to Shop for the Best of What's Old

You love bargains. You love quality. You love distinctive clothes. Even if you hate anything retro, even if you've always turned up your nose at secondhand clothes, vintage clothing or thrift stores may be worth exploring on your next shopping trip.

Vintage clothing stores are the tonier half of this category. Often, they're set up like sophisticated boutiques, offering the most interesting styles of old clothing and accessories. The owners of these shops usually have a passion for vintage clothing and an educated eye, which is passed on to you in the form of a well-edited group of merchandise as well as higher prices.

There are really two distinct groups of vintage clothing stores: antique clothing shops and funkier, more freewheeling vintage stores. Antique clothing stores offer true prizes from the past—beaded flapper dresses and Victorian wedding gowns and estate jewelry—in perfect condition and at top prices. But while prices are often comparable to those for new clothing, they're much less than for new clothing of comparable quality: a 1920s beaded silk chiffon dress, for instance, may cost only a quarter of what a new beaded silk chiffon dress would.

Vintage clothing stores are more concerned with style and fun than with clothes in perfect condition or an impeccable pedigree. In fact, some of the old clothes at vintage stores aren't old at all: they're new versions of popular vintage styles such as Hawaiian shirts or letter sweaters. At vintage clothing stores, you can find everything from real fifties prom dresses that have never been worn to original army coats to torn and faded jeans warehoused since the designer-jean craze of the early seventies.

Thrift stores, on the other hand, make no pretentions to style or quality: they're simply places that sell—usually for charity—anything that anybody gives them. Thrift stores offer the ultimate shopping adventure and the ultimate payoff: if you know your stuff and paw assiduously through the racks, you can come up with a Ralph Lauren cashmere sweater for a dollar or a Harris tweed sport coat for $2.25, the same stuff that you'll see at the antique or vintage clothing store down the block for twenty times the price. (Where do you think vintage store owners shop?)

If you've never shopped at a vintage clothing shop, don't reject them out of hand: you can find pieces there that work perfectly well with a modern wardrobe. But you also have to have a good eye: you don't want to walk out looking like a picture of your mother in 1949. Head-to-toe vintage "costumes" have been out for years; mixing a few interesting old pieces with your new clothes can be a sensible way to dress and shop.

At thrift stores, you can find items that no one would ever guess were old, never mind that they cost a quarter, but it takes a lot more work and a much keener eye. They can be great fun, however, as well as an educational experience—and if you buy something that's a mistake, you're out only a few bucks. The best thrift stores are those in out-of-the-way places—the Salvation Army in Fremont, Nebraska, say, or the church auxiliary in Tunkhannock, Pennsylvania—where the local fashionable people wouldn't dream of shopping. Thrift stores in bigger and trendier cities have usually been picked through by those in the know, who snap up all the "good" stuff the minute it hits the racks.

Any vintage or thrift store shopping has to be approached from the viewpoint of fun: you're not going to buy your winter wardrobe or to complete an outfit, but you might chance on one wonderful something that will make you feel great whenever you wear it—and remember how little you spent for it. Because the nature of the clothing and the stores themselves differ so markedly from any kind of store selling new clothing, your shopping strategy has to be different, too. Some tips:

Men's Clothes Are Better—At thrift stores or flea markets, skip right past the women's clothes—which tend toward polyester pants suits and leatherette peacoats—to the men's clothes, which are apt to be older (men hang onto stuff longer), more classic or appealingly funky, and better quality. Usually findable at even the dinkiest, dorkiest out-of-the-way place, for under $5: boxy Harris tweed sport coats; fifties khaki raincoats; bathrobes (gaudy Liberace style or classic shawl-collar flannels à la Ralph Lauren); slouchy cardigans straight from "Father Knows Best."

Buy Quality—Educate yourself on sniffing out top quality as well as spotting poor quality. Always look at labels—for words like "handmade" or "hand-woven," for designer or brand names, for fabric content (cashmere, alpaca, silk you want; acrylic from the infancy of its development you don't). Check to see how seams are finished, how hems are sewn, how linings are made—all clues to quality, value, durability.

Check for Trouble—Always examine fabrics closely for moth holes, small tears, wear at the collar or cuffs, and pulling or shredding at the seams or in the lining. Check buttons and buttonholes. Look for stains, especially on cuffs and lapels. Instead of assuming the garment is perfect, as you would when buying something new, assume it's not—and then decide, depending on price and how often you'll wear it, whether you can live with its flaws.

Know What You Can Fix/What You Can't—Don't expect to wash or dry-clean stains out of vintage clothing. If the stains haven't come out in the cleaning process most stores put their merchandise through, chances are they're in for life. On the other hand, don't reject something you love just because it's got a defect. Buttons can be replaced, pockets can be relined, beads can be resewn.

Reconsider Fit—When buying vintage clothing, try everything on. Size standards have changed throughout the years, so you can't count on wearing a size 8 in a 1940s dress, even if you always wear a size 8 in modern clothes. If you love something that doesn't fit quite right, consider alterations—they may cost more than the item itself, but can make a thrift store special look like an expensive hand-tailored prize.

Reconsider Price—You have to readjust the way you think about prices at most vintage clothing stores. At expensive, top-quality ones, don't compare value to other used clothing but to what a similar piece would cost new. While $150 might seem steep for a fifty-year-old evening dress, for example, consider that you couldn't buy anything like it new—bias cut, hand-seamed, made of real silk (not polyester, not cotton) velvet—for less than triple that price. And at thrift stores, beware of lowering your price standards too far: when most things cost a quarter, $5 can start to seem outrageous. Remind yourself that that's the price of a package of chicken legs, and let yourself splurge on something just for fun.

Mail-Order Shopping

If the advantages of mail-order shopping are obvious (ease, convenience, often lower prices), so are the disadvantages: ugly surprises that look nothing like the glowing pictures in the catalog.

But as other kinds of shopping have become more sophisticated, so has mail order, and some new catalogs offer levels of style and quality and price not found in most stores.

Two catalogs of note:

Tweeds, featuring classics in natural fabrics with real style, with almost nothing, including coats and jackets, priced over $100. Women's sizes tend to run small; unisex sizes run large. For a free catalog, call 1-800-999-7997, extension C3CB, or write Tweeds, Avery Row, Roanoke, VA 24012-9967.

J. Crew is a tad preppier and more casual than Tweeds, but again, the clothes are well made, wearable, have real style at realistic prices. Wonderful shoes and accessories. For a catalog, call 1-800-782-8244, or write J. Crew, One Ivy Crescent, Lynchburg, VA 24506-9977.

EMOTIONAL ISSUE:

SHOPPING IS HELL

You're invited to lunch with your boss's boss. Tomorrow. You could wear your standby navy blue knit dress, or the suit you wore for your speech last year, but you'd rather find something new, special, wonderful. The problem is that finding something new means going shopping: putting up with the crowds and the salespeople and the overwhelming choices. And spending a zillion dollars. And maybe buying the wrong thing anyway. All things considered, you'll go to the lunch in your navy blue dress.

One interesting thing about women who hate to shop is that they really despise it. The other interesting thing is that most of them have no desire to change. Hating to shop, they say, is a perfectly rational response to something that, in their view, wastes time, drains money, is exhausting, and doesn't offer a very big reward for your efforts.

"I approach shopping with a real loathing," says Molly Friedrich, a New York literary agent, "because I shop in ignorance. I have come to realize that I shop extremely badly. I look for the wrong thing and I inevitably make a purchase that is too expensive and not necessarily becoming. I in fact have not shopped for years except for bathing suits—I have a passion for bathing suits and I look really good in them so I have about fourteen."

"I've always liked other kinds of shopping—food shopping, drugstores—because it always seems so much more successful and you don't have to try anything on," says a Chicago woman. "But I don't get that kind of thrill out of clothes shopping ever, even when I buy something I like. It was so comforting in college when I could toss around that Thoreau quote about not trusting any event that required new clothes."

What exactly is so terrible about shopping? Women who hate to shop have many grievances:

"When I was younger I didn't trust my own taste. Now I do, but even though I have more confidence I'm threatened by the changes in fashion—do I have to get it and how many," says one woman. "It's such a nuisance taking off all your clothes and then whatever you try on never fits. And the mirrors and the lights in the dressing room conspire against you."

"I hate department stores because I'm always hot and lugging stuff and the dressing room feels too small," says Barbara Kasman, who owns a New York public relations firm. "Part of it has to do with doing it for so many years that it gets repetitious. When I was younger I could try on a Chiquita Banana outfit and say, That isn't me but it was fun. Now I've gotten so selective, I know what I like and what flatters me, and that experimental quality is missing. And I can't stand paying the prices, spending $300 or $400 on something that's just okay."

"Physically I don't feel like I have a great body and so I'm always looking for whatever's slenderizing or at least what makes me look less fat," says a Baltimore teacher. "But it's never recreation, it's always a chore, and it's exhausting."

Underneath all those practical objections is often a more philosophical distaste of shopping for clothes: "I think I've acquired this profound passivity in this one area of my life because when the notion of style comes to mind it's often accompanied by substance, and I guess I believe that there's something potentially shallow in caring about style too much," says Molly Friedrich.

The fact remains: women need to wear clothes, and clothes can normally be acquired only by shopping. How do women who hate to shop cope with the fact that they have to?

Well, some of them find ways not to have to. Friedrich, for instance, has three people—a cousin, a friend, and her husband—who buy clothes for her. "My job for the people who shop for me is to supply a reasonably in-shape body for the clothes," she says. "It's worked out very well. It's kept me very trim, a steady size 8, and they're thrilled that they're marrying me up, so to speak, in terms of style."

Other women who don't have such accommodating loved ones sometimes turn to professionals. Department store personal shoppers and image consultants say many of their clients are women who hate to shop but have to look good. Michael Solomon, a consumer psychologist and chair of the marketing department at Rutgers, calls these experts "surrogate consumers." Surrogate consumers for clothes have become popular, says Solomon, because many women don't have time to shop; they're under pressure to "project the right image" but may not feel confident about making the best choices, and "people don't like to put themselves in situations they're bad at."

However, not everyone who hates to shop thinks she's bad at it. To combat her dread of stores, for instance, one woman says she's become a hyper-competent shopper. "I try to do it in what would be dead time—running into a store on my way home from work or on my lunch hour so shopping doesn't intrude on my time with my kids or with my job. I tend to prefer low-service stores, because high-service means someone who's eighteen or like my mother is following me around. I never see shopping as something to do with a friend or, God forbid, my family."

Barbara Kasman says she tried to get around the horrors of shopping by ordering clothes from catalogs, "but it just didn't work." "Now I go shopping at the beginning of the season when my wardrobe needs help; I get one or two outfits and that's it, I don't go anymore. But I don't mind shopping if I'm on vacation or if I just happen to see something, like in the window of a store next to the restaurant where I'm having dinner."

Women who hate shopping because they feel they're bad at it often avoid the experience altogether until they're forced into the store by circumstances—the night before a 9 A.M. job interview, for instance, or the morning of an afternoon wedding. "I call it crisis shopping," says a Washington, D.C., attorney. "The only thing that gets me into the store and out of my clothes in a dressing room is this metaphorical gun to my head. The problem with doing that is I have all these things in my closet I bought under duress and never want to look at again."

Other women sidestep the trauma by finding one store and one type of clothing they like, and then replenishing their stock as opposed to actual shopping. This self-imposed narrowing of one's options can make shopping, if not more pleasant, at least simpler. "Shoes are okay because I can just repeat the styles," says one woman. "And socks. Now there's something that's actually fun to buy."

Nine Secrets of Low-Stress Shopping

If you're one of those women who glide calmly around stores, having the best time of your life, you don't need these tips. If you're one of those women who look with envy at the women gliding calmly around the stores, you do. In lieu of a Valium, try the following stay-calm techniques:

1. **SHOP FIRST THING IN THE MORNING**—The stores tend to be least crowded, the salespeople are in the best mood, and you are less likely to have a sense of being rushed.

2. **AVOID PRIME LUNCH HOUR**—Noon to two is murder in most stores. If you must shop on your lunch hour, try to make it at eleven or after two, when you won't have to contend with as much chaos.

3. **STICK TO ONE STORE, EVEN ONE DEPARTMENT**—Especially if you tend to get overwhelmed by choices, choose a store where you know you like the clothes and, if it's big, limit yourself to one section of that store. This is as much as most personal shoppers will tackle in a shopping trip, so there's no reason to feel you have to push further.

4. **SHOP FOR ONLY ONE DIFFICULT ITEM PER SHOPPING TRIP**—What's difficult will vary from person to person, but almost-universally traumatic and hard to find are a bathing suit, a good pair of shoes, and jeans. If you find one version of any of the above that you like, that fits, and that you can afford in a single shopping trip, you can consider that trip a success. And if you can swing it, buy two.

5. **DON'T SHOP ON BIG SALE DAYS**—Crowds and mass hysteria can be overwhelming, and actual discounts can be overblown. Sometimes, the things that are on sale on Columbus Day are still on sale October 13, when it's saner to shop.

6. **DON'T SHOP WHEN YOU'RE BROKE**—You may feel shopping will give you the lift you need when the mortgage is due, the washing machine just broke down, and the dentist's bill arrives, but spending when you can't really afford it—while it may give you a short-term boost—only adds stress in the long run.

7. **DON'T SHOP WHEN YOU FEEL FAT OR DEPRESSED**—Again, buying a new hat was never really the solution for anyone's woes.

8. **SHOP ALONE**—Don't take your husband. Don't, God forbid, take the kids. And probably don't even take your best friend. You'll be able to get the job done and get out much more efficiently and peacefully if you're alone.

9. **TAKE BREAKS**—Every two hours or so, leave the shopping arena, get off your feet, have a club soda, and read a mystery novel. If your rest doesn't give you the jump-start you need to get back out there, go home.

EMOTIONAL ISSUE:
SHOPPING IS HEAVEN

You have a free day in front of you, or even a few free hours, and there's no question what you're going to do. You're going to go shopping. Shopping is more than productive, it's FUN: you like the people and the windows and the smell of the stores and the vast array of clothes. You like to choose and try on and if you buy, that's great, and if you don't, that's great too. The pleasure is in the process.

One thing women who love to shop have in common is that they love clothes. But it goes further than that: most also think clothes are a worthwhile way to spend money and have confidence in their ability to make the right choices. They like their bodies and the way they look in clothes. And just as women who hate to shop can't fathom why anyone would like it, women who love to shop can't understand why anyone considers it less than a thrill.

"I don't know how people don't get fun out of shopping," says image consultant Joyce Grillo, who likes shopping so much she's made it her career. "I love window shopping, browsing, the whole feeling of being in stores, I love trying things on and the creativity of putting things together. It's like being a little girl playing dress up."

Loving to shop and loving clothes is often a lifelong state of mind. "Both my parents loved to shop," says Grillo, "but my father was the one who was really into fashion and he's probably why I am the way I am. He's the type who checks everything out from head to toe: your hem has to be straight, your shoes polished, everything ironed. I went to Catholic school so I had to wear uniforms until I was twelve or thirteen. I never really had any clothes so when I started as a teenager I said, 'Wow!'"

"I come from a family that put a lot of stock in clothes," says Randi Cone, co-owner of Schecter/Cone Communications, a New York and Los Angeles public relations firm specializing in the entertainment industry. "There were three girls in the family so clothes were something that we talked about a lot when I was growing up. Our mother made all our clothes—she's very unpretentious and could care less about designers, but she liked looking good."

For Cone and many other women who love shopping, looking good is the real payoff. "I have a good sense of style," says Cone. "I've always known what looks good on me, what looks best on my body. I'm sort of dramatic looking and I like making a statement; I guess I like people looking at me and saying, 'She looks good.'"

And like other women who love to shop, Cone is confident about her ability not only to choose clothes that make her look her best but to buy them at the right price. "Because I'm a real good shopper I probably get more for my money than other people," Cone says. "I love a great bargain, but I'll wait until I see something that's right for me instead of buying junk. And I'll buy something that's right for me even when I have no occasion to wear it."

Cone's sort of shopping confidence is key to what makes some people love to shop. "When people feel confident in their ability to be discerning, to know what's good, they enjoy exhibiting their prowess," says consumer psychologist Michael Solomon.

Some people who love to shop are what market researchers call "recreational shoppers," says Solomon. "For these people, shopping is a social and recreational activity, whether they get what they came for or not." Recreational shoppers are the target group for many retailers, producing a sort of chicken-and-egg effect, with recreational shoppers gravitating to stores that make shopping fun, and stores working hard to earn that distinction. "For someone to shop in Bloomingdale's they have to be a recreational shopper," says Solomon. "Shopping in a place like Bloomingdale's is a treasure hunt. You really have to be dedicated to searching out the alleys and byways, and you have to like it."

But other women who love to shop nonetheless hate the noise and confusion of big stores. Especially as women get older, as they have less time to shop and a more clearly defined sense of their own style, they tend to confine their shopping trips to a few favorite places.

Writer Jo Brans has whittled her selection down as far as it can go: "I've sold my soul to a designer," she says. Since moving to New York from Dallas four years ago, Brans shops almost exclusively at the Kenzo boutique on Madison Avenue, and usually wears only that designer's clothes.

It was a mania for discount shopping back in Texas that originally led Brans to Kenzo. "I bought Kenzo first as a dilettante eight or ten years ago when I found these things that were reduced to 25 percent of their original price," she says. "A big new Loehmann's had opened in Dallas that was very luxurious. Whenever I felt the least bit deprived or had an afternoon to kill I would go there and walk around. For me it was the equivalent of what a walk through a museum is for someone else."

While Brans spends significantly more per item at Kenzo than she did at Loehmann's, she says she doesn't spend more money on clothes overall. And, because Kenzo's clothes fit her well and she knows she'll wear them again and again, "even if something costs a lot of money I feel like I'm putting it in the bank, which makes my Puritan blood flow more comfortably."

Women who love to shop say they do everything they can to ensure their shopping trips are good ones. Cone, for instance, doesn't buy anything she can't return, and Brans doesn't shop when she's gained a few pounds or when she needs a specific item she might not be able to find. Another spirit-sustaining trick of Brans's: "I like to get a little dressed up when I go shopping," she says. "I know clothes will look better when I put them on if my hair looks okay and I'm wearing makeup, if I'm wearing hose and comfortable, dressy-looking shoes. If I look my best in the store, then it's not a totally disheartening experience if I don't find what I like."

Control—over how you shop and what you buy as well as over what you don't buy—is at the heart of what makes shopping enjoyable for many women. "I truly feel more accomplished at this point if I don't buy anything," says Randi Cone. "I like going to stores out of curiosity: I like seeing what people are wearing and what's out there and what things cost. Because I know I would always be buying something if I let loose, I feel proud when I can control myself."

"I don't want any bad shopping experiences, because that's one of the things in your life that you can control," says Jo Brans. "There are so many things you can't control—you don't know when your cat will have an inoperable tumor—but you can control your wardrobe, your relationship to your wardrobe, and the way you go about acquiring your wardrobe."

No-Time-to-Shop Shopping Strategies

How you feel about shopping and spending may be beside the point when the overwhelming issue is time. For women with hectic lives, finding the time to shop for clothes may be near impossible; saving time may be the prime determinant of where and how they shop, what they buy.

"When I was a single working woman in my twenties, I'd go to Filene's basement every other day," says a Boston mother of two who now works part-time from home. "I was real thin then and everything looked good on me. I was going to an office every day so I had lots of reasons to wear clothes; I wasn't married so I wanted to look really good all the time, and I had money and time to spend on myself. Now, when I have a babysitter I feel like I should be working or at least exercising. I only shop when I need something specific; I don't have time to haunt the stores or keep track of what's going on sale."

Another working mother says, "I've learned the art of always doing two things at once, so I never go shopping as an excursion unto itself. I'll stop in a store on the way back from lunch, or on the way to the train, or while I'm out buying a kid's birthday present. Actually, I buy a lot of my own clothes while I'm Christmas shopping for everyone else—I'm in the stores then anyway, and the women's clothing departments tend not to be crowded despite the general crush. The trick is never taking off all your clothes in the fitting room, and buying something you like right away."

Having a family isn't the only factor that causes a time crunch: a revved-up career can also make it more difficult to find time to shop. "When I was working in a salon I was near the stores all the time, and when I first started to free-lance I didn't work every day," says Linda Nicholas, a hair and makeup artist. "I used to love to shop but now I don't enjoy it that much, and time is a big factor. I work all the time; when I'm not working I'm tired, and I don't go shopping unless I need something."

Nicholas's solution to the time issue: she uses visits from her mother and sister as an excuse for marathon shopping sprees. "That's what they want to do when they come to New York, so we do all the stores—Ann Taylor, Bendel's, Macy's, Barneys—in a touristy way," she says. When she's on her own and needs a specific item, Nicholas shops at whatever store is most convenient and chooses quiet shopping times—dinner hour on Friday night, for instance, or noon on Sunday.

Stores are cognizant of the fact that women today have less time to shop, and many are trying to make shopping more efficient. Says Michael Solomon, Ph.D., chair of the marketing department at Rutgers, "The big marketing story today is working women who don't have time to shop."

Carson Pirie Scott in Chicago has been a leader in catering to time-pressured women with its Corporate Level. Open from 7:30 A.M. to 7:30 P.M., Corporate Level includes not only clothes but a post office, dry cleaner, shoe repair shop, deli, and gourmet supermarket. And for a $75 membership fee, a Corporate Level image consultant will visit a woman's home twice a year, analyze her closet, determine her clothing needs, and pull together coordinating pieces from Carson's clothing selection.

"It saves women time as well as money," says Janice Locascio, a Corporate Level image consultant. "We gather things for her to try on, do the alterations within twenty-four hours and deliver everything to her office."

Bergdorf Goodman's personal shopper Elaine Mack also says that one of the prime appeals of her service is saving time. "When a woman comes up here she may spend half a day trying things on, but she only has to do that twice a year," says Mack. "In one day of shopping she can buy everything she needs for the entire year."

As with most other personal shoppers at department stores, there is no charge for Mack's services and no minimum budget requirement. A personal shopper at a store will typically interview you about your life and your clothing tastes and needs, and will work around favorite pieces you take into the store, although most won't visit your home or weed through your closet. While many major department stores in cities across the country now employ personal shoppers, it may be possible to work with one even if you live in a far-flung region: Mack says she has clients she's never met who she works with entirely by mail.

Private fashion consultants charge anywhere from $50 to $200 an hour for their services. Why pay for what a store provides free? For one thing, with a private consultant you're not chained to any one store or even necessarily to buying retail, as some private consultants work directly through designers. Also, many private consultants will help you organize and work with the wardrobe you already have.

Wardrobe consultants and personal shoppers can save you the time of hunting down the right departments, the right styles, the right sizes, and the best buys. Because haunting the stores (or one particular store) is their business, they ideally know just where to find the best items. "There are lots of clothes in the store I call foolers," says Mack, "that aren't expensive but look expensive. You have to be very fashion-knowledgeable to pick those out on your own; you have to spend a lot of time searching the stores."

What if you can't or don't want to visit a fashion consultant? How can you save time and shop most efficiently?

Using catalogs is an ever-increasing solution for some women, although many say they've been disappointed when buying work or dressy clothes by mail. However, catalogs from stores or mail-order houses can be a time-efficient source for staples like hosiery, underwear, pajamas, basic sweaters, T-shirts and turtlenecks.

Buying in multiples, from a catalog or a store, is another time-saving trick worth consideration. This makes sense especially with basic items that can be hard to fit, such as bras and shoes. "What's really time-consuming about shopping is finding something you love that fits, at the right price," says one woman. "If I find something that I like that looks good on me I'll buy two or three at a time. That saves a lot of time shopping because when I need to replace a favorite item it's already in my closet and I don't have to go out on another lengthy search."

Making a detailed list of what you need is one obvious but often-overlooked solution, say shopping experts. Taking the time to go through your closet, jotting down what's missing as well as brands of clothes you like and sizes that fit can save you time once you get to the store.

Having a shopping plan—a priority list of what you want as well as where you'll look for it—can also save time by keeping you focused, says personal shopper Vicki French Morris. Morris also advises keeping your energy up by checking your coat, relying on the salesperson to ferry sizes and styles to and from the fitting room, stopping for snacks, and having packages delivered.

Another time-saving measure can be visiting only stores and departments you know and like and buying brands that have been successful for you in the past. "Being a fast and efficient shopper comes from knowing the designers and knowing that most designers season after season are pretty true to form," says Los Angeles image consultant Andrea Sells. "It becomes very easy then to go right through the rack and know which pieces will fit into your wardrobe and suit your body type."

While some women say one visit to a trustworthy color or fashion consultant has made their shopping excursions easier and faster, other women have found the solution in streamlining their wardrobes themselves. "When everything you buy is black knit," says one woman, "it doesn't take much time to go through a store."

Not having time to shop doesn't have to be a negative for your wardrobe, either. One Connecticut executive, who works ten-hour days, has a three-hour round-trip commute, and is on the road one week out of four, says being pressured for time has actually improved her clothing choices. "I used to be such a consummate bargain hunter that I would waste a lot of time looking for something cheaper and then find it difficult to buy anything at all," she says. "Now I actually wait until the night before a trip, one hour before the stores close, and find the time pressure a great motivator in getting myself to buy clothes. I'll know, for instance, that I need a raincoat in a neutral color with a warm lining for Germany that zips out for Italy, and I need it right away. If I ever find myself with more time to shop, I don't know what I'll do."

Eight Ways to Shop Faster

Almost no one has time to shop anymore. But if you really don't have time—if you have to buy a black cocktail dress and you have to do it in the next forty-five minutes—try these fast-forward techniques:

1. **GO DIRECTLY TO THE SHOP OR DEPARTMENT YOU LIKE BEST**—Do not pass the lingerie. Do not collect a supply of stockings for the next millennium. Head right for a place you know, a place you know you like, and don't even look at anything else.

2. **MAKE ONE FAST SWING THROUGH THE AISLES**—The point here is to get the lay of the land, not to look at price tags, not to examine buttons. If something jumps out at you, grab it, but keep on moving until you've given everything available the once-over.

3. **SNAG A SALESPERSON IF YOU KNOW THEM TO BE HELPFUL**—Say something like: "I need to find a black cocktail dress and I've only got a few minutes. It's got to be short, not low-cut, and I'm partial to velvet. I'm also open to navy blue." She can hold whatever you grab, ferry sizes to the fitting room, and maybe—it's a miracle!—find something you've overlooked.

4. **TAKE A SECOND, MORE DETAILED LOOK**—Stop and examine what's on racks you've pinpointed as possibilities in your first swing-through. Grab what you want. Hand them to the salesperson, and head into the dressing room.

5. **DON'T TAKE OFF YOUR CLOTHES IN THE FITTING ROOM**—Basic try-ons can be accomplished without wiggling out of your pantyhose and unbuttoning your blouse. You can pull on skirts and pants right under the skirt you're wearing; you can throw on a sweater or even the right dress over your blouse. Stay organized, putting the don't-fits on one rack and the might-fits on another. If there's something in there you may actually want to buy, then you can take off your clothes.

6. **AS SOON AS YOU KNOW YOU'RE GOING TO BUY SOMETHING, GET THE SALESPERSON STARTED ON RINGING IT UP**—There's nothing more infuriating than actually finding what you want in twenty minutes only to wait another half hour to fork over your money. Attempt to short-circuit this process by handing the salesperson the item and your credit card while you're still in the fitting room.

7. **IF YOU REALLY DO NEED TO BUY A DRESS IN FORTY-FIVE MINUTES, DON'T GET HUNG UP ON PERFECTION**—You may have to settle for a different

collar, a longer hemline, or a higher price than you had in mind. What can I say—those are the breaks when you wait until the last minute. Best to settle and get on with your life.

8. **IF NOTHING'S WORKING, CUT YOUR LOSSES**—Don't look one more time; you'll be frustrated. Don't buy something else to comfort yourself; you'll be disappointed. Use what time is left over to sprint to another store or department, rethink what you've got in your wardrobe, or call a friend with a well-stocked closet.

Eight Things Never to Wear Shopping

What you wear into the store has a lot to do with how comfortable, efficient, and satisfied you'll be with your shopping trip. Think walking shoes, clothes you can move in and get on and off easily. And if you've got any control over the matter at all (meaning if you're not dashing out on your lunch hour), never, ever wear any of the following when shopping:

1. **HIGH HEELS**—Unless you're one of those supernatural women who is actually comfortable hiking a mile in heels, these will kill your feet as well as your enthusiasm.

2. **RUNNING SHOES**—The problem here is that you've got to untie and tie them up again whenever you try something on—not a huge hurdle, but comfortable slip-ons (and offs) make more sense.

3. **A HEAVY COAT**—In winter, they seem to heat stores as if the shoppers were wearing bikinis—tiring and debilitating if you're lugging around ten pounds of down or wool. In the city, of course, you may have no choice, although many big stores have tucked-in-a-corner checkrooms and many boutiques will let you check your coat along with your shopping bags. At a mall, however, or any place you can park near the store, lock your coat in the trunk and run like hell inside.

4. **AN UMBRELLA**—Same issue as above, minus the heat; same solution.

5. **LOTS OF LAYERS**—Having to peel off a cardigan and a pullover and T-shirt and leggings and a skirt, however chic the look, can be daunting and exhausting. Aim for as few and as uncomplicated layers as possible.

6. **LOTS OF ZIPPERS, BUTTONS, BELTS**—Again, same problem as above. It's bad enough to take off all your clothes in the middle of the day in a strange place—why make it even harder on yourself? Elastic-waist pants and a loose-necked sweater and/or T-shirt are ideal.

7. **SOMETHING THAT DOESN'T GO WITH ANYTHING ELSE YOU OWN**—This is antithetical to the concept of building a wardrobe: if you wear the oddball outfit, you'll tend not to be tuned in to items that are consistent in style and color to most of what you have in your closet. And you'll be more likely to make mistakes.

8. **ANYTHING YOU HATE**—It may be comfortable, it may not have zippers or buttons, it may be lightweight, but wearing something you hate will cut into your confidence and may make you feel less good about what you try on. Worse, it can intensify that "I hate all my clothes" feeling and lead you to buy more than you really want or need.

EMOTIONAL ISSUE:

"TRY IT ON, HONEY,
JUST FOR SIZE"

You love to shop. Or you hate to shop. You're drawn inexorably to bargains. Or you shop to give yourself a lift. Or you have trouble buying clothes at all.

Whatever your attitudes toward shopping and clothes, chances are your mother is behind them. Most women either mirror their mothers' manner of shopping for and wearing clothes, or, more rarely, rebel by going in the opposite direction.

Why is mom such a powerful influence? "Shopping is a very private mother-daughter activity," says Ellen Berman, M.D., clinical associate professor of psychiatry at the University of Pennsylvania and co-director of the Women's Center at the Philadelphia Psychiatric Center. "Issues of intimacy and love and jealousy and anger and identification get played out around clothes and shopping."

The reason this link is specifically a mother-daughter one is because there are myriad options for what little girls can wear, and "choices have a lot of symbolic meaning," says Berman. "With a young child the issue is, Does the child have any autonomy. When the child gets older the question is, What does the mother say—We're too poor, you can't be sexual. The mother may have a tremendous interest in having the daughter be pretty, while in adolescence there may be tremendous rage over a daughter dressing in a sexual way."

Whatever the background issues, mother's early influence is often the most powerful motivator in how and why and for what grown-up women shop and spend.

"My mother used to take me to the Art Institute, then we would go to Marshall Field's for lunch or tea and then we would shop, which was very casual, not belabored, no fuss," says Maria Friedrich, an art adviser to private collectors. "As a result I shop the same way. I'm a very spontaneous shopper, I'm constantly snooping; if I'm in the city on business I'll spend a half hour looking in shops, but I don't do it in any laborious way."

"I'm very much a shopping spree kind of person, and this is related to my mother and how she shopped," says a Los Angeles film editor. "My mother was a screenwriter and when she sold a screenplay or a book she would celebrate by buying something extravagant. Whenever I get a job I buy something extravagant with my first paycheck, although my standards for extravagance are much looser than my mother's."

Even when women grew up unhappy with their mothers' ways of shopping and dressing, many say they find it impossible to strike out on different paths. "My mother was a compulsive bargain hunter," says one woman, "and I remember so clearly standing at the sale racks with her while she looked at the price tags first, and if something was marked down far enough she would insist I try it on. One of my most humiliating memories is the summer I was forced to wear this hideous gray bathing suit simply because it was originally $80 marked down to something like $5. For a brief period of my adolescence I went in the other direction and spent all my baby-sitting money on expensive clothes, which my mother teased me about and criticized me for. But now that I'm older I find myself doing the same thing she did, standing at the sale rack looking at price tags, sometimes buying the current equivalents of that gray bathing suit and not being able to stop myself even though I'm very aware of what I'm doing."

Molly Friedrich, a New York literary agent who hates to shop, relying on friends to buy all her clothes, says, "When I think back about shopping and clothes I realize what's led me to this ludicrous passivity is the way I was brought up. From the very beginning I was always raised to realize that we were not like everyone else—we lived in an old house in the midst of this little development; my father was a writer and not a businessman; we didn't get our first TV until I was fourteen—and somehow my parents managed to convey that this differentness was a good thing."

Did she ever shop with her mother? "Never!" says Friedrich. "Oh, no. My mother read Jane Austen and watched the housework slide past and loved her husband and five children, but the notion of a trip to the mall she would meet with absolute horror."

Friedrich's older sister, however, rebelled against the family's nonconformity by developing a passion for shopping and clothes. "My sister eventually installed a padlock on her bedroom door because she was livid that when she left for school I would go into her room, get one of her outfits, and change into it in the girl's bathroom at school."

Just as Friedrich's sister went in the opposite direction from their non-shopping mother, so do other women find themselves pursuing different tacks from their mothers', for better or worse.

"I grew up in a family where looks and appearance were very important. My mother was and is an impulsive spender who always treats herself very well to clothes," says one woman. "But because my parents were divorced I had a very responsible role early in life. I was very controlled and had the practical streak my mother lacked. As a result I don't splurge on myself at all. I wish that I could buy a little more impulsively and change the style of how I dress, but even though I wish it it seems that I can't do it."

Writer Jo Brans says, "My father was a deacon in the Baptist church and my parents' philosophy was that whatever is not absolutely necessary is a sin. My mother wanted me to dress well but it was always based on what you needed for which occasion. I didn't know until college that you could buy clothes just for the sheer pleasure of clothes. My mother had sent me $50 or $100 for a graduation outfit, and instead of buying one I went out and bought fabric. Although I'd never made a thing in my life I made myself all these clothes, and it opened my eyes to the pleasures of being able to express myself with clothes."

Susan Gaynes, a New York dietitian, came by her love of shopping not from her mother, who hated it, but from her stepmother. "My stepmother was a buyer who put me in fashion shows when I was a child," says Gaynes. "She used to love dressing me up. It was exactly the opposite with my real mother, who never shopped. When I was old enough to have my own money, my mother would offer to go with me but I'd rather go by myself."

Even for grown-up women, shopping with mother can continue to be an activity with potent undertones. "It's something you can do with your mother so you don't talk about what's really bothering you," says Dr. Berman. "When you shop together your mother can still mother you; she can buy you a dress even if she can't interfere with your life. But it's a classic kind of interaction which, if shopping together has always been a tradition, can reactivate all the old stuff."

Of course, a mother's power over her daughter's shopping style extends beyond her actual presence in the store, even beyond her presence in this life. Dr. Berman tells the story of a powerful professional woman in her fifties who went shopping with a friend. "The woman tried on a pair of shoes and the friend said they looked great. The woman protested that her mother had always said those were trashy-looking shoes. The friend said, 'Your mother's been dead for five years. Buy the shoes.' Well, she bought the shoes, but she's never been able to wear them."

MONEY

·5·

Spending

·

Y ou go shopping with the intention of buying a new black skirt for under $100 and emerge from the store four hours later with a purple blouse, three bras, a pair of silk pajamas, two pairs of jeans, four pairs of earrings, a strapless green velvet dress, a pound of chocolate chip cookies, and a new lipstick, having spent close to $1,000.

Or you go shopping with the intention of buying a new black skirt for under $100 and once you get to the store you're drawn not to the black skirts but to the sale racks and clearance tables. You emerge from the store four hours later with a purple blouse that was half off, four pairs of earrings from the discount bin, a gray skirt that wasn't exactly what you wanted but was on sale, and a lipstick with a bonus makeup bag, having spent $200.

Or you go shopping with the intention of buying a new black skirt for under $100 and once you get to the store you balk at the idea of spending anything close to that. You find a black skirt for $50 but even that seems too high, and then one for $30, but you still have trouble justifying it. In fact, everything in the store that you could conceivably need or want seems grossly overpriced, and you go home half an hour later empty-handed.

Spending money on clothes for yourself is a potent psychological issue, embracing feelings of self-worth, lessons learned early from mother, and overall attitudes toward money. Whether you spend freely or sparingly, emotionally or rationally, wisely or foolishly can have very little to do with how much money you actually have or what you can afford or even which clothes you want or need. The key to your spending behavior lies not in your pocketbook but in your head and heart.

Stores know this. It's in a store's best interests to get you to spend as much as possible and also—this is important—to make you feel good about it. What stores try to cajole you into doing is spending a little more than you planned on what you need, buying a little extra something that you didn't know you wanted, and having so much fun doing it that you'll soon be back for more.

You already know part of how stores get you to spend from the shopping chapter: store designs that tempt you up the escalators and across the selling floors, displays that entice you into trying new styles or colors or convince you to buy entire outfits instead of pieces, high-traffic first floors stocked with impulse items like accessories and cosmetics.

"Department stores all over the world, even in the People's Republic of China, have cosmetics counters right as you walk in the door, so even if you don't buy anything else because it's too expensive you can usually afford some makeup," says Patricia M. Mulready, a New York University professor of home economics. "In Canton the cosmetics are right next to the tractors."

But there's more.

I have to pause here and say that I don't believe stores are big, evil monsters looking to gyp you out of your money. I'm not telling you to stop buying clothes. Nor am I trying to take the fun out of shopping or to brand buying for pleasure as a mortal sin. The truth is that if you're aware of the forces that are playing on you while you're shopping, if you know what stores do to get you to buy and why clothes are priced as they are and how to make the smartest use of your money, you can have more fun both in the stores and living with the clothes you buy.

It helps to be aware, when you shop, that there are certain things that make you vulnerable to spending. A feeling of fun is one; a sense of understanding is another. Boutiques in department stores have such a dual appeal, tapping into both the child and the adult in all of us. "Boutiques are so popular in department stores partly because they add variety and excitement and partly because they make the merchandise understandable to the consumer," says one former department store vice president. "And of course, if someone understands something—how to use it, how to wear it—they're much more likely to buy it."

You're also more susceptible to spending when you're already spending: at the cash register, with your money or your credit card out, having convinced yourself to buy. That's where you may find all those little things you suddenly remember you need—like pantyhose or socks—or want—a hair bow, a belt, a wallet (while you're reminded of the woeful condition of the one you own).

Also, you tend to spend more at one time when you're using a department store's own credit card: as long as it's out, as long as it's working, as long as you're there, you might as well buy as much as you can.

Your senses are bombarded with "buy" messages every time you shop. The most obvious lures are those you see: from the outfitted mannequins to the Valentine panties that catch your eye as you round the escalators to the fashion show videos in the designer boutiques.

More subtle eye-pleasing techniques may also be at work in the dressing room, says Mulready, where some stores tilt mirrors to make you look ten pounds thinner and install pink lighting to flatter your complexion.

What you hear can also prompt you to buy. Predominantly, that means music: fast-paced supermarket tunes that boost your energy in discount stores or sexy modern music that sets the mood in stylish boutiques or classier and often classical music in higher-priced shops. What you're not aware you're hearing may also be influencing you: "Some stores are experimenting with subliminal messages to discourage shoplifters," says Mulready, "and the theft rate has gone down in stores with tapes that say things like 'Stealing is wrong. Don't be bad.' Stores say they're not using subliminal messages to convince people to buy more, but it wouldn't surprise me if they really were."

Along with your eyes and ears, your nose is also being enticed into buying. Your nose? That's right: scent is a powerful and often subliminal motivator. The fresh-baked chocolate chip cookie kiosks on the main floors of department stores or in the middle of malls are near-irresistible because of their smell. But what you may not realize is that the aroma of grandma's kitchen might not be thoroughly genuine. "They use a chocolate chip cookie spray that permeates the air and makes you think cookies are baking," says Mulready. "Stores also spray handbags with leather scent, which people find appealing."

How you move through the store is also a key to how much you'll buy. According to one department store insider, department stores know that with each higher floor they lose shoppers. That's one reason essential services—such as rest rooms or restaurants—are often placed on upper floors, in an attempt to get shoppers to as high a floor as possible. This phenomenon has also prompted department stores that are renovating to design horizontally rather than vertically, tempting shoppers out and around each floor rather than up another level. One way they do this is by making you walk through the floor to get to the next escalator up or down—and strewing tempting items in your path. Another way is to construct floor plans in circles or "racetrack" shapes that lead you around the floor's perimeter and past all the merchandise rather than to the exit. Patterns in carpeting and linoleum can act as yellow brick roads leading you to the retail Oz: the cash register.

How can the average shopper combat all these sophisticated selling techniques? "Stay out of the stores," Mulready laughs. "I know what they're doing and I still fall for it. Part of it is you're there because you want to be there and maybe you really need something, but it helps to be aware that the store is stimulating you to buy and to keep on buying."

Why Clothes Cost What They Do

Let's go back to that black skirt you set out to buy for less than $100. Let's say you find the right skirt, and it costs exactly $100. Now, you like this skirt, this skirt fits and looks good on you, and this skirt makes sense for your wardrobe—no problems there. But still, you hold up this plain black skirt, with three seams and a zipper, twenty inches square, and you feel that something is not quite right. And what's not quite right is that you can't figure out why this very simple item should cost $100.

If you're buying said skirt at full price in a department or specialty store or an uptown boutique, the first thing you should know is that the store paid, probably, $40 for it. So you're paying $60 of your $100 purely for the privilege of buying it in a store—which may, after all, be your only choice. And half of the $40 manufacturer's price goes to the manufacturer's own overhead and profit, not to anything of value in the skirt itself. Of the $20 that the skirt actually costs, about $15 is for labor and only $5 goes for fabric.

Says Emily Mann, a New York clothing designer and fashion forecaster, "When I was working with offshore goods [clothes made overseas], a pair of pants would land for $8 to $10 [the "landed" price means the production price plus shipping costs and import duty], and would sell [to a store] for $25 to $30 and would then be in the stores for $50 or $60. And $10 landed means that over there they would cost about $5, $2 of which is the factory's profit. So you spend $50 or $60 for a $3 pair of pants."

With a $100 pair of shoes, you may be getting a little more material for your money. A shoe company executive priced out the components of a pair of Italian leather shoes like so: $11 for leather, $12 for labor/workmanship, $6 for the factory's profit, $3 for duty/transportation, $13 for the wholesaler's profit, and $55 for the store—total price to you, $100.

A major factor influencing the price of clothes is the amount of the retailers' markup. "There's a wide variety in the marketplace," says Mann. "Certain stores mark up things three times the price. When I worked in a store as a buyer I would get earrings for $2 a pair and if the earrings looked like they could get $10, I would price them as $10."

"Most stores want to set the price at which they can sell the most pieces," says one retailing insider. "There's usually a reason something starts out at a certain price—it has something to do with where it's made, the fabric—but that may not be the price at which most people want to buy it."

Also, says Mann, the price at which a manufacturer sells an item of clothing may differ depending on the store. "The price a department store pays can be up to 30 percent more than what other stores pay at wholesale."

"There's no such thing as a competitive market, and the consumer really doesn't have a choice," says Mann. "In off-price stores, you see a brand name that looks the same as what's in the department stores. But you as the consumer may not really be getting a bargain at the off-price store because often the buyer has gone to the manufacturer and said they only wanted to pay a certain price and the manufacturer has made something that looks the same but isn't the same quality. When the label is in at an off-price store it often means the manufacturer has worked out such a special program, because manufacturers usually won't allow clothes with their labels to be sold below the wholesale price. If the label's cut out chances are you're getting a better value and better quality."

Smart Ways to Save Money

You want that black skirt, but you don't want to pay $100 for it. Do you really have to? Can you find something comparable for less? Can you afford to wait; can you afford to spend time looking? And if you find what seems like a bargain, how can you tell if it's really a bargain?

There are many ways to save money on clothes. Almost every store runs sales: one-day sales, President's Day sales, end-of-season clearances. And then there are a growing number of stores devoted to selling clothes at a discount over full retail: from off-price places where a bargain may not always be a bargain to outlets where all the clothes are always sold at wholesale or less.

The first thing you should know is that there is a psychology of enticing people into buying at sales just as there is of getting them to pay full price. That untidy, crowded rack of clothes with hand-scribbled price tags in the back of the store may look like an afterthought, yet it's anything but.

"Some retailers will purposely mess up sale racks and clearance tables before the store opens because people think they won't find real bargains if everything's neat," says Dr. Michael Solomon. The message the store is conveying: We can't waste our time and money taking care of this stuff because it's so cheap.

Messy cross-outs on price tags can also be powerful sale tools. One former specialty store salesperson says that at the store where she worked employees were instructed to cross out and write in new prices as many times as possible, to give customers that deep, deep markdown feeling. If a handwrought price tag accidentally fell off a garment, it was reconstructed complete with every cross-out and replaced.

The placement of sale racks in the backs of stores or departments also has a purpose, says Patricia Mulready: "You have to pass by all the full-priced stuff to get to the sale clothes." The retailer hopes that you'll buy something at full price on the way to the bargains.

Some sales, too, are better than others, and it's worth knowing which are which. "Most shoppers don't know the difference between a sale and a clearance," says one department store insider. "A sale is a temporary markdown: the price is going back up. A clearance is permanent. If a clearance item is marked down from $24 to $19.99 the only place it's going is to $14.99 and $9.99 and $7.99." What happens then? "Some stores bring it back next year on a dump table, other stores get rid of it all." Where to? An outlet, or charity.

Also, according to this insider, all sales in the true sense of the word are not created equal. "One- and two-day sales are designed to increase sales in specific classifications in which business is not up to snuff. Twenty-five percent off everything in the entire store is a real desperation move," he says. And a way for you to find good bargains.

The best sales, says this source, are annual events—Columbus Day, Memorial Day—where the shopper will find the best scope and the best selection. "Annual sales are planned into the calendar. The stuff is bought and prepared specifically for those sales. Buyers negotiate with manufacturers for better prices."

If you like to get all your shopping done at once, says the insider, it pays to wait for big annual sales. Still, he says, "certain things never go on sale across the board—you could wait forever. It depends on the manufacturer. You'll never see Ralph Lauren or Liz Claiborne at 25 percent off the whole department. If you did, the manufacturer would be very unhappy with the retailer. You don't see these deep discounts on clothes from manufacturers who have their own outlets [as Lauren and Claiborne do] and you don't see them often on really premium luxury stuff."

The fact that different manufacturers have different discount policies is what makes it worthwhile to comb the store during a big sale—even departments that normally are out of your price range—for the best deals. It can be possible to find an $800 dress from Giorgio Armani slashed to $200, the same price as a far more ordinary dress from a manufacturer who doesn't allow the store to discount its clothes.

Also, in the eternal time-money balance, it makes sense to buy the most expensive items at store-wide sales, to use discounts as an opportunity to stock up on basics, and to pay full retail for lower-priced items. One department store buyer describes his personal and well-educated technique for sale-shopping: "You have to look past the 25 percent off to what that means in dollars. On an $800 suit, you'll save $200, which is worth the wait and the hassle. On a $40 pair of pants, it's probably not worth your hour and a half to save $10, unless it's something you know you'll need and wear for a long time, when it makes sense to buy ten at once."

This savvy buyer holds out for big discounts on private label [the store's own brand] merchandise—"There's a lot more margin for the store to play with, so private label goes on sale more often"—and says one of the most important factors in getting a true bargain is knowing what something should cost. "It's not a bad idea to look through all those catalogs everybody gets delivered to get a comparison, a standard of what things should cost. Catalogs generally have lower markups than most stores do, and can give you an idea of a good basic price for something."

The problem is that there are also many ways to make mistakes saving money on clothes. If you have trouble finding clothes that fit, if you're rushed for time, if you need something for a special occasion or need to replace a staple in your wardrobe, holding out for a discount can be a mistake. If you find yourself continually sacrificing comfort or quality or style to the bottom line, that can be a mistake. And perhaps the biggest spending mistake women make, say fashion and shopping experts, is buying bargain clothes that don't fit correctly or aren't flattering or don't go with anything else in their wardrobes and so never get worn.

"You go through a store and that purple blouse that's on sale attracts you. You don't have any idea what that purple blouse is going to go with but you love that purple blouse. You never wear it, you have nothing to go with it but it was such a bargain you had to own it," says Elaine Mack, a Bergdorf Goodman personal shopper. "If you hadn't done that, if instead of ten purple blouses at $50 apiece you had put the $500 into one item you wear over and over, the $500 is better spent."

Smart Ways to Spend Money

You need that black skirt. Whatever the price, you've got to buy one. And you need lots of other things, as well: it seems that whenever you go to your closet you never have anything to wear. Spending on clothes is in order.

But how to spend wisely? How to devise a clothing budget for yourself, and use it on pieces you'll feel good in and wear often?

I asked several personal shoppers and wardrobe consultants to devise smart spending strategies both for a woman on a tight clothing budget and for a woman with more money. I did not set exact prices, but the concept was the same for both theoretical women: their wardrobes were problematic, perhaps they had a few good pieces but basically needed to start from scratch. How to get the most for their money?

The first surprise was that the experts' spending strategies were the same whether a woman has $500 or $5,000 to spend on a season's clothing. And while different experts had different ways of working, they all agreed on one point: your money is best spent on items that give you maximum versatility.

The strategy:

Set a Realistic Budget—Many women underestimate how much they spend on clothes, says Vicki French Morris, president of French-Haines wardrobe consulting in Chappaqua, New York, because "they're afraid to admit how much clothes cost. Most women are used to spending in dribs and drabs. It's like eating a little at a time; it adds up in the end. I have very rich clients who do that; they spend less for a year than they should for a season." Also, many women have ten-year-old notions of what clothes should cost, or are hooked on bargains to the detriment of wearability, so they'll set too low a budget.

How to be realistic? One way may be to concoct a theoretical wardrobe for yourself, imagining what you might need for every day of the week and taking into account your activities and also a garment's "down time" for cleaning, says Morris. Virtually every wardrobe consultant starts with this kind of "life analysis," detailing your work schedule, your leisure activities, how often and where you go out in the evening, and how often and where you travel, and then finding clothes that will work for your life. "My object is for a woman to go to her closet at any given time and be prepared to go anywhere," says Elaine Mack.

Only after you've pinpointed everything you need should you go to your closet and see what you already own that fits into your wardrobe plan. If you've got a perfectly good navy blazer, a flattering pair of gray trousers, and a pretty new dinner dress, you can cross those off your list. Then calculate the cost of each item you don't have, add up the figures, and *voilà*, a budget.

Of course, you may find you have to work in the other direction, deciding how much money you have and then figuring out what you can afford to buy. Whatever your method for setting your budget, it's smart to give yourself a comfort margin, says Joyce Grillo, president of New York's Impression Management: "I can spend $1,500, but it won't be a tragedy if I spend $2,000."

You've Got to Start Somewhere—Most clothing consultants start with one key piece around which they build the entire wardrobe. Choosing a wardrobe centerpiece to which all other pieces relate helps ensure cohesiveness and versatility. Not only is this a smart strategy, it's a simple one: instead of having to keep your entire wardrobe in mind when you choose something new, you only have to remember a single item.

But which item should you choose for your centerpiece? Elaine Mack of Bergdorf Goodman has one intriguing strategy: she starts with a coat. "The first piece I choose for someone is a coat that's going to work over everything, most likely in black or navy," says Mack. "I want to know I have the right piece to go over whatever's underneath. The wardrobe is hard; the coat is easy."

Jacqueline Murray, who started and runs the FYI/For Your Image personal shopping service at Dayton Hudson in Minneapolis, believes a wardrobe's centerpiece should be something a woman loves. "I always start working from the core of the favorite," says Murray, "and then build a base or underlay for it so it can be used in many ways."

Vicki French Morris takes a somewhat different tack: "The absolute most important item needs to be first, and that should be a top because you always see someone's top. Depending on a woman's needs, it can be a jacket, a sweater or a blouse. That should be the first purchase and the highest-quality purchase, because everything else you buy will be determined by that."

Janice Locascio, an image consultant at Carson Pirie Scott's Executive Level in Chicago, says she starts with a terrific suit. "For a young woman who's, say, an accountant and is building a wardrobe from scratch, my personal spending strategy would be to start with one suit and then expand into separates, and to invest in lightweight wools and gabardines that can be worn through several seasons."

Andrea Sells, a Los Angeles wardrobe consultant, begins by devising with a client a color plan of two basics (say, navy and black), two neutrals (such as ivory and tan), and three "fashion colors" (red, kelly green, and aqua, for example). Whatever the palette, Sells often chooses a black dress as the centerpiece of a wardrobe: "It's the ultimate to get you in and out of any occasion."

Joyce Grillo's recommended wardrobe base:

a skirt and top in the same medium-to-dark tone. "These two pieces can be worn with a cardigan sweater, a tunic, a jacket, or pulled together with a belt to look like a dress."

It may be tempting to use something you already own as the centerpiece of your wardrobe. The problem: "Using a jacket that's in your closet as the kingpin works only if the jacket is truly great," says Vicki French Morris. Unless that's the case, you may do better to splurge on something new for a starter, use what you own as "satellite" pieces.

Then Build Out from the Center— You've chosen the centerpiece for your wardrobe. Where do you go from there?

After the coat, Mack first chooses dresses: "They're easy, they travel well, you can dress them up or down. I like wool jersey, and there's definitely a silk in there." Next, she moves to separates: "My idea is things you can interchange a lot. If you have a great jacket, I'd make sure you had three skirts and two pairs of soft pants to go with it. Then we'd do it with a silk blouse, but we'd also get a great cashmere sweater and maybe a skinny little camisole and a short black skirt for night." Every separate in the wardrobe, in other words, can be worn with the jacket if you so choose.

Sells also goes for interchangeable separates after the basic black dress. "For some working women, a dark suit is extremely important. I'd choose one with pieces that could be worn separately. I'd add a tailored jacket that could be worn for work or for weekends; a twin set with sweaters that could be worn together or separately; wool flannel or gabardine

trousers or a skirt; and two blouses, one dressy and one more casual."

Carson's Locascio also moves into separates from her base of a suit. "If I start with a gray suit I might then add a black skirt, a white blouse, a glen plaid suit, and from there it might go into red."

Whatever a woman's budget, Dayton Hudson's Murray aims for "a minimal wardrobe with high flexibility, with pieces in year-round fabrics and basic colors. It could be a jacket, a skirt, an additional style skirt, and a sweater jacket, in two different colors that make a marriage. From there you could move to a dinner dress, a work dress, one pair of play and one pair of work slacks."

If you always build from a wardrobe's centerpiece, you'll end up with a group of pieces that work together and offer a variety of different looks. Consider Joyce Grillo's method of starting with a dark, matching skirt and top: to those base pieces in, say, charcoal she may add a plum cardigan, to the plum cardigan a black-and-plum silk blouse and a plum skirt, to the plum skirt a navy jacket, to the navy jacket a navy skirt and a gray blue jersey top, and so on. Because every one of these pieces goes with every other, the mathematical possibilities are dazzling.

Don't Forget Accessories— The wardrobe consultants I spoke with say they spend an average 20 percent of a woman's clothing budget on accessories. That may seem high to many women, for whom accessories are an afterthought, tacked on as economically as possible after the main pieces are purchased. In the consultants' minds, however, they're as

important—and sometimes more important—
than the clothes themselves.

"Accessories should be as expensive as
you can afford, because they bring up the whole
look of whatever you're wearing," says Murray.
"To a basic wardrobe I'd add a day belt, an
evening belt, day jewelry, evening jewelry, a
few scarves, and a very good pair of shoes."

"You've got to invest in a good belt, real
skin, because it will make your clothes look
more expensive," says Elaine Mack. "You're
going to have a really good bag and a real
(meaning real wool, real silk) shawl. With
shoes, I believe in black: black suede, black
patent, black silk, and a pair of flats. Not black
leather because it can look bulky and heavy
on the foot. Jewelry should be multipurpose if
possible: you have to have gold and silver
accessories, and if you can't wear one of those
maybe ivory or copper or jet or a colored stone."

Does Money Make Any Difference?—
Not in basic spending technique, say the
experts. While a woman on a tighter budget
may buy Anne Klein II clothes instead of Anne
Klein, wardrobe consultants advise buying the
best clothing you can afford and emphasize
quality over quantity.

"If you buy very, very little but the most
excellent things you can afford, then next time
you're ready to buy you can concentrate on
adding to what you've already got," says
Jacqueline Murray. "You can increase your
wardrobe mobility but stay the same in quality."

Even when a woman has an unlimited
budget, Murray counsels minimalism. "The
principle is the same but you may pay more
per item," she says. "The fewer clothes you
have the better. It's efficient, your closet isn't
overloaded or cluttered, you're not the caretaker
of this huge wardrobe. You can pack for a
month in half an hour."

If you're just starting out and you have a
minimal budget, your money would be best
spent on pieces that are dark (dark fabrics tend
to look more expensive, need to be cleaned
less often), classic (they'll still look right when
you can afford to add to your wardrobe next
year), year-round (choose lightweight wool gabardines, wool jerseys, cotton knits), and solid
(prints are more memorable, can't be worn as
often).

Once you've got these principles and your
core wardrobe down, you can add color, comb
the sale racks, and have some fun knowing
you're spending on things you'll really wear.

• *Style Analysis* •

MIKE LINDNER *is manager of a real estate firm in Westport, Connecticut; wife of a corporate president; and mother/ stepmother to five children. Mike's long leather coat was bought on sale—she is happy to report—at Ann Taylor for $400. Her Lolita Lempicka pants suit was about $1,000 at Mary Jane Denzer in Westport; her neckpiece was $150 at Bonwit's; her Anne Klein patent leather flats were bought at Neiman Marcus in Las Vegas for $160.*

HOW DID YOUR STYLE EVOLVE?

I grew up in Long Island, and went to convent boarding school from the time I was five years old. At fourteen I came out and went to a parochial school, but even at that point it was like a bird being let out of a gilded cage. It was funny, I was always very taken with the nuns' habits. Once we had a little parade and dressed up in all the different habits of the different orders. At one point I was thinking of entering the convent.

In parochial school, we still wore uniforms—the gray skirts and saddle shoes. If we had to go to some function out of uniform, I was very prim and proper, still into the white gloves, because in boarding school we did all those things. It was the only thing I knew.

I spent the last two years of high school at the local public school and so I was very out of place there too. I dressed older than my age, more in an adult style. I never wore pants to school; we wore pleated skirts, the little pearls, cashmere sweaters. I was very interested in clothes, but more to the proper side. I would never do anything avant-garde.

AT WHAT POINT DID YOUR STYLE AS IT IS NOW START?

I was married very young—I had my first child when I was just 20—and by the time my first husband and I were divorced, we owned a restaurant in Greenwich, Connecticut, and lived in Greenwich; and moving from Long Island to Greenwich I found myself in a much more

sophisticated area with people who are very diverse. I was exposed there to a lot of different things, and my style started to become more refined.

By the time I married my second husband and was thrown into the IBM business world, I refined it even more. As my taste gets better and better, unfortunately it gets more and more expensive. When you really love good, well-made, expensive clothes the other doesn't feel as good. If my husband all of sudden couldn't work and I was the sole support of the family, I obviously couldn't buy designer clothes. I'd have to adjust, but I'd hate it! I love clothes. To me, life is a costume party, so it's a tremendous pleasure to me to feel that I'm dressed well.

WHAT SORT OF IMAGE DO YOU HAVE TO PROJECT IN THE ROLE OF CORPORATE WIFE?

*M*y husband is the president of Bunker Ramo, which is owned by Olivetti. I tend to dress toward the elegant, conservative side because my husband is a very, very conservative person. Although he's fine if I want to wear a short skirt or whatever in Las Vegas, he scrutinizes what I wear very carefully for his business. While he has the good sense not to tell me not to wear something, I don't want him to feel uncomfortable in any way. I know instinctively how to dress and what would be appropriate: nothing low-cut; high style but conservative.

HAVE YOU ALWAYS WORKED?

*Y*es. I love my job and I love working. I love goal-setting and reaching my goals. When I became manager of the realty office, somebody told me I'd be so busy I wouldn't care what I wore. Well, I will never not care.

The company I work for is owned by Dollar Dry Dock bank, and when I go up to see them, I still dress very high style, but I would be careful about the length of my skirt, how tight it is, and I wouldn't wear slacks. It would be something like a suit, but I wouldn't feel that I had to wear Brooks Brothers. I would never do that, even if I were at the bank everyday. But I'm also tied into an image now; people talk about the way I dress.

WHAT DO THEY SAY?

*T*hey'll say I dress so well, that it's like a fashion show every day. But I also feel I started them on being more interested in clothes. I've only been managing this office for six months, and I already notice an upgrade in the way they're dressing. I think I'm a very good manager, and when you form a team like that, on a not very conscious level they may want to be more like me. It would be hard for me to stand up and tell people they should dress better, so it's wonderful when it happens on its own.

I was in Colorado for two years, working for a broker there, and the office I was in was jeans and cowboy boots. I stood out like a sore thumb, but I was known for that and I was very accepted. They didn't think I was a snob; my personality doesn't intimidate people. It served me very well in business there. I was different but I never changed my style.

I'M CURIOUS ABOUT HOW BEING IN SALES AFFECTS YOUR CLOTHES.

Sales is a lot of psychology. I will know just by hearing someone's background and talking to them on the phone what they'll be like. I will dress very, very differently for different clients. If I have a client who's very conservative and not interested in clothes, that's when I will put on my plain navy blue suit with a white blouse and pearls. In sales there's a bonding and trust that has to take place. You really have to mirror who you're with; people feel comfortable with people who are like themselves. When they get to know me it really doesn't matter. Once they have that trust in me, that I'm going to look out for their interests and not going to give them a hard sell, then I really can wear almost anything I want.

HOW DOES A SUBURBAN STYLE DIFFER FROM AN URBAN STYLE?

I feel underdressed when I go into New York. I'm kind of awestruck by the way women dress in New York City. Even though Westport is a bedroom community and I would be considered dressed high-style here, I feel in New York they go a step beyond. I love looking at the way women coordinate things, and maybe get ideas for myself. I may be wearing a wonderful suit I've spent a lot of money on, navy blue and a white blouse, and I may wear simple diamond earrings and flat black patent leather shoes. In New York I'll see someone in the same look who's gone steps further, with maybe navy and burgundy shoes from Mario Valentino and the shiny leather bag that would pull in the burgundy and more jewelry and a scarf and I'll say, "Oh, gosh, I look fairly plain."

HOW DO YOU SHOP?

Before, I'd shop at a lot of places with designer clothes at discount prices. Now, I don't have the time to do that. What I tend to do is shop locally and for a short period of time. A few shops I go to that know me very well will let me in after hours, pull things aside, and I'll buy in bulk. Unfortunately, I wind up spending a lot more money. I buy smarter because I'm more careful of what I purchase—it doesn't seem like a bargain to me.

HOW DO YOU ORGANIZE YOUR SHOPPING?

Since I took over this new job six months ago, my time is much more structured and I've had to change the way I shop. If I need a dressy dress I will run out and do that on the spot. I really enjoy shopping; it relaxes me. Just last weekend we went to Las Vegas, and I had the most wonderful time spending hours shopping, but I haven't done that in a long, long time. It's a diversion; I totally forget about problems. It's like some people take cocaine or drink, I like to buy nice things. It is some sort of obsession. When you spend a lot of money on clothes, and you're not a millionaire, then that's probably your little thing that's not so positive.

WHICH DESIGNERS DO YOU LIKE?

Very diversified. I love Anne Klein, I love Donna Karan, although most of Donna Karan is a little too sexy for work, where Anne Klein I feel to be perfect for work. It's very me. Yet I love the French designers, Lolita Lempicka, short skirts. I love pants suits, and probably like them better than anything for work. Last year we spent six months in Italy, and I love Italian clothes. I love Armani, although with the exchange rate an outfit can come to $5,000 and I don't see the value in that.

DO YOU LIKE FEELING SEXY TO SOME EXTENT IN YOUR CLOTHES?

Yes, I do, a little. I don't want to be obvious about it. I might like a strapless dress, although if it's falling down or it's too low, I don't like people staring at me. The funny thing about my look is that, even when I'm wearing a black leather skirt and black lace stockings, I can still look like the girl next door. I wear a lot of black leather; I can get away with it more than someone else.

IS THERE ANYONE WHO'S INFLUENCED YOUR STYLE?

I have a friend in Colorado who's very artistic and very offbeat who puts these wonderful things together, and I admire what she looks like even though it's very different from the way I dress. I take some influence from her for weekend dressing, where I'll wear a black stretch jumpsuit with boots or something, which is not my general style.

We all know the nuns influenced me. My mother was a lady of style, and her look of the forties, with longer skirts and short jackets fitted at the waist with big shoulders, I love that. She was in the army and because she was a model she did the war posters that were all over the subways, and escorted the celebrities. She also speaks Russian and Ukrainian and Polish so she was an interpreter for Eisenhower. I think of her old army uniforms, the fur boa, the pleated wide pants, that kind of look I like very much.

HOW HAS GETTING OLDER AFFECTED YOUR FEELINGS ABOUT CLOTHES?

For a long time when I was younger I felt that I had to dress a certain way, and I've gotten over that. I don't care as much about other people's opinions. That comes with being forty.

The $770 Disaster

Is expensive always better? It can be when a portion of what you spend goes to qualities that upgrade the feel and fit and look of a garment: impeccably matched patterns, expert construction, draping during the design and fitting process to give the garment roundness and life.

But not all expensive clothes share these attributes, and it's possible to pay a bundle for something decidedly not worth the money. How to spot a high-priced disaster?

Lisbeth Riis Albert, a custom tailor and personal shopper who's the president of L. Riis Ltd. and teaches tailoring at Parsons School of Design and the Fashion Institute of Technology, found such an expensive mistake on Macy's designer floor: a $770 suit with nothing going for it.

The problems with the jacket—priced at $540—started with its design. "This jacket has a very curved princess seam and it's also double-breasted. If you wear it open it's going to flounce out and stand away from the back of the body. It's also designed for a full bust so if you open it, the seams will be concave and those dimples look downright silly," said Albert. "It's very restrictive to always wear a jacket closed and it visually gives the body

more weight, but you can't sit comfortably if you don't open the buttons."

Next, Albert's expert eyes moved to the seams connecting the sleeves to the body of the jacket. "Another thing to look for are wrinkles where the sleeve is set in," she said. "If it wrinkles there it will wrinkle on you. A salesperson will say it just needs to be pressed, but fabric has a memory and when it's allowed to relax the wrinkles are back. This happens in the sewing process: the sleeve wasn't eased in properly. The fullness of the sleeve should be at the top for a nice full crown.

"The third thing to look for is whenever there's topstitching—especially when you have a price tag of $540—a red flag goes up. It indicates someone didn't do their homework," said Albert. "Topstitching can cheapen a garment. And if a garment is well constructed topstitching isn't necessary. It's usually there because someone skimped on something, didn't put TLC into it. Topstitching can hide a lot of flaws and keep things in place."

Another problem with the jacket was that the plaids didn't match. "The plaid should continue across the body to the sleeve," said Albert. "At darts and seams, it should make a nice chevron or miter, and the plaids should match at the shoulder and the collar. If I was making this garment I would reject it because absolutely nothing matches up. The back seam should have been cut so it looks like one continuous piece of fabric. The darts should always be placed at the same point in the plaid."

Symmetry and matching are details to look for when buying any plaid jacket, advises Albert. If the plaid on one jacket is mismatched, you may be able to comb the racks for a better version. But be warned: lack of care in matching plaids, an obvious defect, can be evidence of sloppy workmanship that's less evident. If you're thinking of buying an expensive jacket in a solid fabric, it may be worthwhile to check out the same jacket in a plaid for possible clues to hidden faults.

Albert then grabbed the top and the underside of one lapel and tugged them apart. "The interlining is bubbly," she said, "and the lapels stuck together when they were pressed. A tailored garment should look full of life; this one has been pressed flat and lifeless."

Holding both shoulder seams together, she compared the lengths of the two front pieces of the jacket. "You should always measure the front of a jacket like this. This one is off half an inch."

Albert examined the matching straight skirt, priced at $230. "When the zipper goes all the way up to the top of the waistband, that's poor, cheap construction," she said. "It should have had a waistband with an extension and a separate closing. There's no interlining in the kick pleat, so it will never hang straight and will start getting sloppy. And this skirt isn't even lined."

Albert gave the price tag one last disbelieving look. "If they can get the money for it all the more power to them," she said. "But I wouldn't pay $25 for this suit. I really wouldn't."

The lesson: don't assume a garment's price tells you all you need to know about its quality. Instead of examining a higher-priced item less carefully than you would a cheap one, it makes sense to look it over even more thoroughly—using Albert's examination as a guideline—to be sure you're getting value for your money.

Too often, we feel that if we spot what we think is a flaw in something very expensive, the real flaw must be in our own judgment. After all, we think, the manufacturer can't simply charge such an outrageous price for nothing—the piece must have hidden details, subtle qualities we're too unsophisticated to appreciate. Sometimes, that's true. But sometimes, clothes are priced sky-high simply because of fashion, a designer's name, or pure nerve. As with the Emperor's New Clothes, no one has been confident enough to look beyond the hype to what's really there. Until you, that is.

Eight Best Buys

What are the items most likely to make you feel your money was well spent? Those things that, no matter what the price tag, you'll find yourself wearing again and again and feeling great in every time? Here's what women and fashion experts alike cited as best buys:

1. **A PAIR OF BLACK SHOES THAT FEEL AS GOOD AS THEY LOOK, AND VICE VERSA**—Most often these are flats, but dressed-up flats: black patent leather or suede loafers, say. Such shoes can be worn with everything from flannel trousers to velvet skirts, make the daily dressing process infinitely less complicated. If you hit upon such a pair of wonders (and you'll know it when you find yourself wanting to wear no other shoes for a week straight), rush back to the store and buy another pair.

2. **A BIG PLAIN SQUARE BLACK LEATHER TOTE**—How big depends on what you usually carry, but it should accommodate all possibilities, from shoes to notebooks to gym gear to makeup and wallet. It should be completely unadorned, and have two comfortable straps long enough to allow you to carry the bag on your shoulder and short enough to let you carry it in your hand. It should have a zippered compartment for items you need to get at quickly: keys, change, money card. Ideally, it should zip on top (although really enormous ones usually snap) and it should be real leather. It will be expensive, but it will last a long time and always look great.

3. **AN IVORY SILK SHIRT**—This should be a standard style, cut like a man's (but not with a button-down collar), tailored enough for a job interview but with sexy potential. It should be somewhat roomy, so you can comfortably roll up the sleeves or tie it at the waist, but not so big it won't tuck neatly into a straight skirt. The silk should be heavy enough so it won't water spot, stain, or wrinkle easily. Ivory is more flattering on most people than pure white.

4. **A WELL-CUT BLACK STRAIGHT KNEE-LENGTH SKIRT**—If you could own just one skirt, this would be your best choice: flattering on most figures; right with almost every top, every color, every kind of shoe; equally appropriate for work and for parties. One woman says her five-year-old black straight skirt literally was the only one she owned the first winter she bought it: she wore it to work every single day. She's still wearing it. Every so often, one or another of her co-workers, who've seen it a few hundred times, will ask if it's new.

5. **A TERRIFIC COAT**—As your most public piece of clothing, your coat has a lot to do not only with how warm you are but with your mood—if you feel good about how you look coming and going, you're likely to feel good when you're there. What counts as terrific is up to you:

for some women only black leather will do, another woman says she'll never go through another winter without a bright coat to cheer her up, for still another it's the ultimate classic navy polo. A good coat is a steep investment, but keep in mind that you really do wear your coat nearly every day for maybe six months a year, and that a good coat should last three years. That's 350 or 400 wearings: a terrific one is well worth a dollar or two (or even more) per.

6. **A COMFORTABLE, GOOD-LOOKING PAIR OF CASUAL PANTS**—Big, old sweatpants are one thing. Tight jeans are another. Combine the best features of the two—comfort and good looks—and you've got pants you'll hate to wash, the kind you can curl up in as you read the paper in the morning, then wear out grocery shopping and keep on while you cook dinner and still feel good in when the guests arrive.

7. **A GOOD WATCH**—"Good" doesn't have to mean Rolex or even expensive: it could be a man's Timex you buy for $22.95. The point is that you should like, really like, your watch, since it's the item of clothing you actually look at the most. Watches have become accessories instead of mere timepieces, which doesn't mean yours has to be fancy but does mean it should bear some relationship to your clothes.

8. **GREAT UNDERWEAR, AND ENOUGH OF IT**—You're not into frilly lingerie, you say? And what does it matter since nobody sees it? Great underwear can be cotton briefs, if that's what you like, and it matters because it can make a big difference in the way you feel. I mean your spirit as well as your body. It's no fun to begin dressing by rooting around in your underwear drawer and coming up only with underpants that are two sizes too small or ones that have a fly. It's no picnic to be set on wearing your ivory silk blouse only to find the only bra that's clean is hot pink. Not to mention the problems of panties that cut into your stomach or bra straps inexorably drawn to your elbows. A dozen pair of comfortable beige underpants and three skin-tone bras will do nicely for a start.

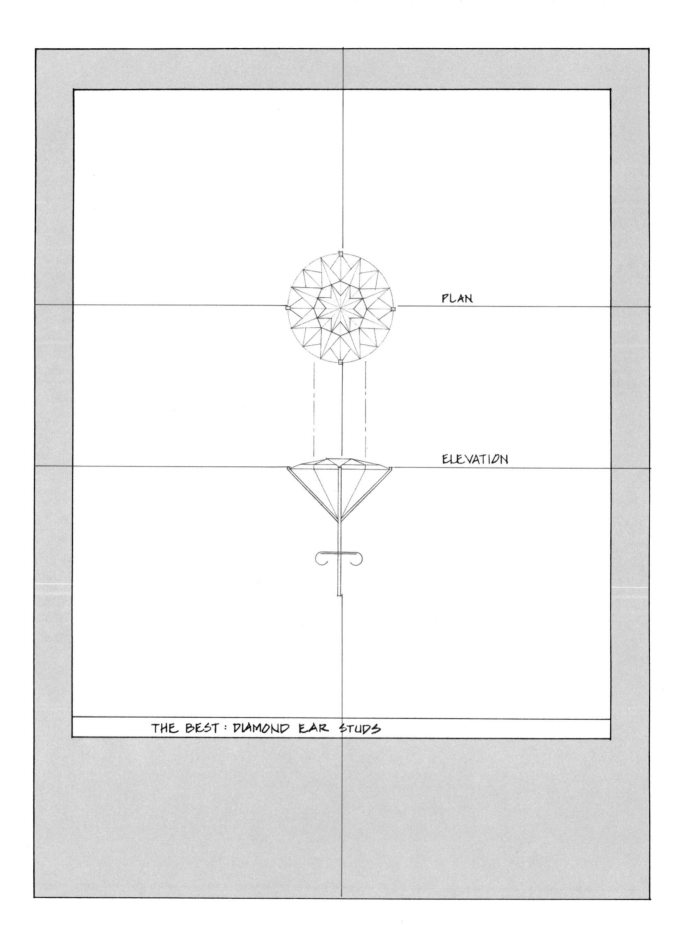

PLAN

ELEVATION

THE BEST: DIAMOND EAR STUDS

The Best: Diamond Ear Studs

1-Carat Diamond—Big enough to see, not so big it looks fake or feels heavy.

Round Stone—Most classic.

Ideal Cut—Not the shape but the faceting of the diamond: the cut named Ideal is the classic 58-facet cut; new and more brilliant are the Princess and the Radiant cuts.

Pure White Color—The whiter the color, the better the stone.

Four-Prong Setting—Optimum for both brilliance and security. A solid setting doesn't let light shine through, makes the stone look duller.

Gold or Platinum Setting—Since the setting shouldn't be visible, choosing 14K rather than 18K gold is a smart way to save money.

French Back—Most expensive, but also most secure, because it locks.

EMOTIONAL ISSUE:
SALE FEVER

You have no problem putting on blinders when you enter a store: you know exactly where you're heading—to the sale rack in the designer department. You actually start salivating when your eyes first light on the silks and fine wools crammed together so that only the hangtags—Armani, Lagerfeld, Anne Klein—are visible. You grab a black cashmere sleeve and examine the price tag: originally $800, it went to $599 and then to $400 and then to $259 and then to $129 and now—Oh God!—$59.

"Finding a great bargain," says one discount devotee, "is better than sex."

Indeed, the mania for shopping sales and off-price and outlets has become so widespread that it no longer can be called an aberration. Some women are turned on by the thrill of the hunt, other women do it simply because it's sensible, and still others find bargain-hunting depressing but addictive.

Women who are confirmed sale-shoppers are known in marketing parlance as "economic shoppers," says consumer psychologist and marketing professor Michael Solomon. "Economic shoppers are sort of recreational but they're not in it for the aesthetic or social value. For economic shoppers it can be like a safari—literally bargain-hunting."

Usually, a penchant for sale-shopping is something women come by early on, often from their mothers.

"There's a gene in our family—a shopping gene," says Nanette Wiser, the editorial manager of Copley News Service in San Diego. "I make a good salary but I don't believe money should be spent for full price. I've become so good at it that I can find the best places in any city when I'm traveling. I ask everyone, Where can I find a cheap tuxedo jacket? where's the best place for discount shoes? and I follow the Russia Rule—when three people agree, that's where I go."

When asked why they shop only for bargains, most women reply, Why not? Money—how much a woman has or can afford to spend on clothes—is often beside the point.

"If I won the lottery and could shop anywhere I wanted to I would probably go full-price, although I do have more money now than I had ten years ago and I still shop at Loehmann's," says Linda Knight, the vice president for employee relations at an international bank headquartered in New York. "I could afford to spend more money at full-price stores but why should I?"

Some women say recent economic history, more than their personal financial situations, is responsible for their addiction to buying at discount.

"It has something to do with living through the great period of postwar inflation," says one woman. "In your mind, you have an idea that a good sweater should still cost $25 and nothing should cost more than $200, so the only way to deal with the reality is to buy things at discount and at the end of the season."

Whether bargain-hunting is a choice or a necessity, whether a woman feels confident about her ability to find both the best and the cheapest has a lot to do with whether she finds sale-shopping fun in and of itself. Those who enjoy it are eager to share their techniques.

"I can remember the years by what I

bought," says Nanette Wiser. "Last year it was a pair of Calvin Klein pumps. This year it was a black leather miniskirt for $45." Wiser keeps notebooks on what she needs, where best to buy things. "I always have a list in my datebook of everything I'm looking for for me, for my husband, and for the house. I carry swatches of everything I'm trying to match: I clip a little triangle out of the hem or the inside of a seam. I also have a notebook full of clips and information on every store that interests me, so when I shop I bring that along."

Linda Knight, who shops at Loehmann's rather than at department store sales, says, "You have to go fairly often and you can't count on finding something. I usually go every other week, on a Saturday or sometimes a Sunday, sometimes only for half an hour, sometimes for two, three, four hours. Instead of buying for a specific occasion, I try to go for classic things that will last a long time and that I will wear often."

Not everyone, however, finds discount shopping so all-out uplifting. "If I come home having bought a $100 sweater for $21, I'm in great ecstasy," says one woman. "But if I find a great bargain and it doesn't fit, that's bad. And I do feel slightly demeaned when I go into a store and imagine the salesperson is looking

at me just looking at the sale stuff. Sometimes I'll look at the regular stuff and pretend to be interested in that too. I'll look at a price tag and if it's real high I'll pretend to be even more interested."

"I have to say that discount shopping can sometimes be depressing," says another woman. "A few months ago I had to go to a wedding and didn't have time to discount shop so I went to this suburban Saks. I was astonished that salespeople would take things out and bring them into the fitting room, that they would bring you the blouses that went with the suit and generally ease the burden of shopping. I didn't like it enough to want to pay for it all the time, but it was a revelation."

For this woman, the whole point of discount shopping is to spend as little as possible on something she doesn't consider very valuable in the first place. "I never feel I should be spending on clothes instead of something else, or instead of investing or saving," she says. "If you spend a lot of money on clothes what have you acquired? A perishable commodity which requires upkeep and cleaning and still doesn't make you look like Audrey Hepburn. And for this you've spent six to eight hours and airfare to Paris. I'd rather go to Paris."

Nine Biggest Money-Wasters

Want to put your money in a paper bag and leave it at the dump? Then you might as well buy one of these items that wouldn't be a bargain at half the price:

1. **A CHEAP SILK BLOUSE THAT NEEDS TO BE DRY-CLEANED**—Tissue-weight, low-priced crepe de chine can look like hell even on the hanger, and it will look even worse after you wear it under a jacket on a ninety-five-degree day. And nearly each time you wear it, you have to send it to the cleaner. At $6 or so a pop. Before long, that $40 bargain has cost you $100, and it really looks like hell.

2. **SHOES THAT DON'T REALLY FIT AND ARE A LITTLE WEIRD, ANYWAY**—So they're uncomfortable, so they're hot pink with a silver heel, they're only $10! It doesn't take a rocket scientist to figure out that a pair of $100 shoes you wear 100 times are a better buy than a pair of $10 shoes you wear once.

3. **A WONDERFUL PIECE THAT DOESN'T GO WITH ANYTHING ELSE YOU OWN**—Unless it's the first step of a radical style change, those great pants for $50 could end up costing thousands once you buy the jacket, the blouse, the belt, the shoes, and the jewelry to go with them. And then you'll have a wonderful outfit that doesn't go with anything else you own.

4. **PANTS (OR A SKIRT OR A SHIRT) THAT ARE A BIT TOO TIGHT**—You tell yourself you'll lose ten pounds. You can pin that button that keeps popping open. So you'll wear a long sweater to hide the bulges. My advice: if you really love it, look for it in the next size.

5. **A BLOUSE (OR A DRESS OR A SKIRT) THAT LOOKS GREAT IF YOU DON'T BEND OVER TOO FAR**—It's a law of the universe: the first time you attempt to wear one of these pieces in which you have to move oh-so-carefully, you drop your purse. Or you trip over the cat. And even if you don't, you're so tense from having to stand just so all day or night that you never want to see the thing again.

6. **CASHMERE AT A PRICE YOU CAN'T BELIEVE**—What will be unbelievable once you actually start to wear this garment is that cashmere could be so itchy, so pilly, and so generally awful-looking. It is not unknown for cashmere to be blended with such unsavory fibers as cat hair and old newspaper, which is probably the case when it's a quarter the price of any other cashmere you've ever seen.

7. **SOMETHING TO WEAR TO A WEDDING**—What is it about weddings that makes almost everyone feel that, like the bridemaids, they have to wear something brand-new? From experience, I can tell you that this is almost certainly a mistake—you'll be stuck with a dress for which you have no use until the next time one of your friends get married (which won't be until the dress goes out of style) and no one really notices what you're wearing, anyway. Everyone is, as they should be, looking at the bride.

8. **SOMETHING FOR SOMEONE ELSE'S LIFE**—It can be difficult to resist an incredibly beautiful beaded velvet evening dress marked down to $45 in January, but if your life does not now and never has included occasions to which you can wear a beaded velvet evening dress, it's not a bargain.

9. **ANYTHING YOU DON'T REALLY LIKE BUT IT'S RALPH LAUREN AND IT'S 50 PERCENT OFF**—Designer labels and big discounts can blind you to the actual piece. Ask yourself: if it was created by Sears, would I still want it? If it were full-price and I were rich, would I buy it? If not, if it doesn't work for your wardrobe or your life or your body, leave it on the rack for some other not-so-smart soul.

EMOTIONAL ISSUE:
CAN'T BUY ME LOVE

You haven't accomplished much at work today. Or you're nervous about that big party tomorrow night. Or you're feeling lonely. Or you lost five pounds. Or you got a job offer. Your first response to any or all of these highs and lows: you go buy yourself some clothes.

And sometimes buying new clothes can be a solution to troubles or an affirmation of strength, when you find something that makes you feel the way you want to feel: thin or loved or successful or confident. But if you don't find something that's right or if you set yourself an impossible goal or if what you buy doesn't, after all, deliver, it can leave you feeling worse than you did before.

"I use shopping as a way to fill myself up, and sometimes it's successful and sometimes it's unsuccessful," says one woman. "One day when I was feeling particularly vulnerable I went to a sale and bought the warmest, cuddliest, heaviest, most intricately designed sweater that made me feel great. I had comforted myself without laying out a lot of cash. But on the same day I tried on a sexy dress: I wasn't feeling sexy and it made me feel like I was in the wrong body."

"I shop when I need to feel better," says another woman. "When I'm completely overwhelmed by self-doubt, aside from taking naps, crying, calling friends, and eating, the only other thing to do is really to go shopping."

Does buying something provide a cure? "It's a little short-lived," she admits. "But I see it as more affirmative than neurotic. It's not helpful to my psychological state to not care about myself, so for me to go out and buy two pairs of trousers I see as an appropriate gesture to get out of this kind of funk. And if I don't find a great pair of trousers, I'll walk down the street and buy flowers or a new lipstick, and that will do it for me just as well."

While spending on clothes can provide some measure of comfort or cheer or self-affirmation, it can become problematic if that's the sole source of satisfaction for emotional needs, say psychologists, or if buying—only to be disappointed—becomes an addictive loop.

"You think this dress will bring you happiness, which doesn't work, so you buy another dress," explains Arlene Kagle, Ph.D., a psychotherapist in private practice in New York. "When the dress doesn't bring you happiness you blame your body, you blame the store, you get the idea that if only you had been able to shop at Bergdorf's instead of B. Altman's, if you could afford Bloomingdale's instead of Caldor's, then it would be okay."

The idea that clothes can bring happiness is not totally unfounded—"If you shop with that in mind three or four times a year, it may even be true," says Dr. Kagle—but is also promoted to an unrealistic degree in ads and magazines, say psychologists.

"If you don't have a lover and you go out and spend a lot of money on clothes, the reason is no mystery when all the clothing ads show a man and woman kissing," says Stephanie Miller, a licensed certified social worker and executive director of the Women's Counseling and Psychotherapy Service in Columbia and Towson, Maryland. "The message is that there's love if you buy this makeup or this coat."

Says Dr. Kagle, "People are taught by the

media that spending money on clothes will do wonderful things for you emotionally and socially and professionally. People then go shopping not out of need but with a secondary meaning, in that buying will bring them happiness."

In fact, some women admit that need—a basic requirement for a specific piece of clothing—has nothing to do with why or what they buy, just as money may have nothing to do with how much they spend. "What I buy has no remote relationship to what I need—I could get by with spending $100 a year on clothes but I spend much more," says one woman. "And for me spending is directly related to not having money; it's a defense against poverty."

"It's not utilitarian," says another woman. "That's the whole point of impulse buying, that it has nothing to do with how much money you have or what you really need. Sometimes, if I see something I love and I know I shouldn't get it—say, a black dress when I already have ten in my closet—I want it even more."

The real need can be a more essential, more emotional one. "I'll get an idea that I need pants or shoes or knee socks but in actuality I've never needed any of those things," says another woman. "With the pants I wanted to look sexy in a casual way; the knee socks were when I was feeling kind of lonely and I wanted to feel strong and sporty; the blouse I wanted when I thought I was going to be on TV and I wanted to look sexy from the waist up."

People who overspend have more active fantasy lives than those with controlled buying habits, according to a study by Thomas O'Guinn, Ph.D., associate professor of advertising at the University of Illinois. Overspenders see their purchases as a way to convey an image of themselves, says Dr. O'Guinn, and sometimes that's an image they have trouble living up to in reality.

If you expect clothes to affect life changes all by themselves, you may be setting yourself up for disappointment. But making a conscious connection between what you buy and what those things say about your deeper desires can set you on the road to real change.

One woman tells the story of how, upon graduating from college and on the eve of heading off to live in the country with her boyfriend, she bought several dresses and skirts, high-heeled shoes, and a black wool coat. "A friend was with me and she said 'What are you doing?' Only then did I realize that I had a subconscious motive for all this buying: I was not planning to stay in a rural community while these clothes were still in fashion. I ended up deciding not to move to the country right away."

This can also work on a simpler level. "I recently bought a new coat—not fancy, a regular down jacket—and it made me feel how much more fun it would be to go outside in the winter, to go sledding and play sports," says a Chicago attorney. "And you know, winter is a little bit more fun this year. I wear that coat almost every day and it's added pleasure to my life."

In a more elemental sense, treating yourself—just because—can be healthy. "I guess there have been times when I bought as a substitute for what I really wanted; when I wanted to leave my job and couldn't get out, it was a positive thing I could still do for myself," says one woman. "I've always been able to treat myself to things even when I had no money; when I couldn't buy expensive things I'd buy little things. I think it's mentally healthy to be good to myself. I've never been afraid of that; it's much worse to be the opposite way."

Indeed, women who find they're unable to treat themselves to anything, even when the need is real, express more concerns than those women who sometimes spend frivolously to boost their morales. "A deep-seated emotional theme for me is not taking care of myself, depriving myself of material things like clothes," says one woman. "The last time I splurged on myself was six years ago, when I bought an expensive winter coat in winter, but even then there was the underlying thing of 'It's practical, it will last a long time.' It has nothing to do with money—I can spend money on my house, or on a trip, but not on clothes."

Why can spending on clothes be different from other kinds of spending? "Very simply, many people perceive clothing as being central to who they are, to their self-concept or ideal self," says consumer psychologist Michael Solomon. "The jargon is 'high-involvement product': clothing is an expression of self and people don't mess with that. Spending money on clothes can be wrapped up in guilt, in wondering whether you've worked hard enough to deserve something. A lot of ads now reassure people that they do deserve things, assuming they can actually afford them."

No matter what your actual budget, spending too much or too little on yourself can both be problems, says Stephanie Miller. "A lot of people get out of control and a lot of people can't spend on themselves, don't feel they're worth it, so they always come last," says Miller. For women who feel they have a spending problem of either kind, Miller has a solution: "I always use that image of a blindfolded woman holding a scale. You can put those things in your life on the scale—your kid's shoes versus your fun fur—and see how it balances out each time."

•6•
LOVE
Men

You are going to dinner at his mother's house. You dress in something he once complimented you on: your pink silk dress, pearls, and black patent leather pumps.

"Uhhhh," he says when he sees you.

"What's wrong?"

"Couldn't you wear something a little . . ."

"A little what? I thought you liked this outfit."

"I do, I do," he says. "It's just that, couldn't you wear something a little more, I don't know, a little more sedate?"

Sedate? This is the guy who bought you a red lace garter belt for your birthday. This is the guy who once referred to spandex jeans as "classy" and "elegant." This is also the guy who, unless you're wearing the red lace garter belt or spandex jeans, usually doesn't notice your clothes at all. You want him to think you look good, but who is he to tell you how to dress, anyway?

A lot of women will deny that men influence the clothes they wear. In fact, whether women are conscious of it or not, whether men seem oblivious to clothes or offer specific fashion advice, men are often the strongest outside influence—stronger than bosses, co-workers, friends, or family—in determining what women wear.

According to the 1984 study in *Glamour* on the psychology of clothes, 75 percent of women say their husbands or partners are the primary influence on the way they dress. Most likely to care what a man thinks: younger women and women whose fathers took an interest in their clothes when they were children. Least likely to be influenced by a man: married women in their thirties or older who rank intelligence as the most important component of their self-images.

"Definitely those results showed that, except for highly paid older executive women, in almost all circumstances women dress for men," says Patricia Mulready, the New York University professor who co-authored the study. "For young women men were number one, and that does not surprise me."

There are several reasons why young women are most likely to dress with men—a specific man, or the general male population—in mind. Young women are more apt to be actively trying to find boyfriends, for instance, and they also tend to be more impressionable, less sure of their own taste in clothes.

"In my twenties I wasn't secure about clothes and I was always hoping to attract someone," says one woman, now thirty-seven and married. "I was in a phase of really wanting to be sexy. I dressed in high heels and really nice dresses and paid a lot of attention to how I looked."

Another woman, now in her fifties, says, "I was married very young the first time and my first husband influenced my clothes a lot. He liked very slinky, sexy kinds of things, and I was perfectly willing to oblige. My mother made me a few evening dresses with his direction, and one of them had a skirt that was so tight I couldn't pull it up to go to the bathroom."

While this woman admits she's "always been influenced in my clothing choices by the men in my life and what they would like," she also says, "I'm less influenced now, because I know what I look good in. My husband loves my clothes but he doesn't talk about them very often; he tries to downplay it because he thinks I'm a fanatic. And I don't always tell him what I spend because he's so grossed out."

Often, how men influence the clothes you choose simply becomes more unconscious, less obvious over time.

"Absolutely men have influenced the way I dress, to the point that it's now just become a way of dressing," says a thirty-two-year-old woman. "I don't mean things that are very exposed, but eye-catching. I like looking attractive."

"If you're fifty and you've been married for twenty-five years to the same man he's probably had an influence for so long you don't even realize that's what's happened," says Arlene Kagle, Ph.D., a New York psychotherapist. "If you're really building a life together, then you're probably going to change your wardrobe because your life will be different. If you marry someone and buy a house in the country, you may find yourself with more work jeans, more mud clothes, than when you had a two-bedroom riverview apartment. If you wear a bright color and your mate says you look terrific, you may consciously or unconsciously buy more, and if you wear a bright color and your mate says, 'What? Another red dress?' you may make a major shift to blue. Clothes can be a way to please someone you love. I don't consider it to be a neurotic tendency."

The bottom line, from Stephanie Miller, a social worker and executive director of the Women's Counseling and Psychotherapy Service in Columbia and Towson, Maryland: "There's nothing wrong with wanting to please a man if he also wants to please you."

Many women say, in fact, that their mates' influence on their clothes has been only positive.

"I live with a man who has very definite ideas about style and I don't agree with many of them, but he has allowed me to be more confident about my own choices," says one woman. "I don't naturally wear much makeup and I feel no pressure from him to do so. I find high heels uncomfortable and he doesn't like them, either. He's so accepting: I like cotton briefs and the same old stretched-out bras, and his idea of sexy is Carter's underpants."

"If you're really absolutely in love with the man you live with and he totally adores you, you just let go and appreciate parts of you that you didn't consider attractive before," says one woman. "I thought I had a big tush and had never worn super-tight-fitting pants, but this man loves my tush and for Christmas bought me the most beautiful water silk pants that fit me like a glove; I poured my body into them. I got myself a tight black velvet vest to wear with the pants and I realized this is an outfit I'm wearing because I feel really loved by this man. Being totally loved had let me love myself."

A man's idea of how he'd like you to dress, and how that relates to your vision of yourself, often becomes apparent only when he buys you clothes.

"My husband's image of me tends to be ahead of my image of myself," says one woman. "He bought me a bathing suit with high-cut legs before it ever occurred to me that I could get away with that style. At first I thought, No way, and spent the first three days I wore it trying to pull it down. Then he said, 'If you'll just look at yourself you'll see that you look really fabulous.' I tend to be more timid in my choices than he is, but so far in the end he's always right."

Another woman says her husband's clothing gifts "have to sit in my closest for several months to get used to my other clothes. He bought me a beautiful purple leather jacket, and when I opened it up I immediately felt shy and unworthy and it was a long time before I could wear it. This Christmas he bought me a black leather miniskirt but three sizes too small. I returned it and they didn't have a bigger size, but it was a very flattering gesture."

Other women, however, say that their husbands' taste is not only ahead of their own but on another planet, and that clothing gifts could (and often do) sit in the closet for a millennium and still wouldn't mix with the rest of their wardrobes.

"My husband travels around the world, and thinks handiwork is pretty," says one woman, who prefers classic, clean-lined clothes. "He once bought me a hand-embroidered blouse from the Philippines that I kept in my closet for six years. I wore it once and I felt ridiculous. Finally, I gave it away and he said I'd never given it a chance."

Another woman says, "My husband is afraid to buy me clothes. It's a combination of him being out of it and knowing he's out of it and me having such specific taste. There are men who can look at an outfit on a mannequin and know it's right and even buy it in the right size, but my husband isn't one of them."

While women often invest great care in dressing to please or attract a man, paying close attention to details of cut and style and color, many men in fact don't notice those subtleties, don't pick up on nuances of fashion. "Most straight men don't notice clothes consciously," says Sheila Jackman, Ph.D., director of the division of human sexuality at the Albert Einstein College of Medicine in New York. "If you showed a man two dresses he could say yes to one, no to another, but our culture has not made it okay for men to pay close attention."

Says Dr. Kagle, "I have yet to meet any heterosexual men who find extremes of fashion pleasant to look at. When a woman is wearing any kind of extreme, she may be intentionally or unintentionally keeping men from finding her attractive. I don't think that you should wander around in pink ruffles, but you should also be aware that most men don't notice if a jacket has the wide lapels of 1985 or the narrow lapels of 1986, or whatever it is that fashionable people find important."

Valerie Steele, Ph.D., a fashion writer and theorist, says many men's ideas of what's attractive harken back to what their own mothers wore. "That's why men are sort of retrograde in their appreciation of new fashions," she says. "If it were up to men we'd still be wearing sky blue shirtwaist dresses with Peter Pan collars."

One woman, who says she suspects that she considers other women above men when she chooses her clothes, says, "Practically anything you pulled together would look fine to a guy, while women are holding you up to higher standards. Women may be judging every detail but I'm surprised if a man ever remarks on something subtle. I wore an antique pin to my husband's company party and two men there complimented me on it. I was amazed that they noticed; I wouldn't expect it of heterosexual men."

What *do* men notice? Often, only what's most extreme. "My husband doesn't influence what I buy," says one woman, "because he can't figure out what I'd like. Sometimes when he points to something in a magazine I'm shocked: it's stuff a real tart would wear."

While there are men who make women feel good about their clothes, and men who are simply oblivious, there are other men whose interest in what their girlfriends or wives wear is not so pure, not so selfless. Some men see a well-dressed woman as an accessory, a status symbol, and conversely, some men may be threatened when their wives or lovers wear attractive clothes.

"In some circles it's very important to some men to have their women dress like they're being kept very expensively," says Sarah Hirshfield, M.S.W., a psychotherapist who practices in Long Island and New Jersey. "Some men may see their women as extensions of themselves, and if you objectify rather than personify someone you're going to get all this garbage: 'Why are you wearing that ratty old thing? ' And of course certain women are chosen by these men very specifically and fall right into the contract. For women who are taught from day one that their mission on earth is to look attractive, get a man, and have a family, then that's what they're going to get when they grow up."

Has the women's movement changed all that? To some extent, but for women's clothes, status and sex appeal are still often intertwined, according to several studies on the psychology of dress. Men who see their wives and girlfriends as status symbols, say psychologists and clothing experts, often encourage them to wear clothes that are at once obviously expensive and obviously sexy. And women who derive all their status from their husbands may either comply or downright insist on wearing those kinds of clothes.

Value judgments aside, the real question here is choice: is a woman choosing to wear the clothes she does, whatever her motives, or is a man literally making all her dressing decisions?

"It's a whole different thing when a man is saying 'Wear this blouse' or 'Don't wear that blouse,' " says Dr. Jackman. "He may really be saying, 'It's okay for me to look at other women but I don't want any other man looking at you,' or 'It's okay for you to wear that in the house but no one else should see that part of you.' "

"My boyfriend was very critical of the way I dressed," says one woman. "One day we went for a walk and I wore an old blouse of my mother's and a fifties skirt that I had worn all the time in the summer for years. He got furious because the blouse was low-cut and other people could see my cleavage and he said that belonged to him. I screamed, 'I've had my body longer than I've had you.' Then I thought, Why am I freaking out? I should be flattered. I'm very unresolved about this whole issue, because I want to be feminist and say it's my body, but on the other hand what I wanted was to be with one person, to have him appreciate me, and not to need all that outside attention."

The source of confusion is often mixed messages from the man himself: he's initially attracted to a woman on the basis of sexy or flamboyant clothes, but then may want her to dress more conservatively once they're together. The underlying issue, again, is control: whether a woman chooses to dress differently postcommitment or whether she feels forced into it.

"It makes sense if you love someone and he's not asking for strange things to try and please him in your dress because he's the one you want to look at you and think you're a sexy, wonderful person," says Stephanie Miller. "But there are men I see in marriage counseling who are very controlling, where it's not a mutual thing. They may want their wives to dress like Muslims because they're jealous. A woman shouldn't give in to that, but then she has more problems than clothes."

EMOTIONAL ISSUE:
STRAIGHT FROM THE HORSE'S, ER, MOUTH

So there you are trying to figure out just what he expects you to wear to dinner at his mother's house. What do men want, anyway?

Theories are fine, but I wanted facts. I thought I'd better go to the source and ask some intelligent men what exactly they thought about women's clothes.

Before you dismiss the comments that follow as the babbling of idiots, I should say in defense of the men I talked with that they have all done a lot of thinking—thinking about computer software, thinking about the stock market, thinking about poetry, thinking about law, thinking about baseball. They just, as you will discover, have not done much thinking about women's clothes, as least not what women would call thinking.

"Do you notice women's clothes?" I ask one man, a stock market analyst.

"Yes," he says decisively.

"What do you notice?"

"I notice," he says, hesitating, "I notice a lot how women's bodies look in clothes."

"Women's clothes are sex," says another man bluntly. "When you talk about a woman's clothes you can't use neutered words like 'pretty' or 'stylish.' When you're looking at a woman you're so caught up in sexual imaginings, and clothes are so much a part of that, unbuttoning, touching. They're some sort of distillation, a real expression of sexuality."

Most women, I tell him, don't view their clothes quite so unilaterally.

"Oh?" he says. "Really?"

Another man says he prefers clothes that are "distinctive, classy and unusual." Like what? "I like earrings. Black anything. I'm really big on sweaters, angora or bright colors. Shoes never did that much for me. But I do like see-through blouses and fishnet stockings."

Sigh.

"I like my girlfriend to dress as sexily as possible, within the bounds. I don't want her to look like a hooker," says a lawyer. What sort of outfit would be to his taste? "Oh, a slinky dress, tight-fitting, slit up the side of the leg, low-cut, no bra."

Doesn't he think that get-up might cross the bounds of what Grandma would call decency?

"There is a line," he admits, "but it's at the 40 instead of the 10."

Are these guys for real? Would the lawyer truly be delighted if his girlfriend showed up at his firm's Christmas party in the dress he described, or is all this just fantasy?

Truth be told, most men have a far heartier appetite for blatantly sexy clothes than women do. On the other hand, many men have trouble describing exactly which clothes they find attractive, and when pressed for details often cite comic-book-obvious items. In real life, men may be entranced by women wearing silk pleated skirts or cashmere turtlenecks, but most would be hard-pressed to recall the specifics of the clothes or articulate their appeal.

In fact, the very mystery of women's clothing is exactly what many men like. "There's a women at work who has such a great sense of dressing," says one man. "She wears wild things; she has an endless amount of clothes;

I never see her wearing the same thing twice. I'm not sure how it's done and I can't even remember anything specific, but what I like is that she always looks different."

Part of what he admires, he says, is this woman's mastery of a skill he finds so unknowable. In contrast, he offers the example of another woman he knows: "When I first met her I thought she was attractive, but as time went by I decided that she dressed herself in the worst possible way. I remember one thing she wore: a brownish dress that was a little too big not in a good way. It tells you so much about the person that they never learned to do those dressing things."

Still, there's learning and there's learning. A woman who is too involved in her clothes is as likely to turn some men off as one who is oblivious.

"I might be attracted to someone who was overly dressed, who was really into makeup and fancy jewelry," says one man, "but I wouldn't want to be involved with her for more than a week." Why not? "It suggests a strong sense of herself based on material or outside things; someone who looks outside instead of inside herself to find out who she is."

Another man claims that a lack of interest in clothes is precisely what attracts him to a woman. He talks fondly of an ex-girlfriend who hated to shop, wore castoffs from friends, and never really looked right. "I'll never," he says sadly, "find another woman as unfashionable as she was."

Some men say they have philosophical objections to conventionally attractive clothes . . . but. "I always say how ridiculous it is that women wear confining and impractical things that don't let them move, like high heels," says one man, "yet I like the way they look."

One man, after searching for words to describe the clothes he likes, finally gives up. "I know women put a lot of effort into clothes as an element of attraction," he says, "but to tell you the truth, most of the time men have no idea, not a clue, what women are wearing. Most guys don't even know what *they're* wearing."

Five Fashion Options for the Nontraditional Bride

Maybe it's your second marriage. Or maybe you're an adventurous dresser. Or maybe you just feel too damn old to get into one of those elaborate white wedding dresses.

Today, there are lots of just-as-appropriate alternatives for the bride who wants to wear something different. Not only do these options often look better than traditional wedding dresses, most are far less expensive.

If you want to wear a nontraditional outfit for your wedding, consider the following:

1. **AN ANTIQUE DRESS**—Not the well-preserved white lace Victorian dress that's become almost as common as the filmy polyester getups in every corner bridal shop: something that shows a little more imagination. Consider a twenties flapper dress, something slim-cut and tea-length in silk chiffon or with wonderful beads. Or a fifties ultra prom dress—pastel, off-the-shoulder, with an outrageously full net skirt and three crinolines beneath. For the vampy bride: a Jean Harlow-esque, bias-cut thirties evening gown in silk charmeuse or silk velvet. Or how about his-and-hers tuxedos—à la Elvis, of course.

2. **AN UNSUITABLE-FOR-BUSINESS SUIT**—There was a time when many a bride felt compelled to make a feminist statement about marriage by showing up for the wedding as if it were a conference at IBM. She wore a suit—a businesslike, garbardine suit (maybe it was ivory instead of gray) with a plain white shirt. Now, that look is wrong but the idea is right. Instead of a blazer, think curvy little peplumed jacket. Instead of a baggy, knee-length skirt, think short, tight, and slit, or long, pleated, and silk. When considering a suit as possible wedding garb, ask yourself if you could wear it to any conceivable business event. The answer to this question must be no.

3. **SOMETHING NAUTICAL**—Take a cue from one hip bride who marched down the aisle wearing a pink-trimmed white sailor dress, complete with straw boater. The groom wore a navy blazer and white pants, a tastefully polka-dotted tie, and a boater. And the flower girl (if you go nautical, you've got to have one) wore a proper navy-and-white sailor dress . . . and a boater.

4. **ONE WONDERFUL NON-WEDDING DRESS**—Think of all the dresses you've fantasized about buying if you only had someplace to wear them. Realize that now you do. Compared to the price of a run-of-the-mill wedding gown, a fabulous body-hugging evening dress from

Norma Kamali, say, or a billowing silk outfit from a Japanese designer will not seem so outrageous. Then after you're married, you get to think of places to go so you can wear the dress again.

5. **TWO WONDERFUL NON-WEDDING DRESSES**—You're having a small private ceremony and a low-key reception for family in the afternoon, and a wild party for friends at night. Instead of trying to find one dress that both won't shock Aunt Mildred and will wow your pals, buy two dresses. For the wedding proper, look for something feminine and demure—ecru or pale pink silk with pearl buttons in back and a softly pleated, mid-calf skirt. At night, play out every fantasy of the not-so-innocent bride: wear red, wear strapless, wear sequins. Wear black, for that matter—just be sure the groom realizes you're making a fashion statement, not a statement about him.

LOVE

7

Sex

You're in love, or maybe just in lust. No matter: the point is, you've planned a romantic evening with the object of your attraction and you want to wear something sexy, something that makes you feel sexy and also that he will find appealing.

Possible? Of course. Clothes have an irrefutable power to elicit sexual feelings: you know that from experience. Foolproof? Hardly. One element of confusion is that there's no such thing as sexy clothes per se. What's perceived as sexy has a little to do with fashion and more to do with culture and a lot to do with the individual: the body and mind of the wearer as well as the eye of the beholder. The fact is, people often disagree about what's sexy. The clothes that you find sensual may leave your best friend cold, and what both of you agree is sexy may be very different from what a man finds attractive.

Let's backtrack a little. How do clothes, which, after all, cover the body, further the desire to uncover it?

There's the basic animal theory of the sexual appeal of clothing. "The females are the less brilliantly colored in the animal kingdom so they get their partners by scent," says Sheila Jackman, Ph.D., director of the division of human sexuality at the Albert Einstein College of Medicine in New York. "We've kind of wiped out our pheromones so we attract with this plumage we call clothing."

Some experts say that clothes act as literal sexual symbols: high heels accentuate the curve of the calf to create a "breast" on the leg, for instance, or purses represent vaginas, ties stand for penises. Other theorists base the sexual appeal of clothes on neophilia—the love of the new—claiming that fashion changes because men are most stimulated by "new" body parts. After a few years of tight, low-cut shirts and long skirts, the theory goes, men get tired of breasts and yearn to see legs, and so turtlenecks and miniskirts are reborn.

While all these theories may contain elements of truth, the real reason clothes have sexual power is probably at once larger and simpler than any of the individual theories. "It's silly to say that men get tired of breasts. Men never get tired of breasts," says Valerie Steele, Ph.D., author of *Fashion and Eroticism* (Oxford University Press, 1985) and professor of the history and social psychology of dress, in the graduate division of the Fashion Institute of Technology. "The trouble with a lot of sex appeal theorists is that they assume clothing functions as a basic sexual lure or sexual code, and I think that's nonsense. While some kinds of sexy clothes are an overt lure, like prostitutes' clothes, most women dress up to look pretty or sexy not with the overt intention of seduction but to create an image of sexual beauty."

If fashion doesn't change simply to satisfy a male desire to see legs, say, instead of breasts, new styles and shapes are nonetheless often trumpeted as sexy, sensual, alluring, or at least feminine. Ads and fashion layouts often give a stronger impression of sexiness than of the clothes themselves. The message: wear these clothes and you will look sexy, he will find you sexy, and you will . . . well, the logical conclusion to that sentence is "have sex," but the implication and draw for many women is more likely to be "fall in love."

"Today sex and love go together," says Patricia Mulready, a New York University professor specializing in the social psychology of clothes. "If a woman is dressing to sexually attract someone she's probably trying to make him love her."

Whether and why a woman wears sexy clothes, and what she considers sexy, undeniably has something to do with the times. Women who came of age with feminism, for example, often have more negative feelings about dressing sexily, at least for public consumption, than younger women do.

Susan Kaiser, Ph.D., an associate professor at the University of California at Davis whose focus is the social and psychological aspects of clothing, has been working on a study about college students' attitudes toward sexy or attractive clothes. "We asked them if they ever felt people were really enjoying looking at them, and the female students said, 'Oh, sure,' " says Dr. Kaiser. "When we asked them how that made them feel, they said it didn't really bother them, that they liked being viewed as attractive. We didn't get comments about being on the street and having people ogling you; they viewed it as fine. I'm thirty-four, and I would respond very differently to those questions than they did. Feminism is becoming less prevalent among younger women."

An older woman, with feminist notions intact, may prefer a more self-oriented kind of sexiness in clothes—things designed not specifically to attract, but to make her feel sexy, independent of an audience.

"Hand a woman a mink bathrobe and I think you would get a sexual response," says Arlene Kagle, Ph.D., a New York psychotherapist. "It has something to do with what we've been trained to think of as luxurious. You have to be an expert to tell the difference between real silk and certain high-grade synthetics, but we've been trained to think of silk, satin, and mink as more luxurious and sensual."

"Recently advertising has educated American women that being sensuous is not directly connected to a man," says Sheila Jackman. "I'm thinking about ads for lingerie, cosmetics, stockings, that say this will make you feel sexy for you, not just for him. Nice fabrics feel good against your skin. Some women knew that all along, other women are just being given permission to realize that silk feels good, yucky pantyhose do not."

It's no accident that psychologists use words like "trained" and "educated" when talking about sexy clothes. Knowing which clothes make you feel sexy and carry sexual messages, they say, is not something you come by naturally; it's something you learn from sources as diverse as Barbie and *Vogue* and dear old mom.

"Sexual arousal is not an automatic biological response to the sight or touch of another person's body," says Valerie Steele. "You have to be conditioned to find a particular kind of clothes and a particular kind of body attractive. As we're growing up certain kinds of clothes become identified with eroticism and femininity or masculinity. I'm sure Uncle Sigmund is right and a lot of the time we're responding to things we saw and felt twenty years ago."

Identifying certain clothes as sexy or attractive starts early . . . very early. "By two years of age children have a good sense of sex differences based on clothing symbols," says Susan Kaiser. Very young children, says Dr. Kaiser, have an easier time telling males and females apart on the basis of their clothes than of their genitals. "If you put a wig and a dress on a doll with a penis, children will say it's a girl," says Dr. Kaiser. "Young kids see the sex differences in black and white; they don't tolerate the ambiguity we do later." For young children, what's most attractive are usually clothes that make sex differences most pronounced: ultra-curvaceous women in form-fitting, flouncy dresses, muscled He-Men in army uniforms.

"Part of the reason kids get into these stereotypes is the question of 'Who am I?' " says Ellen Berman, M.D., clinical associate professor of psychiatry at the University of Pennsylvania and co-director of the Women's Center at the Philadelphia Psychiatric Center. "The other thing is that being pretty is very powerful in this society, and when you're small that kind of power is very intriguing. It's fun for a little girl to dress in feminine, pretty clothes and get noticed. How many sources of power do you have when you're four?"

While children grow out of these exaggerated images of sexual allure by age six or seven, says Dr. Kaiser, that doesn't mean those ideals vanish forever. "A lot of ambivalence even on the part of people who reject sexy images is because we're still socialized to value those things in early childhood," Dr. Kaiser says. "That image is still there as to what our culture deems attractive, and it hasn't changed."

If a little girl dresses in hyperfeminine clothes at four, emulating a Barbie or Cinderella, and then wears nothing but jeans at age seven or nine, she may again become enamored of sexy or attractive clothes as a teenager, partly because she's newly obsessed with boys, partly because wearing grown-up clothes can take the place of actually growing up, and partly because her parents are likely to disapprove.

"Most teenagers want to feel older and more sexual and many parents are somewhat appropriately terrified of their children's sexuality," says Dr. Berman. "Wearing sexy clothing in adolescence is a wonderful way to have a fight."

Not only her parents' attitudes toward sexy clothes but their social status may influence a woman's ideas on what's sexy. "To working-class or poor people there are traditionally two ways out—athletics and entertainment—so women may dress like their favorite entertainer," says New York University professor Patricia Mulready. "For working-class women, a sexy look à la Dolly Parton or the young Farrah Fawcett may be what's considered attractive."

For middle-class women, according to Mulready, there's a wider range of acceptable choices. "And with old-money families in New England there is the Katharine Hepburn look and everything else is pretentious or overdone, New Rich or Texan, whatever the stereotype is of how you're not supposed to look," Mulready says. "That comes from the 1880s, which was the heyday of prescriptions on how you were supposed to dress at certain times of the day if you were a lady."

However a woman's idea of sexiness varies according to her age, class, upbringing, and politics, chances are it will also differ from a man's idea of what's sexy. For one thing, men tend to see all women's clothing—even items like nursing shoes that to women are decidedly nonsexy— as sexier than women do, according to Dr. Kaiser. "Part of that is that males view females as sex objects to some extent," Dr. Kaiser says. "And males will think there's some degree of sexiness in anything a woman could wear simply because a woman is wearing it."

For women, nuances of style and color can make the difference in whether clothes are sexy or attractive or not, while men may not notice those details. When clothes have more obvious sexy qualities—sheer fabric, a plunging neckline—women may judge them moderately attractive, Dr. Kaiser says, while men may see them as downright erotic. The bottom line, according to Dr. Kaiser, "There's room for a lot of misinterpretation."

When sexual messages have to cross not only gender boundaries but class ones, those misinterpretations can be serious indeed. In date rape cases involving middle-class men and working-class women, says Patricia Mulready, the man's defense is often that the woman was "asking for it" by wearing sexy clothes. "He may have grown up hearing his mother say that any woman who dressed like Madonna was cheap, a tramp," says Mulready, "when in her culture those clothes are a standard way to look attractive."

Another dilemma is that the clothes men judge as most attractive are also often the ones women see as least functional and comfortable, according to studies done by Dr. Kaiser. What's at work here is the old notion—still alive—that helplessness is sexy.

Also still thriving is the late James Laver's "Erotic Principle," which says that sex appeal is the dominant force in women's clothing, while hierarchy is dominant in men's clothes. In a study of the semiotics of shoes, Dr. Kaiser found that, "The woman's shoe that was thought the most sexy and attractive was also judged the highest in status. That was what surprised me the most, that people still equated sexiness with status so strongly."

Kaiser says her findings suggest that women still often have to make a choice between looking competent and appropriate or sexy and attractive, that it's difficult for women to find clothing that—at least in men's eyes—does both. However, Dr. Kaiser says, what most women want their clothes to project is, in semiotic parlance, "neither–norism": "Women neither want to be strictly sex objects nor competent without any attractive qualities. The shoe study suggests, though, that it's difficult for women to be viewed as competent without being thought of as cold."

The good news: "Since I did that study there have been more colorful shoes with lower heels, attractive but still comfortable," says Dr. Kaiser. "In semiotics this is a 'both–and' kind of solution: clothes that are both attractive and functional."

Meanwhile, your decision about whether to wear those high heels or the suede flats for your romantic evening has become infinitely more complicated. The suede flats expose a little toe cleavage, but will he even notice? He'll definitely like the heels, but do you really want breasts on your legs, and are you willing to sacrifice the ability to walk? Will opening one extra button incite him to bestial behavior? And what, after all, would your mother say?

Ah, sex. And you thought it was going to get easier.

• *Style Analysis* •

LIISA MARGOSIAN *is a makeup artist, aspiring actress, and sometime baby-sitter who lives in Los Angeles. She's wearing a cropped jacket by Vedra of Ibiza, bought at Sara in Santa Monica for $10 (marked down from $158); a Betsey Johnson bandeau that was $25; a lace-and-linen skirt bought in a Big Sur shop for $80, over lace Betsey Johnson leggings, $28. Liisa's boots are Kenneth Cole, purchased at Sacha of London in Los Angeles for $110. Two of her silver bracelets are from Arizona, gifts from her father; the other— featuring famous French monuments— was brought from Paris by a great-uncle more than fifty years ago.*

YOU SEEM TO HAVE AN EASY TIME DRESSING IN A WAY THAT'S SEXY OR FEMININE, AND I WONDER WHAT THAT'S ABOUT FOR YOU.

I was really influenced by dancers. Before *Flashdance* even came out, the clothes I was most comfortable in were falling-off-the-shoulder shirts and pants pulled up really high with belts around them. I love boots, and again, I think that's from dancing. I've always liked the feeling of lacing up toe shoes, and so I love lacing up boots and have lots of those kinds of boots.

I have lace tights that I wear underneath a lot of things, and I think they make things sexy. I'm not afraid to wear something where the slit is ripped a little too high.

IT'S INTERESTING THAT YOU USED THE WORD "AFRAID," BECAUSE FOR A LOT OF WOMEN IT'S SCARY TO WEAR SOMETHING SEXY OUT ON THE STREET, AND IT DOESN'T SEEM SCARY FOR YOU. WHY?

It's risky for me because I don't feel I have this great body that I want to show off. On the other hand I feel that this is the person that I am right now and why cover it up. My mom used to say wearing really bagging clothes lets you not face up to who you really are and what you really are. It's not like I wear things that show off my body necessarily but that I'm not trying to cover it up.

HOW DO YOUR CLOTHES EXPRESS YOU?

I don't have a big budget for clothes, and if I can't change my wardrobe I can change my accessories. It's in the accessories that I express myself. I'll find a really great tie-dyed big scarf and I'll throw it over something that I've been wearing for years or I'll tie it around my waist and change the whole look of the outfit just to say, "Well, I've got a little bit of this hippie in me."

HOW DO YOU MANAGE TO FIND THE KINDS OF THINGS THAT YOU WANT ON A TIGHT BUDGET?

There's a great store in L.A. called the American Rag Company, that's a combination of vintage clothing and designer clothing. You can find a great black dress for $110 and a vintage jacket to go with it for $15. If I start out with a dress for $100 and I have $40 more to spend I can completely change the look by adding things to it.

I shop at The Limited a lot: I can get ideas from a more expensive shop and buy something similar at The Limited for $150.

IF YOU HAD A LOT MORE MONEY, WOULD YOU DRESS DIFFERENTLY?

It used to be when I saw a skirt that was $500 I would think it was outrageous, the worst capitalism imaginable, and that if I had $500 I wouldn't buy that skirt. But now I think I would, because when I go to interviews or auditions I have to be dressed in a way that says I'm worth the money they're going to pay me for the job. I can't go in looking like I don't have the money to support that statement. At the same time, I also want to look put together so somebody will trust my judgment and my work.

When I first moved to L.A. I bought a cream full-length silk duster for $350, but it's the greatest thing I've bought because I can wear it over anything and make it look like a million dollars. A lot of times on interviews I don't take it off, because it doesn't look like a coat. I usually wear it over a rayon black blouse with cream flowers that was $29, and a pair of off-white rayon pants that I bought at The Limited that look like silk pants, that were about $30.

A LOT OF WOMEN WHO LIKE TO SHOP CHEAP SHOP AT OUTLETS OR DEPARTMENT STORE SALES. IT SOUNDS AS IF YOU DO IT DIFFERENTLY. WHY?

I don't get a regular paycheck every week because I free-lance. I'll get a lot of money all at once and then I go for weeks without any money. I keep track of what I need—for instance right now I need an oversized black wool cardigan—and if I find it I'll spend $200 on it. But then I'll wear it with a Hanes T-shirt. I'll spend a lot of money in one area and not much in others.

I'm not a budget shopper, but then again I don't have a big budget. I read a lot of magazines and I look at a lot of catalogs, and I'll see what they're showing and then go into my closet and try to put it together. Once or twice a week I'll put something together in a way I never have before. My dad got me this shirt and skirt for Christmas two years ago, which never really worked as an outfit, but I wear the shirt to work all the time with a pair of pants and just recently I put the skirt together with another jacket that I already had and a belt and a pair of boots and those lace tights and discovered this great little outfit that I didn't think I had.

HOW MUCH DOES FASHION INFLUENCE WHAT YOU WEAR?

In my closet I've got mini mini mini skirts and I've got skirts that go down to my ankles, and I wear the whole spectrum. If something short's appropriate, if I'm going to a beach party, I might wear a short miniskirt over capri pants with an oversized sweatshirt belted in. When I go to work the next day I'll wear a skirt that goes down to my ankles.

HOW DO YOU DECIDE TO MAKE THOSE CHANGES, TO WEAR A VERY SHORT SKIRT ONE DAY AND A VERY LONG ONE THE NEXT?

I'm really influenced by theater, by films, and by musicians. If I went to see some movie that has to do with living out on a farm, the next day I might wear my peasanty clothes. It all has to do with what I'm walking into and what I've walked out of.

WHAT WAS IT LIKE MOVING FROM NEW YORK TO L.A. IN TERMS OF HOW YOU DRESS?

When I first moved to L.A., no one understood my style. I was wearing black stretchy pants and black lace-up boots and a black Norma Kamali shirt with shoulder pads. In a way those clothes work for me here, but it's so hot here. You become more body-conscious because you can't wear so many layers and scarves; you have to wear things that are sleeker.

People here have great bodies, and because of the industry you have to keep up with what's going on in the film business. It's very superficial; it's very silly. Some of the L.A. style is silly—very short, layered lace skirts, but I do have a couple.

WHAT WERE SOME EARLY INFLUENCES ON YOUR WAY OF DRESSING?

I grew up in a very conservative suburb of Boston, but when I was about eleven years old I went for the summer to live on a commune in Canada. It was 1975, so it was still the hippie free-thinking seventies. That really was the thing that changed my style. Up until then I was wearing what everybody else was wearing in the seventies. Up there, everybody was running around in bell-bottoms and hip-huggers and gauzy things tied around their heads, and I came back to the suburbs three months later with my hair in these hippie braids. That gave me this real feeling of independence.

I was raised to be conventionally pretty, and that made me very self-conscious. Now, putting on really funky oversized glasses or really nerdy glasses or something that actually makes me look uglier gives me a certain freedom with my style. By wearing something that's a little bit weird or a little bit offbeat allows me not to be that woman that everybody thinks is so pretty.

IT SEEMS AS IF, BY COMBINING CLOTHES THAT ARE MORE CONVENTIONALLY PRETTY WITH THE OFFBEAT ONES, YOU'RE SAYING, "YEAH, I'M PRETTY, AND I ENJOY IT, BUT ALL OF ME IS NOT INVESTED IN THAT."

The other day I was going out to dinner with my boyfriend and I said, "Maybe I better go home and change," and he said, "Change? What are you going to change into? You're just going to look as funky as you do now." I had just come out of a yoga class. I was wearing sweatpants that have seen a million apartment paintings with this wonderful leather bomber jacket and I was wearing my hair in a baseball cap with a huge velvet ribbon in the back. I was wearing these shoes I bought in London last year that now are the rage here—thick-rubber-soled suede shoes. Together, this definitely made a statement, but I wasn't trying to.

EMOTIONAL ISSUE:
THE SECRET POWER OF LINGERIE

You are in the audience of a large conference on world banking, wearing just what everyone else is wearing: a tailored navy blue suit, a white shirt, sensible black shoes. An interesting-looking man approaches the podium, and you shift in your seat to get a better view, when something happens. Something only you are aware of, something slightly uncomfortable but not quite unpleasant. Simultaneously, the strap of your lace bra has slipped off your shoulder, one of your garters has popped, and your silk tap pants have what can delicately only be called "ridden up."

This is a fantasy, this is only a fantasy. Or is it? Much has been made in recent years of the image of the conservative businesswoman with a personal secret. Under those serious suits, beneath that corporate exterior, she's wearing the most feminine, most luxurious, sexiest lingerie imaginable.

One thing is for certain: sales of sexy lingerie have boomed since the bra-less, back-to-nature era ended in the mid-seventies. And the design of lingerie—mass-market as well as expensive, basic as well as whimsical—has reached never-before-explored regions of both sensuality and playfulness.

The question remains: Are women really wearing elaborate lingerie? When, exactly? And why?

"I have a very curvy figure, and when you have a body that already gives itself away, you want to save something for the one who really gets to see you," says one woman. "I'm totally obsessed with sexy, lacy, provocative bras, but that's my secret."

"I would love to be into lingerie," says another woman. "My husband bought me a black silk teddy for my thirtieth birthday, and I like the way it feels, I like the way it looks. I'd like to be the kind of woman who walks around in lace teddies and pomponned mules all day, like Jerri Hall. But the truth is, I'm not."

"I have this enormous drawer underneath my bed," says another woman, "that is completely packed with sexy lingerie, all stuff my husband bought for me before we got married, when we first got married, and once in a while now, although he's pretty much given up. I'm strictly a comfortable cotton underpants and stretch bra woman, and I've worn each of those sexy things at most one time for five minutes."

"I love lingerie," says another woman. "It feels really nice if I open my underwear drawer and see a lot of lace. But I'm not so much into panties as different kinds of bras. I have one black lacy bra that makes me aware of my body in a different way, because it tends to come unhooked. Frilly stuff gets me thinking about my body more than normal underwear does."

Indeed, wearing sexy lingerie is, for most women, an entirely different enterprise than wearing regulation underwear. Sexy lingerie can call up issues like body image, sexual pressure, and—not incidentally—a lot of ambivalence.

"Women's negative body images make it impossible for lots of women to put on lingerie that says 'Stare at me,'" says Sheila Jackman, Ph.D., a psychologist and sex therapist. "If you're not comfortable with your body, feeling like you're under a microscope is not a turn-on, it's a turn-off. It's also 'What am I supposed to do now that I have it on?' A lot of women would like to try it, and then feel stupid, and then wonder what's wrong with them. Another feeling that's very pervasive is 'I'm not enough myself, I need this extra.' "

Whether a woman likes sexy lingerie or not, there's often a man's opinion to contend with. And his feelings, surprisingly, may be just as ambivalent as her own, can affect her feelings if she's wearing lingerie partly to please him.

"Right after college I lived with a boyfriend for three years who loved sexy underwear," says the woman who loves it too. "We were pretty young and innocent and it was fine. I know men who only get turned on by the thought of underwear, and that makes me feel like a whore. I had another boyfriend who was totally embarrassed by the fact that he might or might not get turned on by my underwear. For my birthday I asked him for sexy underwear and what I got was a milk steamer."

The reason lingerie incites such varied and complex responses? Ads about serious businesswomen wearing lingerie for their pleasure only, aside, most people still associate sexy underwear directly with sex, a complex issue in itself.

"If you ask people whether they wear sexy lingerie, some women will say they like it and some don't; some men like it and some feel pressured by it," says Patricia Mulready, a New York University professor specializing in the social psychology of clothes. "But anytime you see lingerie on TV or in a movie you know sex is going to happen or someone's seducing someone. It doesn't always happen that way in real life."

"Breasts and vaginas are supposed to turn men on so they can procreate, and the mystery—dressing it up so you can see or not see what's under the lingerie—is an extension of that," says Dr. Jackman. "It doesn't mean there's something wrong with you if you don't like it. It's just more plumage."

The Best: Silk Negligee

Spaghetti Straps—Sexiest and slinkiest, although flat half-inch straps will be more comfortable.

V Neck—Most flattering, best fit.

Tailored Facing at Bodice—Indicates better quality than a simple hem.

No Lace—Unless it's very fine imported or antique lace, lace at the bodice can cheapen the look of a silk negligee, may wear faster than the fabric itself, can pucker and pull and itch.

Silk Charmeuse—Charmeuse is the kind of silk that resembles satin: it has some weight and a sheen. There are some quite good synthetic charmeuses, but none that truly live up to the look and feel and quality of real silk.

Solid, Not Patterned, Fabric—Jacquards or prints can make you look heavier.

Bias Cut—This means the fabric is cut on the diagonal, which makes it slink over your body, move when you do. Charmeuse cut on the bias is what made Jean Harlow look so great.

Tailored but Generous Shape—A charmeuse negligee should not pull or be uncomfortable, but should look as if it were pinned to fit your body. Good silk, cut on the bias, should do this effortlessly.

French Seams—Seams are sewn twice, so no edges at all are visible on the inside.

Hand-Rolled Hem—A rolled hem has a "soft" edge, is doubled under, is sewn with tiny stitches.

Ankle Length—The most classic and luxurious; as long as you've gone this far, you might as well go all the way.

A Note on Caring for Silk Lingerie: Most fine silk lingerie is labeled "Dry Clean Only" or sometimes "Dry Clean or Hand Wash," which can be enough to make you run for the polyester. What you should know is that those care labels are primarily for the protection of the manufacturer, who understandably does not want people returning shriveled silk undies that went through the "Heavy" cycle with the towels and blue jeans. In fact, says designer Sami, who makes some of the best silk lingerie around, "I've had my charmeuse negligees for almost nine years, and I really abuse them because I want to know what they can stand up to. I put them in the washer on a gentle setting with mild detergent; when I take them out I shake them to get them going the right way, and then I let them dry a bit on a line and iron them when they're damp. They come out beautifully and they don't have that dry-cleaner smell."

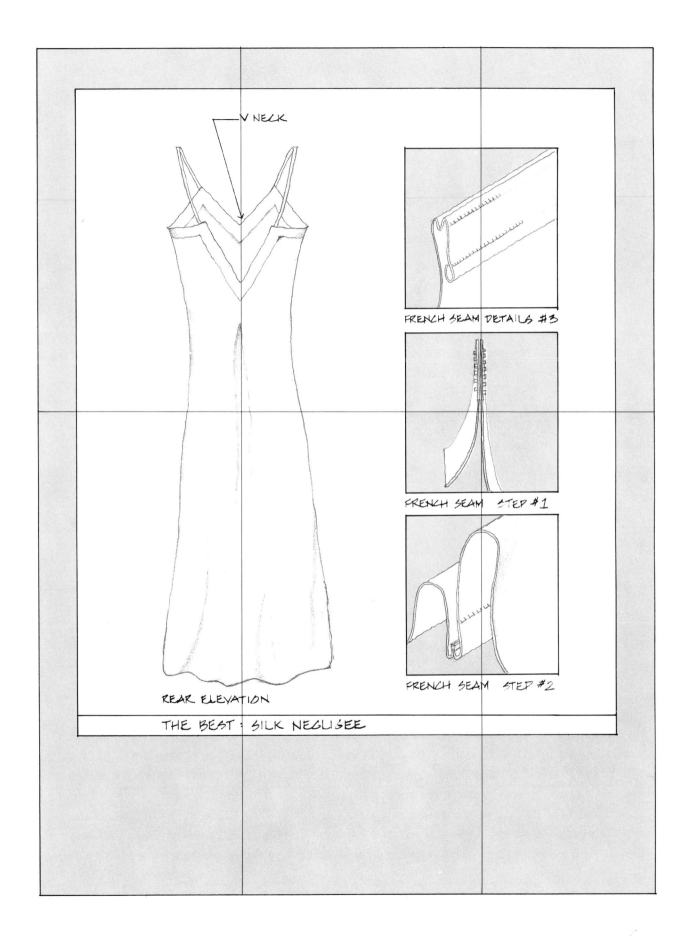

V NECK

FRENCH SEAM DETAILS #3

FRENCH SEAM STEP #1

FRENCH SEAM STEP #2

REAR ELEVATION

THE BEST : SILK NEGLIGEE

8

Kids: How Pregnancy and Motherhood Affect Style

•

When you contemplate having a child, you imagine that you'll get big and have to wear some sort of maternity clothes, and then after the baby's born you'll go back to wearing your old clothes.

You don't imagine the baby spitting up on your silk blouse. You don't imagine mashed peas on your white skirt. You don't imagine that your white skirt will no longer fit even when you've lost all of your pregnancy weight because your hips are slightly but irrevocably broader and your stomach is unalterably rounder. You don't realize you will no longer have time to shop for a replacement for that white skirt. Or time to make sure your shoes match before you leave the house. Or—now that you're paying a baby-sitter $700 a month and a mortgage that's double the rent on your pre-child one-bedroom apartment—you will no longer be able to afford to buy many clothes, even if you had the time and energy to do so.

Just as having a baby can spark a revolution in the way you live, so can it bring a dramatic change in the way you dress.

What surprises many women is that dressing for pregnancy can be infinitely simpler and more fun than dressing after the baby is born. For starters, being pregnant gives you a mandate to go out and buy new clothes. And the different physical requirements of pregnancy—needing clothes that are more comfortable, that let you move, that don't define your figure—can lead women to explore ways of dressing they haven't tried before, new styles that may carry over to their postpregnancy clothes. Rather than finding pregnancy clothes restricting to their style, many women find them liberating.

"I loved dressing for pregnancy," says one woman. "I loved having a limited number of outfits and feeling like I was excused to wear them all the time. I should have been Catholic, because I discovered I love wearing uniforms. And after I went back to work, and even now that my son is three, I got into that concept of uniform-dressing much more than I had before. I have five great things and I don't mind wearing them every day."

Susan Gaynes, a New York dietitian and the mother of an infant son, gave up high heels and figure-hugging clothes when she was pregnant and now—partly for practical and partly for aesthetic reasons—continues to wear more comfortable clothes. "I didn't wear maternity clothes when I was pregnant. In the winter when I was getting large I wore long sweaters with elastic-waist pants or skirts I bought in my regular size or one size larger," she says. "Now I've kept that style because I like it."

Other women also say they got hooked on comfortable clothes after discovering them while pregnant. "Now I just can't wear anything that's physically uncomfortable," says one woman. "I won't wear shoes that don't feel good, I won't wear anything that's too tight in the waist, I won't wear itchy material, and I will never do it again."

"As soon as I got pregnant I started wearing sweatpants and I kept wearing them until my husband threatened to kill me if he saw me in them one more time," says one woman. "Then I started branching out into other kinds of knit pants, but being pregnant totally devastated my desire to get dressed in anything that wasn't totally comfortable."

What most women don't like—however comfortable—are conventional maternity clothes. "I was appalled by the selection," says one woman. "It's almost impossible to avoid bows, flowers, ruffles, and fake polyester crapola."

"I can't stand pregnancy clothes and the way they make women look like little girls," says Maria Friedrich, an art adviser to private collectors, who became pregnant with her second child when her daughter was only five months old. Instead of conventional maternity clothes, Friedrich bought a turquoise coat "to cheer me up," a two-piece wool outfit that stretches over her belly and looks like a jumpsuit, and a pair of pants. "I care about keeping my style when I'm pregnant and I'm not at all embarrassed about my shape: I'm not waddling around in muumuus," she says.

"When you're pregnant another person really is in your body, and although that person will probably wear pastels, it doesn't mean you have to," says Judy Newmark, editor of the St. Louis *Post-Dispatch* Sunday magazine and the mother of two young daughters. "It's difficult because a lot of manufacturers miss that point. I hate things that make you look like the baby. I am not a chicken-print woman."

During her pregnancy with her first daughter, who was born in August "of the hottest summer in St. Louis history," Newmark relied on "real thin cotton Indian dresses like we wore in the sixties. They were so lightweight that one of the few maternity things I bought was a maternity slip. I wore these dresses all the time: they were extremely cool, colorful, big, and long enough to be fairly graceful and to look right with flats."

Her favorite outfit when pregnant with her second child, who was born in mid-winter, was a black turtleneck dress "cut like a trapeze" that she wore for everything from delivering speeches to attending business dinners. "The one extravagant thing I bought was $250 cowboy boots that I'm still wearing. They're very comfortable but they have just enough lift so they don't look clunky. Also, I wore huge earrings all the time. I never had a denim or a corduroy jumper, and I think the idea of a maternity power suit is ludicrous—what are you supposed to be, a pregnant man?"

Finding decent-looking pregnancy clothes can be no simple task, however. Some women said that when they did hit upon something that worked, they bought it in multiples. Weekend clothes are easier than work clothes: most women wore their husbands' shirts and sweaters (or bought men's clothes of their own) with knit pants, maternity jeans, big overalls, or sweatpants.

After the baby is born, the first fashion problem many women face is that all their prepregnancy clothes are now not one but at least two years old. An entire year has passed during which they gave no thought at all to the trim skirts, knit dresses, and silk blouses hanging in the back of the closet, and upon resurrection some of those clothes may be found to be out of date, ill-fitting, even moth-eaten or otherwise damaged from neglect.

"I started trying to get pregnant in the fall and finally succeeded in March, so I didn't buy anything new that winter," says one woman. "My child was born in December, and I went back to work in March, so again I didn't buy anything new. The next fall when I started rummaging through my clothes I found that the newest ones were three years old, and a lot of the things I thought of as fairly new were in fact five years old. I'd been thinking I had this fully stocked wardrobe, and discovered I had to start virtually from scratch."

If a woman returns to work before she's lost all her pregnancy weight, she's often forced to keep wearing her maternity clothes (which can be depressing) or to buy new clothes that fit but nevertheless seem like a waste of money. Hobbling by on a "transitional" postpregnancy wardrobe can be fine for a few months, but some women finally cave in and accept facts when they still haven't lost all the weight a year later. "I finally threw out all my old clothes and bought bigger new ones," admits one woman.

Even when all the weight comes off, size and shape can change. Some women say that a rounder stomach, broader hips, or larger breasts have forced them to change the way they dress: "At least my legs still look the same, so I just choose things that are shorter and looser through the middle," says one woman. Another common development: larger feet. "I had to buy all new shoes because my feet are a size bigger," says one new mother. "But all my old ones are still in the closet because I can't bear to throw them out."

Then there's the issue of breast-feeding. Women who continue to nurse their babies after they return to work find they have not only newly enormous breasts—the buttons on that prepregnancy blouse no longer close, that knit top is suddenly so tight it's indecent—but a problem with, well, leakage, at least for a while. Good-bye silks, linens, anything that stains. While nursing pads are designed to protect clothing from milk, many women find them bulky and uncomfortable: if pads keep milk from staining a crepe de chine blouse, they can also show through the blouse, so what's the point? A vest, a loose cardigan, or a well-buttoned-up and not-too-delicate jacket may be the only solution until feeding schedules and your body stabilize.

Mothers who are staying home with their children can wear hardier clothes to begin with, but still can't escape the style problem caused by breast-feeding. "I nursed my daughter until she was twenty-six months old, and for all that time all my clothes had to be nursable," says Sue Yellen, who works part-time as a lawyer in Chicago. "I wore lots of shirts with buttons, dresses that buttoned all the way from top to bottom."

After baby, cleanliness can be a dressing problem many women face for the first time since they were kids themselves. "When my kids were little I never really felt clean for a while," says Judy Newmark. "I would get to work and find spit-up or worse on the back of my shoulder. I changed clothes much more often and I looked at how I was going to wash something in a way I never had before."

So too can changes in roles and in activities prompted by motherhood—working woman to stay-at-home mom, social butterfly to homebody—influence the way women dress. "Since having the baby, I live in pants, I never shop for pantyhose, and my high heels are in a drawer," says Susan Gaynes. "I used to go out to restaurants a lot and now I don't go out. I have one strapless evening dress hanging in the back of my closet."

Women with young children find they have little time to shop, and less money to spend when they do have the time, which also prompts changes in the way they dress. "Having a kid hasn't affected the way I dress," says one woman, "but I shop less and spend less money, so as I result I have less clothing. It's the same kind of clothing that I wore before, just less of it."

"Now I don't have the time to shop as much as I would like and when I do it's in stolen moments when I could be with my son or working or otherwise doing something worthwhile," says Andrea Higbie, an editor at the New York *Times*. "Also, I can't indulge as much as I used to because of expenses from having a new house, of buying things for Paul, and paying for the nanny. Clothes are not on the priority list—they seem so self-indulgent and I feel I have to justify the expense every time."

Looking back on the time before her son was born, says Higbie, "It seems now that I had all the time in the world. I used to think about what I would wear to work the next day as I was driving home in the afternoon. Now I only think about it in the shower right before I get dressed, but that's an improvement over when he was first born, when I would only think about it standing in front of the closet."

Other women agree that time pressure may be the single most important factor affecting the changes in what they wear postchildren. One new mother's solution for work is to wear only dark knit clothing that doesn't have to be ironed or dry-cleaned often, to use the same accessories with everything, and to wear only black pumps—she has two pairs that are exactly alike so she doesn't have to worry about wearing two different shoes. Another woman has reduced her wardrobe to only clothes that, she says, "let me get dressed without thinking at all. Every single jacket I have goes with every single skirt, and every shirt goes with every combination."

Even when time doesn't bring changes in what a woman wears, it often influences how she gets dressed. "Getting ready in the morning is a nightmare," says Judy Newmark. "Before 'Sesame Street,' I don't know how any working mother got ready with three people to dress. I didn't give up anything in terms of what I wore to the office when I had my kids, but now I get them dressed and give them breakfast and while they eat watching 'Sesame Street' I run back and forth and put on my underwear and makeup. I don't put my clothes on my body until my mother shows up to take the kids to school."

For some women, psychological issues connected with motherhood can influence style. Women may find themselves deemphasizing their sexuality, feeling conscious of how a mother, as opposed to a just plain woman, "should" dress. As one woman put it, "I was feeling so protective of my child, I didn't want to think at all about my clothes. When I was pregnant and when she was smaller, I didn't want to dress in any special way at all because then I'd feel so constricted."

Ultimately, though, kids get older, mornings get less hectic, budgets and time loosen up, and mother's clothes are not so influenced by the fact of her motherhood. One woman, planning to return to work now that her child is four, says, "I just recently took out some clothes I used to wear to work before I was pregnant, and I loved the way I looked in them. I looked so together, so feminine, much more vivid than I do now. I guess I've been dressing not to be vivid, not to be attractive or sexual or get noticed. Suddenly I liked the feeling. I'm ready to start dressing up again."

EMOTIONAL ISSUE:
"MOMMY, WHY DON'T YOU WANT TO LOOK PRETTY?"

Mothers of daughters know that there comes a time, round about age three, when most little girls reject all the nice Oshkosh overalls and striped T-shirts in their dressers in favor of ultra-frilly, hyperfeminine, pink-and-purple getups. For many three-to-six-year-old girls, a dress or a skirt is de rigueur, stockings—preferably lace—must be worn, and the shoes of choice are patent leather and bowed.

"Where did I go wrong?," the blue-jeaned or sweatsuited mother wails. "I gave her a baseball glove for her first birthday, I painted her room blue, I don't wear makeup or high heels or dresses. Where is she getting this from?"

Could this early predilection for stereotypically feminine trappings be somehow inborn? Or is the culprit still society, which—despite mother's example—purveys the ideal female as one wearing elaborate and often impractical clothes?

"Little girls are looking at the world and deciding what's pretty," says Arlene Kagle, Ph.D., a New York psychotherapist. "There are other models besides mother: pictures in books, pictures on television, toys that they get. I've never seen a book of *Cinderella* where Cinderella goes to the ball in blue jeans. Everybody wants to be a princess."

At home, what inspires little girls to dress up may be not mother but daddy. A Freudian would call the three-to-six-year-old's pink-and-purple passion a manifestation of the Oedipal complex, and even most non-Freudian psychologists would say a little girl's adoration of daddy—and vice versa—at this age is appropriate and healthy. "All the research on sexual difficulties points to it as a father–daughter issue," says Dr. Kagle. "It's crucial that at two, three, four, and five, a girl's father thinks she's the most wonderful thing in the world."

Whatever the style inspiration, the fact remains that little Jordan, getting ready for nursery school, is likely to fling herself on the floor and kick her feet if you try to make her wear those blue denim overalls. And if you don't buy her the dresses and accessories she craves, you'll have a very difficult time explaining your chronic lateness to your boss.

The enlightened mother will swallow her opinions on style and allow her daughter to choose her own clothes—a boost to the child's confidence and self-expression as well as to the mental health of the entire family.

"The year my daughter was two, I thought I was being really smart and bought her ten pairs of overalls for the next year at an end-of-season sale," says one mother. "You have to understand that even on sale this was an investment of a couple of hundred dollars. And then the next year she refused to wear them, simply wouldn't. After a prolonged struggle, I finally caved in and took her shopping. It was torture to stand there and let her pick out these tacky dresses with gold lamé stars and pastel cats on the front, but not as torturous as trying to wrestle her into those overalls every morning."

One problem remains: the little girl who has accomplished her own fashion goals will next turn her attention to her woefully underdressed mom.

"One day as we were walking to nursery school, I in my usual sweatpants and my daughter in her usual pink dress and party shoes, she looked up to me and said, 'Mommy, why don't you want to look pretty?'" says one mother of a five-year-old. "I felt terrible."

The woman explained that the clothes she wore were more comfortable and practical than dresses and heels, which held no water with the daughter's fashion dictum of prettiness *über alles*. The only time her daughter approves of her clothes, this mother says, is when she's dressed up for an evening out.

"One night I was all dressed up for a party. My daughter said, 'Mommy, you look pretty,' and her friend, who was staying over, said, 'Yeah, a lot prettier than you really are.' "

Even mothers who habitually dress in skirts and heels for work don't quite pass muster with their hyperfeminine little girls. "My daughter's standard for attractive business clothes is Office Barbie," says one woman. "If it's not a gold lamé blazer and four-inch mules, it doesn't make it."

While most women say that they ignore their little girls' fashion advice (as the little girls ignore theirs), some admit that having a daughter in an ultra-feminine phase allows them to reembrace their own femininity. "Watching my daughter get so into her ruffled skirts and Mary Janes made me see that all this stuff can be pleasurable for its own sake, not just to please some man," says one mother. "It's not like I'm trading in all my tailored jackets and gabardine pants, but I'm sort of having more fun with stuff like pearls and pretty shoes, stuff I haven't allowed myself to be interested in for years."

In fact, despite their ambivalence, many women discover that they themselves had the same predilection for lacy lavender dresses, say, or hair bows when they were little, says Susan Kaiser, Ph.D., an associate professor at the University of California at Davis who specializes in the social psychology of clothes and who has been studying how mothers and preschool daughters negotiate clothing choices. "When women look at pictures of themselves at the same age," says Dr. Kaiser, "they often find they had the same haircut, wore the same kind of clothes."

How does Kaiser, the mother of a four-year-old daughter herself, handle the fashion issue? "I finally decided to let her father help her get dressed for nursery school," she says. "It goes a lot more smoothly with him."

At about age six, the tables turn again, and the same little girls who insisted on skirts will now wear only pants and sneakers. Freud might explain this as the symbol of a natural progression from the Oedipal to the latency period, and maybe it is. In any case, mother no longer has to feel conflicted about femininity versus feminism, and can resume wearing jeans free from the tyranny of her in-house fashion critic. Until, of course, her daughter turns thirteen, and insists that mom—once again, no matter what she's wearing, totally out of it—walk ten paces behind her at all times.

• *Style Analysis* •

MELISSA DAVIS *is a mom, a work-at-home part-time book editor, and, last year, was a student at Harvard where her husband had a fellowship. (Recently, she and her husband had their second child and moved to Miami.) Her black-checked skirt is from Ann Taylor and cost $50; her pink shirt was $20 at Benetton; her suede shoes were $125 at a small shop in Soho. Melissa is also wearing a jeans jacket she bought seven years ago in California, a Hermès scarf that was a gift from her mother, and twenties' Jensen silver jewelry that was given to her by her mother-in-law.*

AT WHAT POINT DID YOU START DRESSING IN THE STYLE IN WHICH YOU DO NOW?

Probably around '78. I suppose I wanted to maintain a certain amount of iconoclasm but I was too chicken to go all the way. One foot was rooted in middle-class suburban America, knowing the comfort in that and knowing how well that translates throughout your life because you look normal and you look safe. Another part of me was saying, "I don't really want to be safe." If you're completely outrageous and flagrant people don't take you seriously as a human being, but if you're so straight you don't have any identity, you're just another speck.

HOW DO YOU FIND THINGS FROM BOTH WORLDS THAT MEET IN THE MIDDLE? IS THERE SOME COMMON THREAD?

I like things that are unadorned; really, really plain things. If something's unadorned and it's black, I will buy it. If it's a black miniskirt or a black pullover sweater or a black headband, I'll buy it. The place I get the weirdest are shoes. I love shoes. Because your feet are extremities and not quite as noticeable, you can wear weird shoes. I have about forty pairs of shoes, but I only wear four pairs with regularity. When I get shoes that I like I wear them to death.

HOW DID YOU DEAL WITH DRESSING FOR PREGNANCY?

I pretty much wore what I always wear. I loved those Naf Naf jumpsuits, because when I was pregnant with Max we were living in Florida and it was always hot. I bought about four of those. They're real lightweight cotton and they look like scrub suits surgeons wear and have buttons down the front. I adjusted them accordingly. I'd wear goofy socks or pinch the sleeves and legs in and roll them up and wear them with a pair of silver sneakers. I probably dressed more outrageously when I was pregnant, because I looked so absolutely repulsive, what the hell, what could hurt?

WHEN YOU WERE STAYING HOME WITH THE BABY, HOW DID THAT AFFECT THE WAY YOU DRESSED?

It was in Florida and I was fat for a year afterward, so I wore shorts and T-shirts. When Max was six months we moved to New York. I kind of slobbed out. I didn't have any time, waking up four times a night I was sort of out of it. I don't remember in New York dressing particularly well, except when I went back to work, when Max was two. I dressed up up up, more than anyone else in the office.

WHAT WAS THAT ABOUT?

Grown-up self-assertion, I suppose—wanting to be a real person rather than somebody's mother. I weighed 115 and I finally had a little bit of money and someplace to go and I wanted to be chic. I got a fur, a Hermès scarf; I got uptown a bit.

DID THAT FEEL LIKE YOU?

Yeah. But I also wore my Hermès scarf with a blue-jean jacket, and my mink coat with a nightgown underneath if I had to go out and move the car.

WHAT'S IT LIKE MOVING FROM NEW YORK TO BOSTON AND GOING TO SCHOOL AGAIN?

Once again, I'm trying to react against everybody else. Most of the people in the seminars I go to are dressing like students, and I'm usually the only one in a skirt or a dress. I see it as a sign of respect. If someone is going to be so nice as to come and talk to us for an hour, I'm not going to sit there in a T-shirt and blue jeans. I think that diminishes the person's kindness and authority.

TELL ME ABOUT SOME OF YOUR FAVORITE THINGS YOU HAVE NOW, WHERE THEY CAME FROM, AND WHY YOU LIKE THEM.

I like my black mink coat, because it keeps me warm and people wait on me in stores. It's power, it is, it's a power coat. My husband tried to completely spoil it for me but it was absolutely worth the money I spent on it. I don't even think it was that much money—$1,900. Of course that's my yearly clothing budget. I think we still owe $300 on it.

I have a dress that's a black-and-white tattersall, real beautiful, real plain. I have black shoes I bought in Soho that I have not parted from. They're suede, cut up high over the instep, with little elastic inserts on the sides. I bought this black cotton fisherman's knit sweater that's about twelve sizes too big, which I like because it's warm and comfortable and it covers my bum. I really love my Hermès scarf; my mom gave it to me for Christmas but I gave her explicit instructions. I have a navy blue blazer with gold buttons that's real long, that I got at The Limited, that's a spin on a classic double-breasted blazer. I wear that with a short black leather skirt or with corduroy trousers.

DO YOU HAVE ANY PERSONAL RULES ABOUT DRESSING?

Yes, strong ones. No revealing of the chest. I'm always covered up, even at night. You know, your mother said, "Don't show your arms after you're thirty." I believe that. I love turtlenecks and always wear my shirts buttoned up like David Byrne. I don't even wear camp shirts with open necks. When I wear miniskirts I wear tights. I never wear anything that fits real tightly, especially around my waist. Even when I had a really great figure, when I was exercising all the time, it made me uncomfortable to show my body.

My bathing suit is an old lady bathing suit—white pique with a skirt. My mom wore them and I thought, I'm a mom now and I'm going to wear them.

HOW MUCH DO YOU SPEND ON CLOTHES IN A YEAR?

A lot of money. Probably about $2,000 or $3,000.

WHERE DO YOU SHOP?

I do a lot of shopping at The Gap and at Benetton. The clothes fit and they're often all-cotton—I don't wear wool except for sweaters. Everything's real plain. Everything always comes in black. You can try one thing on once and if it fits you can buy it in four colors.

AT WHAT POINT IS A SKIRT OR A SWEATER TOO EXPENSIVE?

I won't spend more than $100 for a skirt, and a sweater—since I make so many of my own—I really balk at spending money for sweaters. I have an inherent suspicion about things that are on sale, that the reason they're on sale is because nobody wants them. On one hand I could say that if nobody wants them that's because they're unique and interesting, but usually that's not the case. Things that are on sale look like somebody's worn them for a week, they have this kind of sad, limp, tawdry look. I like things all crisp and new. If I buy a shirt I always get the one in the plastic bag, that hasn't been opened, with the pins all in it.

DO YOU TEND TO WEAR MOSTLY NEW STUFF, OR MIX NEW STUFF WITH OTHER THINGS THAT HAVE BEEN IN YOUR WARDROBE AWHILE?

I tend to wear almost all new stuff, except for a blue-jean jacket I've had for ten years or jewelry that's all old, like the Jensen silver from the twenties that I got from my husband's mom. I hate old clothes, thrift store stuff. They're imbued with somebody else's spirit. It gives me the creeps; it feels like grave-robbing.

WHAT DO YOU DO WITH YOUR OLD THINGS?

I put them in plastic bags and put them in the basement or I take them to Goodwill. If I were more organized and had more time I'd get rid of everything. The rule in our house is that if it hasn't been used for six months it gets thrown out. That's true for my clothes as well, and if I don't get rid of them it's because of guilt—if something's hanging in the closet it's somehow serving some utilitarian purpose; at least it's being clothing.

TELL ME ABOUT A MISTAKE YOU MADE.

The biggest mistake I made was on a whim in Florida; I had to go to something formal and went on my lunch hour to a department store and bought this red-sequinned cardigan. It was $250 and you can buy them now off a rack for $59. I thought, I'll buy it and I'll always have it, but I've tried to wear it for other formal things and I look gross, absolutely gross.

I've made a lot of mistakes with shoes. Once I bought a cheap pair of black shoes that I loved and wore every day but the heels started wearing down so I went back to the store, where they didn't have the same ones but they had similar ones. I bought four pairs at $20 each and they just didn't do it so I never wore them.

AT THIS POINT IN YOUR LIFE, IS THERE ANY WAY IN WHICH YOU'D LIKE TO CHANGE YOUR STYLE?

I suppose I should wear things that are outside the rather narrow confines of my style. I don't want to, but I think I should. I've really gotten it down to a uniform. It certainly makes my life easier; I can get up and get dressed without much thought and look presentable. I know what jewelry to grab and what scarf to grab. I don't have to figure it out, because everything pretty much goes with everything else. I never bought an outfit in my life.

I get really upset when I see rich women who are all wrong. That drives me crazy. I want to take her and say, "If I had your money . . ."

IF YOU HAD HER MONEY, WHAT WOULD YOU DO?

I would dress properly. I think there ought to be a law against being done up in an unnatural way. I'd buy a Chanel suit. I'd get really really really good fabrics. The thing about very expensive clothes is that you can roll 'em up and throw them in the back of your closet and they still look great.

But I'm not the kind of person who would be all decked out. Can you see me in a Chanel suit? Give me a break. I like to mix things, like shoes from Fayva and my Hermès scarf. It's like our car: we've got a Harvard sticker on it and we've got fuzzy dice. It's the offbeat. When I was little my mother always used to say, "All you have to do is learn to walk like them, talk like them, and look like them, and you can do whatever you want." People don't really look any deeper than that.

Eleven Alternatives to Conventional Maternity Clothes

1. **BIG MEN'S SWEATERS**
2. **BIG MEN'S SHIRTS**
3. **FAT MEN'S TROUSERS WITH SUSPENDERS** (from antique clothes stores, thrift shops)
4. **COTTON-KNIT PANTS OR LEGGINGS, LONG KNIT TOPS**
5. **LAURA ASHLEY DRESSES AND JUMPERS**
6. **DRAWSTRING COTTON PANTS**
7. **MEN'S PAJAMA BOTTOMS** (Old ones are nice for summer pants)
8. **SWEATS, SIZE EXTRA LARGE** (cut off the ankle elastic, roll up the legs)
9. **OVERALLS**

For the hospital/nursing:
10. **CLASSIC MEN'S PAJAMAS**—Drawstring Waist, Buttoned Top
11. **STRETCH LACE BRA, LOW-CUT WITH FRONT CLASP**

Seven Things That Don't Work for Most Working Moms

If you're a new working mom, you may find that you have to purge the following items from your wardrobe for about five years . . . or your child will purge them for you:

1. **ANYTHING WHITE**—Okay, maybe you can get away with a white blouse.
2. **ANYTHING LINEN**—Especially in white.
3. **ANYTHING SILK**—High moisture spot potential.
4. **DANGLING EARRINGS.**
5. **LONG NECKLACES.**
6. **SKIRTS THAT CRIMP YOUR STRIDE.**
7. **ANYTHING THAT REQUIRES A LOT OF TIME AND ENERGY**—You won't have much.

Flattery: How to Choose the Most Flattering Clothes for Your Size, Shape, Looks

·

You try on clothes in the fitting room, or get dressed in the morning, and the first thing you do—assuming that the zippers zip and the buttons close—is look at yourself in the mirror. What exactly are you looking for? Well, you want to see if you look good, of course. Do your hips look slimmer, your stomach flatter, your skin more glowing? Is this outfit doing anything to bring out your best features, minimize your worst ones?

While there are some rules on which clothes are most flattering, there are just as many theories—often conflicting. One expert says navy blue is the most flattering basic color; another says it's the most deadly. One fashion consultant recommends long blouson jackets for large-hipped women; another says short jackets work best for that figure type. The only absolute judge of whether clothes are flattering is the mirror, but it helps to know what you're looking for your clothes to do.

The fact is, you can't consider flattery without talking about what's called "ideal body image"—the current standard of physical perfection you want clothes to help you approximate. "Current" is an operative word here: the ideal changes over time, and so do the criteria for flattering clothes.

"It really starts with the body," says Elaine Mack, Bergdorf Goodman's personal shopper. "Society has given women very negative body images. If they're not this tall and this skinny, then they don't fit the ideal mold. A hundred years ago, Rubenesque was the ideal and if you were tall and skinny you didn't fit in."

Why the changes? Patricia Mulready, who teaches a New York University course called "The Unfashionable Human Body," explains, "Generally in our history, whenever women become more equal to men the ideal silhouette becomes more similar. Beyond that, if there's a move back to the feminine body we may be seeing a move back to more traditional women's roles." The ideal body right now is a combination of the two: tall and streamlined with broad shoulders and slim hips as well as full breasts and a delineated waist.

Right or wrong, healthy or not, that ideal becomes the standard for judging whether clothes are flattering. Based on today's ideal, says Mack, the optimum clothing silhouette is "an inverted triangle, which makes women look tall and chic and slim. I'm 4 feet 11¼ inches and I want to look taller."

Styles with Universal Flattery Power

What flatters almost everyone, given that the definition of flattery is what makes you look tall, lean, fit, and feminine?

"Shoulder pads are the best thing that ever came out because they accentuate the top of you," says Elaine Mack. "I always want to bring something to the face because the face is the focal point. Also, shoulder pads deaccentuate the hips."

"Shoulder pads balance out so many problems," says Los Angeles fashion consultant Andrea Sells. "If a woman is pear-shaped a wider shoulder makes her look smaller on the bottom."

"Shoulder pads," says New York image consultant Joyce Grillo. "As long as you bring out the shoulder you'll look smaller on the bottom. If you're big in the bosom, shoulder pads can balance out the bust. And shoulder pads are also great for short women."

"I don't think shoulder pads will ever go out because the American woman feels so strongly about balancing her figure," says designer and trend consultant Emily Mann. "Although I think they will get smaller, more rounded, shaped like an actual shoulder."

The reason the right shoulder pads are so essential, says Julee Spencer, owner of the shop Julee Julee in Westport, Connecticut, is that they can determine the fit and proportion of the entire outfit. "A major element of proportion starts from the shoulder. A garment has to fall or hang from something and generally that's the shoulder," says Spencer. "If you balance your figure by the way the clothing hangs from the body at the top it solves a lot of problems. We rework a lot of shoulder pads to be right for the person."

Beyond shoulder pads, is there anything else that is flattering on a variety of bodies? Here the experts begin to, if not exactly disagree, at least differ.

"An oversized tunic or sweater-knit with shoulder pads is flattering on just about everybody from smaller women to those who wear large sizes," says Emily Mann. "A trapeze jacket over a short skirt can be flattering on a lot of women, because it hides what women are most self-conscious about: the stomach, behind, and thighs. The most democratic neckline is a plain jewel or crew neck."

"Larger, longer jackets over shorter skirts are very flattering to a lot of women," says Andrea Sells, "but it depends on the type of jacket because a double-breasted jacket can make you look bustier and boxier. A single-breasted unconstructed jacket with shoulder pads worn with a shorter, slim skirt works really well."

"A blazer looks good on everybody in this world," says Richard Assatly, who, with Maurice Antoya, designs Anne Klein II. But what kind of blazer? On a woman with a pear-shaped figure, Assatly says, a short jacket that fits well throughout the top may be more flattering than a longer jacket that can pull across the hips.

Says fashion consultant Vicki French Morris: "One shape that is flattering on almost everybody is a long blousey overblouse that comes in a little bit at the bottom. Turtlenecks can be more of a problem than a solution; cowl necks are a lot easier to wear."

Elaine Mack's candidate for most-flattering garment: "A loose chemisey dress, although a lot of slim women are afraid of it because they think it makes them look pregnant or fat, and fat women don't always like it because they think it's hiding them. But it's really a very flattering silhouette because when you move you see a body and when you don't it's soft and flowing."

Designer Mimi Loverde says owning a shop has given her a new perspective on flattery: "When you're designing clothes you're trying things on someone who has a perfect figure. When you have a store you suddenly see your clothes going onto all kinds of figures and you realize you always have to consider that. It's made me design more things that can be universally worn."

One dress in her line that looks good on a variety of bodies has a fitted top, slightly empire waist, and a softly gathered below-the-knee skirt, says Loverde. Another near-universally flattering item: a loose, long, tailored shirt.

The ultimate conclusion of most experts is, however, that there are very few pieces that truly are flattering across the board. Even among women with the same general figure type, flattery will vary depending on subtle differences in proportion and shape of both body and clothes.

Andrea Sells begins her fashion consultations by measuring a woman's body: at the neck, bust, shoulders, arms, waist, hips, just about everywhere. "It's not scientific but the tape measure is straightforward," she says. "The measurements become a factual thing; on paper you can see that you're thirty-six inches across the chest and thirty-two across the hip. I can figure out what kinds of clothes are appropriate by doing a body analysis, but in truth a lot of people can get away with wearing a lot of clothes they don't think they can. The key is balancing out color and texture and proportion and silhouette."

Good fit is also an important element of good looks. At Julee Julee, an in-house tailor reshapes garments for optimum flattery. "It's amazing what happens when you start tailoring something," says owner Julee Spencer. "Sometimes raising a shoulder or putting in a different shoulder pad can work miracles." Spencer also believes a main component of flattery is proportion—not how long or short or loose or shaped a skirt or jacket is, but how those elements are put together, down to the shoes.

There is also a psychological element to flattery, say some experts: it can take a certain amount of confidence to embrace those clothes that are most flattering. Says Elaine Mack, "Women dress like cookie cutters because it's safe: they don't want to stand out, they don't want to bring attention to themselves. I like to get women to try something they wouldn't have tried on their own and get a reaction from other people. Almost 100 percent of the time they will come back and say 'Oooh, I love that red dress. Let's go that way: let me look at myself with shoulder pads, with a shorter skirt, with more color, with a scarf at my throat.' "

Flattery Shortcuts for Different Bodies

While there are few flattery absolutes and many dressing "rules" have recently flown out the window, experts say there are certain styles you may want to try first, some flattery shortcuts to consider depending on your figure:

Pear-shaped—The most common figure "problem," and the opposite of the slim-hipped, broad-shouldered ideal. The aim here is to emphasize your top as well as to deemphasize your bottom. Shoulder pads (surprise!) can greatly increase the wide-hipped woman's dressing options.

"A lot of women think if they're big on bottom they can't wear knits but they can if they wear shoulder pads," says Joyce Grillo. "Clothes should be a little looser, sizes a little bigger."

Long jackets can be flattering, say most experts, if they fit at both the top and the hips and don't delineate your broadest point. A long, straight jacket or cardigan, worn open over a belted skirt or pants, can also be flattering.

A to-the-waist, strong-shouldered jacket can also be flattering with the right skirt, meaning one that's not too tight, not too full. A soft dirndl, say in wool jersey, can be flattering, as can a skirt with stitched-down pleats; avoid skirts or pants that balloon out over hips. The most flattering skirt length has more to do with how long and slim your legs are and the proportion of your outfit than with the width of your hips.

In general, wearing a lighter or brighter color on top than on bottom will be more flattering than, say, a black jacket and a white or hot pink skirt.

Short-waisted/Long-waisted—"One of the most common figure problems is being short-waisted," says Joyce Grillo. "A lot of women don't realize they are and wear things that emphasize rather than flatter." How do you tell if you're short-waisted? The length of your body from your armpit to your waist ideally equals its length from your waist to the bottom of your derriere. If your armpit-to-waist measurement is less than that from waist to bottom, you're short-waisted; if more, you're long-waisted.

What's flattering on short-waisted women are styles without a defined waist: long, straight jackets or cardigans, tunics, chemise or dropped-waist dresses. "Short-waisted women shouldn't wear anything belted, or tight tops tucked into skirts," says Grillo. "Particularly if you're big in the hips, emphasizing a short waist will make you look bigger."

Being long-waisted can make it easier to find flattering clothes. "Long-waisted women can really look fabulous and elegant in belts," says Grillo. Problems come in, depending on proportion: a woman who's long-waisted but has large hips should not wear a belt, even if her waist is slim. And calling attention to a long waist can make short legs look shorter.

Big Bust—Large breasts may not be considered a figure problem by many women, but they can present dressing problems. Says Joyce Grillo, "When you're big in the bosom the most flattering things will have soft fabrics and simple lines. I usually recommend nothing with a collar or lapels. Jackets can be disastrous because even if they're flattering they tend to be uncomfortable."

Andrea Sells advises large-busted women to avoid breast pockets, ruffles, and horizontal seams across the chest. Modest V-necked tops and blouses can be flattering, as can deep V-necked, not too tight cardigans.

Narrow Shoulders—The obvious and oft-repeated flattery solution is shoulder pads in everything. Beyond that, says Sells, narrow-shouldered women should avoid dolman and raglan sleeves, full skirts, and halter tops.

Round Tummy—The point here is to stay away from anything—be it pants, jacket, sweater, dress, or skirt—that defines the shape of your stomach. Long, straight-cut tops tend to work well; pleated pants and skirts can be either flattering or a disaster, depending on the cut and the fit. If your stomach gets significantly rounder late in the day or for two weeks every month, try on clothes then to get a realistic picture of whether they're flattering.

Heavy or Short Legs—To make legs look slimmer, stay with simple, nonclingy skirts and pants, says Sells. Hem a dress or skirt where your legs are slimmest (right below the knee, below the widest point of your calf). If ankles are a problem or if you want to elongate your legs, keep shoes, hose, and skirt in the same dark color. If you have short legs, proportion the length of your skirt so the hem doesn't bisect the lower half of your body—either a little shorter or a little longer is fine, depending on the proportions of the rest of your figure and outfit.

Large Bottom—To slim a big bottom, dresses are usually better than skirts, says Sells. Avoid a defined waist, wear easy-fitting longer tops over not-too-tight pants.

Large Women—The "large-size" market has in recent years undergone a revolution, with many wonderful new styles and stores for women who wear over size 14. So, too, has much of the fashion wisdom on large-size dressing been revolutionized, with good-looking options far beyond the standard black tent dress.

The first thing to remember if you're large is that dressing tricks for your specific figure type may be more valid than general advice. What's flattering will vary depending on whether your weight is all in your bottom or all in your top, whether you're short or tall, whether you're evenly proportioned or short-waisted and large-busted. While a woman who's both short and heavy may look better in similar-toned pieces, a taller woman may look terrific in bright colors.

Most of the designers making large-size clothing have gotten away from the idea of trying to make large women look skinny. Still, they say, the most flattering styles are those that fall away from the body, even when the silhouette is shaped. Many of the flattery secrets are in the cut: jackets and tunics a bit longer, narrower waistbands, a tad more coverage on bare pieces.

Petite Women—Just as large-size clothes and fashion rules have gone through a dramatic change, so have petite clothes. No more tiny prints or little girl styles, but "regular" styles scaled down for the petite body—generally defined as under 5 feet 4 inches and less than 125 pounds.

The old notion that wearing things smaller—clothes with minute details, teeny jewelry—would make petites look taller has been replaced by the idea that big and bold can confer presence and stature. "All those old rules don't add that much height," says Grillo. "Bigger jewelry and shoulder pads and a bit of lift in your hair can help, but high heels can make you look ridiculous."

Again, petites may do better to consider their own particular bodies than the general fact of their height when looking for flattering clothes. What looks best on a short-waisted, big-busted five-foot-two-inch woman can be very different from what's most flattering on a woman of the same height who has large hips.

Wearing toned clothes—a taupe jacket with an ivory blouse with a beige skirt, hose, and pumps—can be more flattering than a high-contrast outfit—a red blouse with a black skirt with white hose and black shoes, for instance. But that doesn't mean you can't mix colors in similar families, such as plum and navy, or wear a white blouse with a navy jacket and skirt.

What's Color Got to Do with It?

Color consultants, experts who tell you which colors will be most flattering on you, are big business. Indeed, many women who've had their colors done say it's made shopping easier, given them more fashion confidence, garnered compliments not on the color of their clothes but on their overall looks.

Many fashion consultants who don't subscribe to one of the strict color theories—grouping women into the seasons of the year, for example—nonetheless believe that color can be an important component of flattery.

"One thing I have a real bug about is color theory," says Vicki French Morris. "It's had ambivalent acceptance in the world of fashion but I buy it as a directional thing. You can dress from catalogs in flattering colors and really look good, and you can dress in Armani and Lacroix in colors that are unflattering and look terrible."

"I'm not a believer at all in color consultants who break you down into winter, spring, summer, and fall," says Andrea Sells. "Most people fall into all categories, and depending on the tone and fabric—most people can wear most colors."

I once researched a story on color consultants for *Glamour* by visiting five different consultants with five different theories and having my colors done five different times . . . with five different results. There were some cross-overs—navy was more flattering on me than black, the consultants agreed; ivory better than white, peach better than red—but there was also a lot of disagreement. One consultant provided me with a wide array of browns, for example, while another warned me against ever wearing it. One color chart was heavy on the purples, another vibrant with greens.

I came away confused about whose advice to believe, and full of cautions for women about orienting their entire wardrobes to one consultant's theories. At the same time, there's no doubt that some colors are more flattering to each person than others, and a good color consultant can help guide the way to those choices. While I continued to rely on black after my color experience, I added new pieces in navy as opposed to gray and also became a devotee of peach, unexpectedly flattering with my auburn hair.

Short of having your colors done, is there any way to tell which shades are most flattering to you? Well, you can attempt to analyze yourself the way a good consultant would: sit in front of the mirror in natural light and drape your shoulders with large fabric swatches. Alternate tones in the same family—a bright red with a burgundy, for example, peach with rosy pink, navy with black. You may be able to see some dramatic differences; then again, you may not. It's sometimes difficult to be objective about your own looks, although it's also possible to pay a consultant whose eye is no better than your own.

Most color theories are based on warm versus cool undertones in complexion and also on the amount of contrast in your coloring. If your coloring is obviously what consultants would call warm (golden hair, tawny skin) you'll look better in warm colors such as orange; if it's cool (ash brown hair, pink skin, blue eyes) you'll look better in cool colors like periwinkle blue. However, it can be difficult to judge which category you fit into, and you may in fact be a combination of the two. Personal shopper Lisbeth Riis Albert advises clients to choose colors with the same amount of contrast and the same intensity as they see in a black-and-white picture of themselves.

All these techniques aside, are there some colors that are generally more flattering than others?

"The first are corals," says Andrea Sells. "They're wonderful on almost any skin tone."

From there the experts diverge. Mann thinks navy is the most democratically flattering basic, as does personal shopper Albert, while Sells calls navy "a very difficult color. It makes most people appear dead."

Sells says that off-white is flattering on the majority of people, while pure white can be difficult because "nobody truly has white on their skin, their teeth, their eyes."

What other colors does Sells think are difficult? "Camels are horrible on a lot of people, and brown can be hard to wear depending on the shade—that's where skin tone and hair color come into play. Grays are hard colors to wear. For many people red is too dramatic. Some women tense up; in a color like that, they feel self-conscious."

While choosing the right colors can play an important part in flattery, it can also be a negative if you get attached to them to the detriment of other considerations. "So many women are so stuck on their colors that they don't realize they have no shoulders," says shop owner Julee Spencer. "Color is only a small part of what's going to make something flattering or not."

• Style Analysis •

MARY MOEN *is the owner of Pacific Entertainment, a Los Angeles publicity firm which represents actors and musicians. Moen was photographed wearing an Anne Klein suit she bought at Ann Taylor for $350 ("It was something I needed for meetings"); a deep blue Emmanuelle Khanh silk blouse she bought in Paris for $180; suede pumps found for $30 at a designer discount shoe store; sterling-and-onyx earrings Moen bought at Bullock's as a treat for herself for $50; and a sterling bracelet from Hong Kong, a gift from a friend.*

YOU WORK IN THE ENTERTAINMENT INDUSTRY; WHAT'S THE GENERAL STYLE OF THAT BUSINESS?

For the people who I work with, managers and agents, it runs the gamut from tailored suits and Miss Marple clothes to lace leggings and flared crinoline skirts and wild Maud Frizon shoes, and that's on women who are extremely successful, who handle major actors. You get to a point where it doesn't matter what you wear, you're so successful. People here more than anywhere dress how they feel best. You're not constrained by weather and there's an anything-goes attitude.

HOW DOES THAT WORK FOR YOU?

Well, today I had an appointment with a potential client, a woman who has been a model for years and is now acting. I thought about what I was going to feel comfortable in today.

I feel a little plump because I went to a big family dinner last weekend, so I wore black wool gabardine pants, a silk blouse, flat shoes and a gabardine jacket, all black and all matched, buttoned up, and completely covered. That to me felt very secure. I didn't have to worry about skirt heights or adjusting anything; I just wanted to present myself intelligently and not worry about my clothes and I knew I would feel good in that outfit. I've had the pants for two years, they're Valentinos that were $100 in Loehmann's. I can't believe I ever dressed without them. When I wear them I know I'm fine, that I can have a bulge here and a bulge there and it won't matter.

HOW HAS STARTING YOUR OWN BUSINESS AFFECTED THE WAY YOU DRESS?

It hasn't affected it at all; I dress the same way as I did when I was an employee. I have to watch my money a little bit more: I have overhead and employees, so I'm more conservative when it comes to shopping. I'll buy wardrobe staples rather than a purple suit. But while I shop more carefully than I did in the past, it hasn't changed my style.

WHAT THINGS LOOK BEST ON YOUR FIGURE?

I have large breasts, so particularly when I'm dressing for business I don't want to be concerned that part of something is showing. That to me is heart attack time. I generally avoid T-shirt necklines, Peter Pan collars or round necks: this cuts me off and makes me look out of kilter. Sleeveless is really bad on me. I try to stick to button-up, turtleneck, and usually something with a collar as opposed to none.

I lost about twenty pounds a few years ago and started going to a trainer three times a week, and became much more comfortable with clothes. I never used to dress to show off my legs. Short skirts certainly aren't a daily diet but I do feel very powerful when I wear a suit with a skirt above the knee. I feel, Okay, get out of the way; I'm comfortable and self-assured. It's a great combination of masculinity and femininity.

WHAT'S A SHOPPING TRIP LIKE FOR YOU?

I usually go to a mall, and I always look for shoes first. I have a real shoe thing. I'll try and find a couple of really good shoes first and figure out from there what I want to do next. I don't have to think and contemplate about shoes; if I see them and they fit I buy them. With clothes it's a decision-making process for me, so I would rather get the shoes out of the way first because I'm usually real sure about the shoes.

I usually take a list with me of the things I really need to have, like a new white shirt or a black silk short top. I know specifically what I need for my closet. I usually go on a Saturday and give myself maybe three hours, four hours at the most. I love to do it but I don't like dragging it out. I try to avoid the big stores. Smaller stores that cater to quality stuff are usually what I find works for me, things that are a little bit unusual.

HOW OFTEN DO YOU DO THIS?

Three or four times a year. Spring and fall are the big times, and then in summer I usually do something pretty major.

HOW MUCH DO YOU SPEND ON CLOTHES IN A YEAR?

Probably between five and seven thousand.

WHAT DO YOU LOVE?

I love Anne Klein and I love Donna Karan. Her clothes fit me really well and her style is really terrific. I love Katherine Hamnett, although it doesn't look great on me. It looks great on tall, tall, bone-thin people. Byblos is wonderful too.

Most of my shoes are Charles Jourdan. A lot of times I'll find wonderful things on sale. I find I can skimp on clothing but I try not to do that on shoes. I can always tell a bad pair of shoes. You can get by with not spending a fortune on clothes if you've got great shoes and a good handbag.

WHAT KIND OF BAG DO YOU CARRY?

That's one thing I do look for in department stores. I carry big leather bags, but I don't buy them too often. I keep one until it's so old and ratty that I have to get a new one.

IS THERE ANYTHING YOU BUY CHEAP?

Summer clothes I never buy expensive, ever, because I don't really need to dress in the summer. It's so hot here, that less is more. I wear real cool big boxy shorts, short tops, very loose-fitting clothing. There's such a wide range of stores that cater to that here.

CAN YOU WEAR THAT TO WORK?

*N*ever. In summer for work I wear cool, long things. I try to avoid hose if I can but often that's impossible, if I'm having a meeting or going to a studio or something. I wear white big baggy shirts with a long skirt.

The whole style changes in California in the summer. When it starts to get a little cooler everyone's eager to get their jackets out and everyone's dressing more in a controlled way.

DO YOU VARY YOUR CLOTHES DEPENDING ON WHO YOU'RE MEETING WITH?

*I*f I'm meeting with a male actor, I'd wear a turtleneck and look very corporate. If it's an actress I wouldn't be quite as conservative. If you have a man he wants to know you're going to do a great job for him and it's not going to be about the way you look. I don't want to confuse people, and I think people tend to get very confused sometimes in this business. With women that sexual element doesn't come into play. Women are more apt to see me as a professional person no matter how I'm dressed.

DO YOU HAVE A WIDE RANGE OF DIFFERENT THINGS IN YOUR WARDROBE?

*Y*es, I do.

HOW DO YOU MANAGE TO MAKE THEM ALL YOU?

*T*here's a lot of different people in me. I feel differently each time I go out shopping. One shopping expedition doesn't necessarily have anything to do with another. A lot of times I'll look in my closet and say, "Oh my God, when did I get that, when am I ever going to wear it?" and then two or three weeks later it will be perfect.

WHAT WOULD SOMEBODY SEE IF THEY LOOKED IN YOUR CLOSET?

*T*hey'd see an eclectic mix of stuff. It all works, it's all in the black, red, white, blue range, everything solid. I think I have one blouse that has a pattern on it. I don't like busy stuff, like florals and checks and squiggles. I like plain colors with good fabric. But it all looks like it works.

IS THERE ANYTHING YOU HAVE A PASSION FOR?

Probably stockings. I like dark-colored stockings. They're coming out with so many new wonderful kinds of stockings now it's fun to shop for just that. I love cotton tights I wear with skirts and flats. There are beautiful silk stockings that come up to the thigh that have a grip on them that just stay—I love those.

DO YOU HAVE A FAVORITE OUTFIT?

A suede skirt and matching jacket I got in Paris. The jacket is a bolero with piping on it with small, padded shoulders—it's black and white. I wear that with flats, tights, a white shirt, or a white camisole. I wear it out to dinner or to a film, anywhere but work. That must mean something.

WHAT DO YOU USUALLY WEAR GOING OUT IN THE EVENING OR TO A PARTY?

If I know a lot of business people and peers will be there, which is 60 percent of the time, I wear things that are perhaps striking, that may stand out a little bit. That does not necessarily mean a plunging neckline and a short skirt; usually something I know I look good in and feel good in. It's always black; the only other color I wear often is real deep blue. My mother calls me Johnny Cash.

I NEVER ASSOCIATE CALIFORNIA STYLE WITH BLACK CLOTHES. IS THAT NORMAL THERE?

There's not too much normal out here. But at a party the other night, it was a sea of black, particularly the women. Black is really prevalent here now, and in some stores it's almost the only thing that's being shown. Black is it; if you don't like black, you're sunk.

Ten Pieces That Add Ten Pounds to Your Hips

Go to the grocery store. Pick up a ten-pound ham. Imagine this hunk of meat plastered to your hips and thighs. That's the effect of clothes that add extra weight to your figure—weight that nobody needs, no matter how thin or fat you are to begin with.

Avoiding that extra ten pounds is as simple as avoiding the following pieces:

1. **DIRNDL SKIRTS**—Any skirt that is gathered at the waist, whether short or long, has the effect of adding bulk where most women need it least. The conundrum: full-cut skirts can make you feel thinner, because they're comfortable and seem to hide below-the-waist bulges by their very fullness. While this offers psychological relief, it's not the physical reality. The exception may be a loosely gathered skirt of fine material such as silk or lightweight cotton. In general, however, infinitely more slimming than most dirndls for even the most bottom-heavy woman is a slim, straight skirt—and if you don't believe me, have someone take a picture of you in a gathered skirt and a slim one, and judge for yourself.

2. **ANYTHING PLEATED FROM THE WAIST**—Skirts, dresses, and even some pants that have pleats starting from the waist can have the same effect as gathered skirts: emphasizing rather than camouflaging a rounded belly, bottom, hips. What happens is that the pleats tend to pull apart (they're supposed to lie flat) and fan out. If you like pleats, look instead for the kind that are stitched down (how far down depends on what you're trying to disguise) and buy the piece large enough so pleats stay smooth.

3. **TO-THE-HIP BLAZERS**—Suit jackets that are nipped in at the waist and end at the widest part of your hips tend to broaden your beam. In general, avoid any piece that creates a horizontal line at the widest point of any part of your body—a skirt that's hemmed at the broadest point of your calves, for instance, or sleeves that stop in the middle of your upper arm.

4. **SKINNY-SHOULDERED TOPS**—No matter what the fashion status of shoulder pads, breadth at the shoulders helps balance width at the hips. If you don't have naturally broad shoulders, avoid skinny-shouldered T-shirts and sweaters, halter tops, strapless dresses. Soft shoulder padding, boat necklines, set-in (as opposed to raglan) sleeves, button detailing at the shoulder can all help add the width that balances the bottom.

5. **CINCHED-IN WAISTS**—Don't wear anything that accentuates your waistline, despite the fact that you may want to show off its slimness. Wide, tight belts, dramatically nipped-in jackets or dresses, or waist-hugging sweaters can all make your hips look even wider in contrast.

6. **ANYTHING BALLOON-SHAPED**—This goes for long blouson jackets that end in a tight band below the hips; knit dresses and skirts with ribbing at the knees; even long sweaters that are loose over tummy and hips but hug in at the thighs. Even if the balloon shape is not pronounced, it is one of the least flattering styles if you have wide hips. Infinitely better: any piece that falls straight from waist to hem.

7. **BULKY SHOULDER BAGS**—This may seem a bit extreme, but a pouchy bag that rests against your hip adds inches where you want them least. If you like shoulder bags, look for one that lies as flat as possible against your side, preferably above or below the widest part of your hips.

8. **DOWN COATS**—The only potentially flattering down coat is a huge one that's cut straight up and down and falls to your ankles, one so voluminous that no one can tell where the coat ends and your body starts. Some of the worst offenders: princess-style down coats, to-the-hip jackets, bombers. Acceptable jacket style: straight cut, to mid-thigh.

9. **ANYTHING TOO TIGHT**—Too-snug clothes—blouses with gaping buttons, jeans that reveal panties beneath, skirts that crease across the hips—tend to make you look heavier than you are. Aim instead for an easy fit that doesn't hug your form.

10. **ANYTHING TOO BAGGY**—Likewise, baggy clothes of any sort can add the illusion of bulk. The problem is the same as that with dirndl skirts—too-big clothes can make you feel more comfortable and often thinner, but in fact can make you look heavier.

The Best: Straight Skirt

1½-Inch Waistband—Most secure, most comfortable, most flattering.

Waistband Extension with Separate Closing—Button or hook.

Darts from Waist—For smooth shape.

Two Slash Pockets—Choose either flat, unobtrusive pockets or none at all.

French Lining—Attached only at waist, seamed and hemmed invisibly and separately.

Near-Invisible Zipper in Back—A side zipper can disturb the line of the skirt.

Medium-weight Wool, Gabardine, Silk, or Cotton—If fabric's too lightweight, bulges can show through. If too heavy, the skirt will add bulk. Not recommended: flimsy silk or wool crepes, thick tweeds.

Straight Cut—Should neither bell out at hem nor hug the knees.

2- to 4-Inch Overlapping Slit—Should be almost invisible, but allow you to walk freely—take a large stride in dressing room. Some very well cut straight skirts don't need a slit.

Length—Optimum length depends on your style, your figure, your proportions, and where you're planning to wear the skirt. However, the most classic, most flattering straight skirts are never longer than right below your knee.

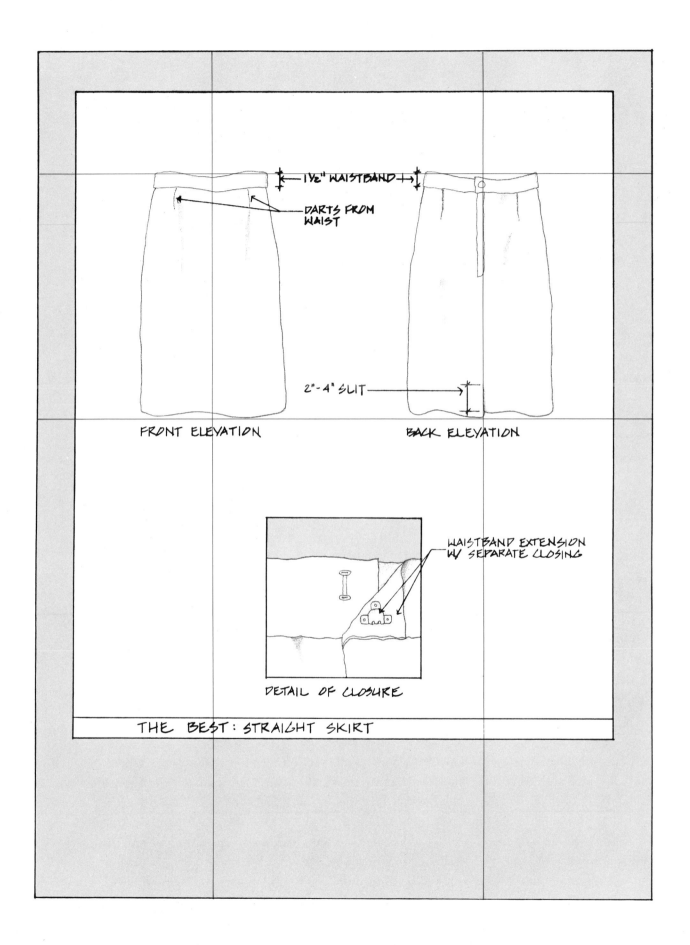

1½" WAISTBAND

DARTS FROM WAIST

2"- 4" SLIT

FRONT ELEVATION

BACK ELEVATION

WAISTBAND EXTENSION
W/ SEPARATE CLOSING

DETAIL OF CLOSURE

THE BEST: STRAIGHT SKIRT

GOOD LOOKS 10 Fit

You need some gray flannel trousers, and you find a pair in your price range and your size and bring them into the dressing room. However, the fit isn't really right: the waist is too big, gaping at the back, while they're too tight across the hips. You go out and find another pair in the same size and a similar style from a different designer, which turn out to be too big all over. You go out onto the floor once again and find yet another pair of pants. These fit, but somehow they make you look fat.

Finding clothes that fit well can be an arduous and baffling process. Why does one size 10 fit differently than another? Why do you take a 6 in one brand and a 12 in another brand? How is it possible that one version of a standard item will make you look bulky or feel uncomfortable, while another version that seems to be exactly the same will nevertheless be slimming and feel wonderful?

The only absolute about good fit is that it's essential to looking terrific in your clothes. Fit is really a subspecies of flattery, in that clothes that fit you perfectly can make you look like you have a perfect figure.

But what counts as great fit is different for each woman, depending on both her tastes and her body. Different designers fit their clothes differently, partly because of their individual philosophies on fit and somewhat due to their perceptions of who they're dressing and how those women want their clothes to fit. And the actual fitting process, as well as construction details that influence fit, varies from one manufacturer to another. Add to these variables the fact that government size standards are only nominal, no longer truly adhered to by clothing manufacturers, and you have the answer to why fit is such an elusive quality.

"Fit is absolutely 100 percent relative to the body," says Lisbeth Riis Albert, a custom tailor and personal shopper who is president of L. Riis Ltd. and teaches tailoring at Parsons School of Design and the Fashion Institute of Technology. "Good fit doesn't mean the same thing for everyone because we're all so different. You want fit to overemphasize your strong points and deemphasize your weak ones."

To illustrate the relationship of fit to the body, Albert used me as a guinea pig. My strong points, said Albert, were the shape of my face (a long oval with a pointed chin), my bust (round), and my waist (slim). And now for my weak points: my shoulders (narrow and sloping), my hips (broad), and my arms ("skinny," said Albert).

"You should be looking for things to round you out," said Albert. "You want to wear something that does the opposite of your face; you want to broaden your body or your face makes you look too skinny."

Too skinny was something I hadn't been called since I was twelve. Was Albert actually saying I should be looking for clothes that made me look fatter? Not exactly. My ideal fit, as with every woman, varied for different parts of my body. Albert lifted the unpadded shoulders of my blouse into a higher, squared-off shape and pulled its cuffs tight at my wrist. I instantly looked better.

"The squareness at the shoulders makes you look more erect and slims your hips," she said. "By wearing your sleeves full and then tight at the wrist it gives you a little fullness at the arm and emphasizes the femininity of your curly hair and round bust."

Albert then put me in a long, shaped, double-breasted jacket. "There are forty-seven reasons you should not buy this jacket," she said. "The V neck makes your face look much too long and your body look much too narrow. The coat is much too long for your proportions: the first button falls below your waist and makes you look like you borrowed your father's coat. The sleeves are too wide, which overemphasizes your skinny wrists. And it's too big, which you can see because the fabric is collapsing in the front [between the sleeves and the lapels]."

It's in this way that fit and flattery go hand-in-hand: while the sleeves were the right length (to the wristbone above my thumb) they were too wide to be flattering; while the jacket's length and shape were right for my hips, its long waist and too-big shoulders cancelled out its bottom-flattering potential. And, according to Albert's analysis, even if the jacket had fit my body perfectly, its low V neck was wrong for my face.

Albert says she tailors 95 percent of the clothes she buys for herself off the rack. "I have a sway back so skirts usually hang longer in the back, the side seam shifts forward, and I get a fold of material between my legs. If I take off three-quarters of an inch in the back of the waistband the skirt hangs straight and all the folds are gone, which makes me look like I have a perfect figure, which I know I don't."

Having your own clothes tailored is the only way to ensure perfect body-specific fit. "With real couture clothing individual body quirks can be easily disguised with darting and seaming and padding," says Patricia Mulready, a New York University home economics professor. "That's why many rich and famous people look far better than the poor and not so famous."

Ah, there's the rub. True couture or custom-made clothing is astronomically priced, and alterations beyond rehemming are expensive. While more women's clothing stores are following the lead of men's stores by offering free tailoring, most women still have to try to find optimum fit off the rack.

Whether or not a ready-made garment will fit you, says Albert, starts from the shoulders. "You can think of your shoulders as a coat hanger. The slope of your shoulders affects the basic hang and fit of a garment." There are three general shoulder types, Albert says: sloped, regular or natural, and square. If you buy something made for a shoulder type other than your own, she says, fabric will bunch up in back, the garment will be imbalanced, and the sleeves won't hang properly.

Another standard body variation affecting fit is the shape of your pelvis—broad versus round—according to Albert. On women who are round and full in the rear, skirts will tend to hike up in back, while women with broad pelvises may have to contend with creases (smile lines) across the fronts of their skirts or pants.

There are, per se, some garments that are easier to fit than others, and some items in which good fit can be found at a lower price. Not surprisingly, knits, which have some amount of give, are generally easier to fit than wovens, and unconstructed clothing is easier to fit than that which is shaped. Jackets and pants are generally harder to fit than skirts, but separates are easier to fit than one-piece garments, such as dresses or jumpsuits. "Anything that's made proportionately to the body, that has a defined waist, is going to be hardest to fit," says Albert.

The High Cost of Good Fit

Usually, the best-fitting ready-to-wear clothes are the most expensive. And the reason is simple: "It's expensive for a manufacturer to spend a lot of time on fit," says Michael Kors, a designer whose clothes are both high-priced and known for their superb fit. "There's the cost of changing the pattern constantly and getting the fit model in constantly. The same straight skirt will react differently in different fabrics, so if we do the same skirt in 250 different fabrics, we refit it 250 times. And a good fit model costs $200 an hour. In production the model's here a good thirty hours, and a runway model at the same price is here at least as much time."

Designers who make lower-priced clothing agree. "The fewer sizes I make the better, because if you have a lot of sizes you have to hold a lot of inventory," says Don DelCollo, who designs the reasonably priced Outer Limits line. "I've been doing more fitted items but it's very time-consuming. Shoulders and sleeves look so simple but from a design and fit point of view they're so hard. In one design of a sleeveless knit top I wanted it not to be revealing but not tight under the arm, but by opening up the arm I created a pucker, and then to get rid of the pucker was an amazing thing. I had to work on that pattern fifteen to eighteen times before I got it right."

One factor affecting the fit, and the expense, of tailored clothing is whether it's draped or flat-cut. "In draping you transform the muslin right on the mannequin, adding a little piece here and a tuck there, and make a garment to fit before you make the pattern," explains Albert. "A blouse, jacket, or pants that are draped will always look and fit much better than one that's cut on the flat, which means a pattern is made and the garment is cut before it's fit on the body. It's very difficult to take a garment that's cut on the flat and put three-dimensional ease and flair into it."

Michael Kors not only drapes his designs; he drapes them not in muslin but in the fabric in which they'll be made. "It's hard to guess what a drapey crepe will look like when you start with muslin," says Kors. "Unless the fabric's a million dollars a yard we cut right into it."

Is there a way for you to tell whether a garment's been draped or flat-cut? Draped clothes generally look rounder, almost as if a body's inside, even on the hanger. And the price tag will give you some indication—most, but not all, of the designers making high-priced clothing start by draping their garments. And everyone agrees that the master of off-the-rack fit is Italian designer Giorgio Armani: it's worth looking at and trying on his clothes, even if you can't afford to buy, to get a fit standard against which to compare clothes in your own price range.

"What distinguishes the fit of an Armani from a cheap mass-market garment is partly the attention taken in the sewing," says designer and fashion consultant Emily Mann. "He doesn't have to knock out 500,000 pieces a day. Sweatshop laborers get paid by the seam, so if they take an extra quarter-inch off or take a chunk out of the side, it doesn't matter, it will still go out. Cheap fabric doesn't drape properly so no matter what you make it won't look as good. And lining, which adds cost, can make a difference in whether something hangs properly because if it's lined it doesn't rub up against your skin or your stockings. Also, lower-priced clothes tend to be skimpier because you can cut more pieces from each yard of fabric. Some designer size sixes will really be government standard size tens, because the woman feels more comfortable spending that much money if she sees herself as a 6."

That's How You Fit a Dress

With government size standards largely fallen by the wayside, wide swings in sizing and cut, based primarily on the fit philosophy and process of the individual manufacturer, have become the norm. "There are general standards in the industry, but every house fits differently," says Richard Assatly, the co-designer of Anne Klein II, known in the industry as a moderately priced line that generally fits "real people." "It's just what you feel the woman you want to be wearing your clothes is shaped like. Anne Klein II is not couture-minded; we want to fit a little smaller and fit more people across the board. We add a little room in the hip, because most woman are hippier, but our biggest sales are between sizes 8 and 12. Another house may feel its customer is skinnier or may fit larger. It comes from the customer in and from us out."

How does designer Michael Kors see his customer? "Since I've been in business her shoulders are bigger and her back is broader, probably from working out. But a lot of women now, even if they're in terrific shape and a size 6, still have a little stomach and don't want their clothes pulling across that. And there are very few women who are 5 feet 10 inches and a size 4. If our customer is a size 4 and narrow she's probably a smaller woman, and if she's a size 12 or 14 she's a taller woman. But stores tell us that our customer likes a trimmer look, that she wants to show off her figure."

Ready-to-wear fit is, in short, a chicken-and-egg process in which women have no choice but to participate. Designers visualize their clothes on a certain type of woman, choose a fit model who embodies that type, and judge the success of that fit by the sales of their clothes. The good news is that, if you find a brand of clothing that fits you well, chances are it will keep fitting you well season after season, because designers tend to retain the same fit models and the same fitting processes year after year.

"We always fit on the same model, and it's very hard when she's not around," says Richard Assatly. "Another person who comes in may still be a size 8 but she's different."

It all goes back to the quirks in each individual body. Says Michael Kors, "When I started I fit everything on just one person, and if you had that figure, great, and if not you were in trouble." Kors says his views on fit were broadened by traveling around the country, making personal appearances at stores and seeing his customers as well as hearing their opinions on fit.

Now, says Kors, "each garment goes through three fittings. The initial cut is to fit a runway model with a fantasy body—she may be 5 feet 11 inches and a 12 in the shoulder and a 4 in the hip. The production fit is done on a fit model who was picked because her body is like our customers': she has a nice figure but it's not perfect; she has curves; she's round; she's an 8 but she's not skeletal; she's 5 feet 7½ inches. Once a garment is fitted on her we cut the first stock and it's generally tried on by someone who works here who it's likely *not* to fit. I like to see something I think will have fit problems on a body it will be a problem on— a bare dress on someone curvy or pants on someone who's straight up and down. The women who work here are from sizes 2 to 16, from 5 feet to 5 feet 10 inches, and any of them may be pressed into service."

Even when a designer tries his clothes on several other people, the fit model is key. "A good fit model is not just a perfect body," says Kors. "She's very vocal. She'll say, 'I know you wanted oversized, but this is huge' or 'I feel I look fatter than I should in this.' "

"A mannequin can't tell you that the armhole's too high," says Anne Klein II's Assatly. "It's the fit model's job to tell you it's too tight, it's too loose, she can move, it's balanced properly."

Assatly's first fit model (fit is later adjusted on a differently proportioned stock model) is Stephanie Robbins, a popular Seventh Avenue fit model who's a fiftyish mother, in great shape but not perfect. "She's round, which we like; she's evenly proportioned; and she has a little stomach [as does Assatly himself]. I fit things to disguise that, because I want my own clothes to hide my stomach. I wouldn't want a model with a completely flat stomach, because if you're older than twelve and if you don't do leg raises every morning, it's not realistic," Assatly says.

Assatly is fitting a knit dress on Robbins. "How does it feel on?" he asks. "It looks tight across the bust. Is it? It's a little snug across the rear."

"In front I keep wanting to grab it," says Robbins, tugging at the fabric under her bust and then twisting around to check her back in the mirror. "I can see my bra in back."

"It needs a little shape under the bust and a little room in back," says Assatly as an assistant designer pins the dress's bodice.

Robbins keeps studying her rear view. She frowns. "This makes me look like I've got the biggest ass you've ever seen."

Assatly laughs. "See?" he says. "That's how you fit a dress."

• *Style Analysis* •

LYNN KUTSCHE *is a pediatric cardiologist and director of the residency program at a hospital in Gainesville, Florida. For her picture, she wore a silk-and-linen knit dress by Laura Biagiotti she bought for about $400 in New York three years ago in preparation for a summer in Europe. Lynn's Donna Karan bronze earrings were bought during her stint as a salesperson at Saks for $90, considering a markdown and an employee discount.*

WHAT KIND OF THINGS DO YOU LIKE TO WEAR?

I like a personal style that's my own. I'm tall—I'm 6 feet tall—and I find I can carry a dramatic look; I can wear big jewelry. I like to either wear my hair very full or pull it back severely, something dramatic. It took me a while to appreciate this. When I was very young I thought of myself as tall and skinny and now I think of myself as tall and fashionably thin. When I discovered more expensive and more stylish clothes, after I got out of medical school, I discovered I looked good in them.

Where I really started to discover this was California, in San Francisco where I went to do my cardiology training. From the first moment, I loved it. I'd see all these women in wonderful clothes on the street, and I started to imitate them, to try the things they were doing.

WAS THIS NEW FOR YOU?

Yes. I grew up in a suburb of Detroit, and went to undergraduate school and medical school in Michigan, so San Francisco was really different, much more adventurous in terms of clothes, really fun. In California, it's accepted to really be yourself, and people liked it that I was trying all these new things with clothes, that I was very interested in clothes. In the three years I lived in California, my style really changed: it became much freer, much more experimental.

WHAT WAS IT LIKE TO GO TO GAINESVILLE FROM CALIFORNIA?

It was culture shock. Gainesville was much more conservative. When I arrived here, people would actually stop to stare at me. My whole style sense faltered. I realized, for instance, that if I was going to fit in here, I would have to wear a bra. At first it was boring, I wasn't having as much fun with my clothes, but then I realized that I like my job here and I wanted to fit in, and that's when I developed what is more or less two different wardrobes. I have my conservative Gainesville wardrobe, and then I have my big-city wardrobe; big-city meaning Jacksonville as well as New York. In my Gainesville wardrobe I have things like long denim skirts and nice white shirts.

DO YOU SHOP IN GAINESVILLE?

Not really. I shop in San Francisco or New York, where I have friends, or in Miami, or in Jacksonville. In Jacksonville I can find the basics I wear to work, like little cotton knit dresses. I wear a lot of those, because it's so hot here.

DO YOU LIKE TO SHOP?

I love to shop. I like the atmosphere of the stores, trying on different things, imagining where I'd wear them, trying out different looks. It doesn't matter so much whether I buy, but if I go into a store and don't find anything that I like, that's not much fun.

TELL ME ABOUT THE YEAR YOU SPENT IN NEW YORK.

I was working on a book about cardiology, and I could live wherever I wanted as long as I had access to the research, so I chose New York. I'd been feeling like, after living in Gainesville for so long, that I'd lost my flair. Part of the reason I wanted to live in New York was to get my sense of style back. What I did was, over the Christmas season, I worked part-time in Saks, in the Calvin Klein department. I just watched what people were wearing and got ideas from them.

WHAT A GREAT IDEA!

It was wonderful, plus I was right there when things went on sale, and with the employee discount I was able to buy a lot of new clothes. I felt like I got my style back; I went to the makeup counter and had my makeup brought up-to-date. It was a lot of fun.

YOU WORK WITH KIDS. DOES THAT AFFECT HOW YOU DRESS?

*Y*es, it does. At work I like to wear things I can move around in easily, that allow me to get down on the floor if that's what I should be doing. Also, kids like color, so I'll wear brighter colors to work.

WHAT THINGS WOULDN'T YOU WEAR?

*A*nything cute.

WHAT'S THE AVERSION TO CUTE?

*A*t 6 feet tall, you're not cute. Anything cute, pastelly, any obvious polyester look; I dislike the Dress for Success look, the navy blue suit and the white shirt. It doesn't look good on me, and it's boring.

DO YOU HAVE A CURRENT FAVORITE OUTFIT, SOMETHING YOU JUST LOVE?

*M*y favorite outfit is my Valentino jacket; that's a tan, black, and red plaid with elastic at the waist. It's comfortable, it's perfect for traveling, it works with almost anything I put underneath it, with black, with white, although I tend to wear ivory instead of a pure white. It looks great with my favorite skirt, which is an Anne Klein black straight skirt with a leather yoke at the waist.

DO YOU PAY ATTENTION TO DESIGNERS?

I do, in that it's hard for me to find clothes that fit me correctly, because I'm tall and very thin and I have broad shoulders. When I find a designer whose clothes fit me, it makes shopping much easier and I tend to go back to that person's clothes again and again. Anne Klein fits me well, Calvin Klein, Valentino. They're just wonderful, because when I try them on they always fit perfectly.

DO YOU HAVE ANY IDEA HOW MUCH MONEY YOU SPEND ON CLOTHES IN A YEAR?

I don't know the amount, but I try to buy one good thing in the fall and in the spring and then buy cheaper things to fill in. I keep my good things for years. I still wear some things

I bought in '76 and '77. I have a collection of clothes at this point, and each year I just add a little bit to it.

DO YOU FEEL EXPENSIVE CLOTHES ARE WORTH THE MONEY?

*A*bsolutely.

WHY? A LOT OF WOMEN WOULD SAY, "HOW CAN A JACKET POSSIBLY BE WORTH $500 OR $600?"

*O*r $1,000. It's the fabric, the fit; you can throw it in the corner and when you pick it up and shake it out all the wrinkles disappear immediately; it lasts for years and years.

WHAT ABOUT ACCESSORIES AND SHOES?

I love shoes, but my foot is very hard to fit. I wear a 10½ or 11 AAAA. As a result almost all my shoes are Ferragamo, which I like but which doesn't allow me to be that adventurous. I love jewelry: I love gold and pearls and Chanel things. I love to find unusual things, handmade earrings or pins, in out-of-the-way places.

IT SOUNDS LIKE YOU PUT A LOT OF TIME INTO YOUR CLOTHES.

*I*t's a hobby for me. I enjoy everything about it. I enjoy getting dressed, deciding which shoes I'm going to wear and which necklaces and how many should I put on. The whole process is fun, deciding if I'm going to wear a belt and which one.

HAVE YOU EVER THOUGHT OF GIVING UP MEDICINE AND GOING INTO THE FASHION BUSINESS?

*T*he only thing I've thought of seriously is—I started to play golf here, and I can't find any golf clothes I like, so I've thought of marketing a line of great golf clothes. If you don't want to be cute in everyday life you don't want to be cute while you're playing golf.

I'm also interested in fashion and health. I mean in a physical way, things women have done to themselves in order to be fashionable, corsets and high heels and things like that. I think there's also a connection between fashion and psychology—that your clothes affect your mood and your mood affects the clothes you choose. I'll notice if I'm depressed I'll wear things that are more dull, whereas if I'm feeling good about myself I'll take more care getting dressed.

WAS THERE EVER A TIME IN YOUR LIFE WHEN YOU DIDN'T ENJOY CLOTHES?

Back in high school, when I didn't appreciate the way I was built. It seemed to me then that the great-looking girls were short and overdeveloped, and I was tall and underdeveloped. I just didn't have the kind of body that looked good in little plaid skirts and knee socks. If your knee socks fell down in high school, your boots are going to fall down for the rest of your life.

Nine Signs That It's Too Big

1. The waistline drops below your waist.
2. You can grab a handful of fabric someplace you shouldn't be able to.
3. It goes askew all by itself (i.e., shoulders drop toward the back, skirt twists around).
4. Long sleeves approach your knuckles.
5. It's got folds where it shouldn't have.
6. The neckline doesn't lie flat against your neck.
7. The darts pucker.
8. The seat droops.
9. You could wear it if you were nine months pregnant.

Ten Signs That It's Too Small

1. The button line pulls open, even slightly.
2. Hip pockets gap rather than lie smooth.
3. It creases at the bust, waist, hips, thighs.
4. Buttons or snaps pop open when you sit or bend.
5. It feels tight in back when you cross your arms.
6. You have to take a deep breath to zip it.
7. Underwear lines are visible.
8. It doesn't move when it should, i.e., pants legs hug thighs rather than slip up when you sit down.
9. It has long sleeves . . . that end above your wrist bone.
10. It pinches, presses, or tugs at you . . . anywhere.

EMOTIONAL ISSUE:
IF IT'S A SIZE 12, I DON'T LIKE IT

You're shopping and you see a pair of nice gray trousers with a hangtag marked size 6. You usually wear an 8 or, on bad days, a 10, but these look like they might fit and you take them into the dressing room. Sure enough, they look terrific. Feeling not only triumphant but transcendentally thin, you practically fly out of the pants and head toward the cash register. As you eagerly hand over your credit card, you pick up the trousers to give them one last satisfactory look when you notice something. Something terrible. There, inside the waistband, on a teeny, tiny little tag, is the real size. Size 12. You drop the pants on the counter in horror and rush from the store, your shopping trip ruined.

How does a simple number become invested with so much power? How can the size of a garment override the true size of your body? Why does a size 6 dress have infinitely more appeal than the same dress in a size 12?

"Sizes are a form of self-definition," says Patricia Mulready, a New York University home economics professor who specializes in the psychology and sociology of clothes. "People constantly refer to themselves as their sizes: I'm a size 8, I'm a size 10. A size 12 used to be considered fit but now it means you're overweight or obese or not a good person. By going into a 12 it makes someone feel that way about themselves, especially if they've been dieting or exercising."

Indeed, many women admit that size completely colors their feelings about clothes as well as themselves. "I'm a sucker for size," says one woman. "I will go completely by the number. Most of the time I wear a 10 but sometimes I can only fit into the 12 and I get really depressed and won't buy it. If the exact same thing were sized a 10 I would buy it."

Everything is relative, and each woman has her own definition of what size passes into the forbidden zone. "My mother has great clothes but if she offers me something, even if I really like it, that's a size 6 or 7 I won't take it," says one woman who usually wears a size 4. "Clothes in a larger size are tainted no matter how great they are."

Considerations of fit and flattery can be totally subservient to size. "If I tried on something and didn't know what size it was and it fit and turned out to be an 8, not only would I like it less but I would be disgusted with myself and my whole day would be ruined," says the size-conscious size 4 woman. "On the other hand, I bought these pants that are hideous, that I can't even wear, purely because they were a size 2 and they fit me."

The reason a number can distort one's perceptions, says Patricia Mulready, is that "people are already seeing themselves distorted. Research shows that women actually see themselves larger than they really are." If body image is out of whack, then, size can offer an "absolute" measure of how small—or big—you really are.

While most often only the wearer is privy to the size of her clothes, some women say they suffer from the fear that other people will see the size and form an opinion of them on that basis. "I bought this coat that was cut very slim in a size 14," says one woman, "and the first thing I did when I got it home was cut out the little inside tag with the 14 on it. I didn't want to have to look at that size every time I put on the coat, and I didn't want anybody else to see it."

In some cases, letting other people know your size is not a fear but a reality. If size vanity is strongest for bottoms and eases for tops (it's okay to have large breasts and broad shoulders; not okay to have big hips), then the ultimate size-conscious garment is a pair of Levi's with a size patch on the outside.

"When I was in college and my jeans got so faded you couldn't see the size, I'd want a new pair," says one woman. "My roommate used to buy her jeans two sizes too big and I thought she was a lunatic. Once I thought of borrowing a pair of her jeans and then I thought, Oh, no, what if someone thinks that's my true size?"

"Size 28 was the coolest and size 30 was not shameful," says another woman. "When I went to a size 32, I stopped wearing jeans altogether because if you weren't wearing the ones with the size on the outside everybody knew it was because you were too big. I just pretended I liked khakis better."

Clothing manufacturers are well aware of women's size consciousness, hearing about it from retailers. "Retailers say it's so difficult," says Gayle Dabal-Potter, the designer and co-owner with her husband and brother of Cotton Colors. "If they say a top only comes in one size, then people ask what size is that, and if the retailer says extra large, people will pull back and say 'Oh no. I'm not an extra large.' If you mark something 'One size fits all,' then the person thinks it means her instead of an extra large."

Other designers who make unconstructed clothing are also cognizant of size vanity when they name their sizes. Mimi Loverde, who makes unstructured hand-dyed garments that she wholesales to stores across the country and also sells from her own shop in New York's Tribeca, often starts with oversized pieces that shrink during the dyeing process. "With our tights we have to start with a large and an extra large. We first started calling them large and extra-large and people said no," says Loverde. "Then we called them small and medium. When someone comes in the store and says they take a large and we say we only do a small or a medium and the medium fits up to size 12 or 14, they like that much better. They like knowing they're not a large or an extra-large."

Don DelCollo, who like Loverde both wholesales and retails his Outer Limits clothing, avoids labeling items simply "large." "If something says 'large' people won't buy it even if it fits," says DelCollo. Instead, he calls his three sizes S–M, M–L, and S–M–L.

Some manufacturers avoid the entire small versus large, 6 versus 12 issue by creating a new sizing system for their clothes. At Nancy Heller, a new size has recently been added to the standard sizes 1, 2, and 3 . . . size 0. "Psychologically it's better because you don't know what size something really is," says Sue Marx, Heller's design services manager. "I'm very tall and big, but I take a 3, which feels great."

This big-is-small concept is also used by The Forgotten Woman, a chain of shops for large women, which sizes its clothing 1, 2, 3, 4, 5, and 6. The theory: it's depressing in itself for a woman to try on a size 24, uplifting if that same garment is called a 6.

Retailers and fashion consultants who have some control often avoid letting clients know the size of a garment. "I try not to tell clients what size something is," says Vicki French Morris. "I don't discuss it until it either fits or it doesn't."

Julee Spencer, who owns the shop Julee Julee in Westport, Connecticut, says, "In our dress section we don't merchandise according to size; we just get people into the dress. Size is not an issue because we make it not an issue."

Size vanity is not necessarily a gender-specific trait. "When I shop with male clients and they tell me their suit size, I'll bet them a thousand bucks right on the spot that they're wearing the wrong size," says Joyce Grillo, president of Impression Management, a New York image consulting firm. "They're so sure they know their size and then we'll go to the tailor and they're wearing something that's two sizes too small." Ever two sizes too big? "No," Grillo laughs. "Never, never too big."

The irony of all this is that, while the government sets size standards to be followed by all manufacturers, those have changed over time and vary from designer to designer, sometimes store to store. The notion that clothing size is any standard measure of body size is a false one. In fact, the women with the least size consciousness are often those who work in the fashion industry.

"I know that size is so imprecise and that there are so many variations from company to company that it doesn't influence my buying decision," says one fashion executive. "If something fits me in a lower size I know it's because some companies put smaller sizes on larger clothes. Size wouldn't go into my buying decision and wouldn't change my evaluation of how something fit or what it looked like. Mentally healthy? No, just realistic."

The Best: Jeans

Major Seams, at Seat, Side, Inseam, Double Stitched—Stronger where there's pressure.

Finished Edges on Exposed Seams—Neater, stronger.

Heavy Zipper or Metal Buttons at Fly.

Metal One-piece Button—Much stronger than sewn-on button.

Five to Seven Belt Loops.

Pockets Reinforced with Rivets and Burrs—Again, for strength.

Contrast Stitching.

Back Pockets—Flattering rear view.

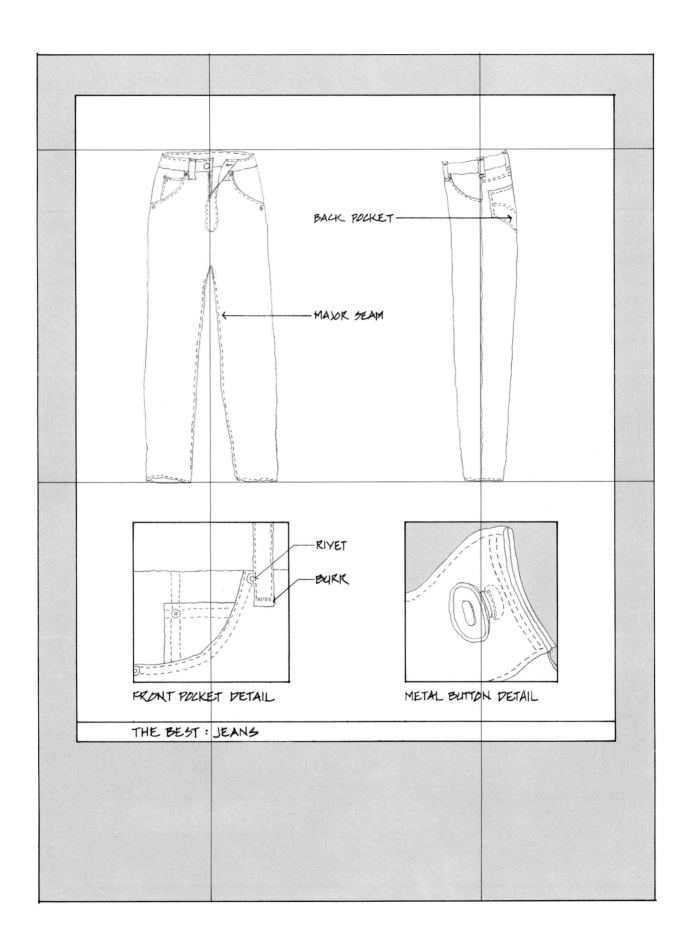

BACK POCKET

MAJOR SEAM

RIVET

BURR

FRONT POCKET DETAIL

METAL BUTTON DETAIL

THE BEST : JEANS

A Note on Denim: The best jeans are made with fourteen-ounce denim. Rinsing or stone-washing—for a soft, year-old look—has taken over from unwashed denim as the classic choice. Today, the finish on rinsed or stone-washed jeans looks natural, as if it got that way through wear and your own washer and dryer.

A Note on Fit: The optimal fit of jeans depends partly on your taste and partly on what's most flattering to your body. Whether you like your jeans baggy or snug, the best fit is consistent throughout the pant—not tight in one place and baggy in another. Beware of a waistline that gaps at the back, jeans that ride too low on your hips and so sag at the crotch, and tightness through the thighs that can emphasize weight there and cause the pants to bell out at the bottom. If trading up or down a size doesn't solve fit problems, try another style or size range (misses instead of juniors, for instance) in the same brand or a different brand altogether.

GOOD LOOKS

11

Comfort

·

You are getting dressed for a dinner party, and before you are two choices. The first is a draped silk blouse, a leather miniskirt, pantyhose, and high-heeled pumps—attractive, maybe; sexy, definitely; but you know that before the night is out, your feet will be killing you and your stomach will be straining against the waistband of the pantyhose and the skirt and you'll be clutching at the folds of the blouse. Your other choice, a big black turtleneck and loose black knit pants you can wear with socks and flats, is certainly comfortable but may leave something to be desired in the way of attractiveness: it makes you look a little bulky, a tad flabby, a bit like a slob.

Sometimes, it seems as if clothes fall into two groups: those that look good and those that feel comfortable. Combining the two qualities can seem like a difficult feat. Is it true, then, that you have to suffer for beauty? That dressing for comfort means looking dowdy or sloppy? Not at all, if you're tuned in to what makes clothes comfortable, to the nuances of fit and construction and style that let you put clothes together in a comfortable and good-looking way.

The first thing you should know is that many designers, even those who are making relatively structured clothing, aim to invest their clothes with comfort. The reason has as much to do with philosophy as it has to do with good business.

"Unless something is comfortable there's no need to own it," says Richard Assatly, co-designer of the Anne Klein II line. "I don't feel we have the time today to be uncomfortable; it interferes with thinking."

"Comfort is absolutely a basic priority in everything I make," says Joan Vass, whose clothes are known for both their comfort and their good looks. "You want to be able to forget your clothes but feel as if you look wonderful. I attempt to make clothes for modern life, for the woman who's active, busy, who moves around and works. Even when she's out in the evening she should be able to get in and out of the car comfortably. If you look as beautiful as you can and feel as comfortable as you can you gain as much confidence as possible."

"When you feel comfortable you feel confident; one feeds the other," says Gayle Dabal-Potter, who designs Cotton Colors. "I get dressed up once in a while and I do own a nice sexy black dress, but I wouldn't wear it if I was uncomfortable." How does one find a nice sexy black dress that's also comfortable? "You have to try on a lot of them."

How something feels is, of course, the only true test of whether it's comfortable. That's why many designers who are oriented toward comfort try their clothes on themselves as well as on several other women with various kinds of bodies.

"After I make a sample and wash and dye it, I put it on," says Dabal-Potter. "I'm a good person to try stuff on because I don't have your average phenomenal body and I'm high-waisted, so if something fits me it will fit a lot of people. I also try clothes on the woman who runs my showroom, who's a 10, and my pattern-maker, who's a 12."

Joan Vass says she tries her clothes on "at least five different people, short and tall, and then I ask them how it feels. I come from an academic background where one is accustomed to checking things a lot, and the more people who check something the better it will be."

Usually, designers who make comfort a priority in the clothes they make also value comfort in the clothing they wear. "I personally don't want anything to take my attention away when I'm working, and if I'm doing nothing I don't want my mind to be on anything, certainly not on my clothes," says Richard Assatly. Don DelCollo, who designs the Outer Limits line of clothing, says, "I buy clothes for comfort, but I won't buy anything that doesn't look good. I get out of the dressing room and walk around and see how I feel. If I feel constrained I put it back, because

I know once I buy it I'll be pulling and yanking on it until I rip it. If I can move around I feel more agile and I have a better mental attitude."

While physical feel has a lot to do with the comfort of clothes, attractiveness can influence your perception of a garment's comfort. "The psychological can sometimes outweigh the physical," says Patricia Mulready, who worked on a study for DuPont on the relative comfort of various kinds of jogging bras. "There was a pretty jogging bra that felt nice and even though the bounce was more it tested higher for comfort than another bra that kept the breasts in place but didn't look or feel as good. There's some level where construction and tactile feel are combining subconsciously with appreciation and that affects the comfort rating." Conversely, says Mulready, if clothes look uncomfortable (but in fact aren't) people often feel uncomfortable wearing them.

Optimum comfort, then, comes from clothes that look good as well as feel good. How do designers combine the two, and what should you look for to get both? There are three main components of comfortable, good-looking clothes, say the experts:

Fabric

"What makes clothes comfortable is first of all always the fabric," says Mimi Loverde. Loverde likes natural fabrics, primarily cotton, but says comfort varies depending on the type of cotton that is used. "We test lots and lots of cottons, and find many we can't use," says Loverde. "It's very important that it doesn't pill, and you can see that as soon as you wash or dye it."

However, says Loverde, if you're buying something that hasn't been washed or garment-dyed, it can be difficult to tell how it will feel once it goes through your own washing machine a few times. "It's very hard for the consumer, because it's almost impossible to tell how a fabric will feel and hold up until it's been washed," says Loverde. "That's a lot of the success of washed and prewashed garments, because something that's been broken in is going to be a lot more comfortable."

Other designers who make comfortable clothes also prefer natural fabrics: cottons for year-round wear, pure cashmere, sweatshirting. There has also been much experimentation in recent years: washed silks and linens, wools blended with silk for softness, cottons shot with Lycra for ease, all manner of knits. The reason designers like natural fibers is that they tend to feel better next to the skin, and they also breathe, keeping you cooler in summer, warmer in winter, drawing moisture away from the body.

Is more expensive fabric more comfortable? "Not always," says Loverde. "You can go buy Chinese cotton underwear T-shirts for $2.50 that are as nice as $24 cotton camisoles in lingerie stores."

Construction

How a piece of clothing is put together can have a lot to do with how comfortable it feels and how good it looks. Some construction details you can see; others are hidden but will make a difference on the body.

"When clothes are designed well, they're more comfortable because of the nature of the sewing," says Loverde. "When you put on an expensive European jacket and it feels great, that has a lot to do with the way it's sewn. They'll take the time to sew a curve in a garment because that's the way the arm moves and that's the angle at which the sleeve should be put in.

On a cheap garment, they cut straight up and down and throw the seams in. Good construction costs money."

Loverde points to the way jeans are made in France as opposed to the way they're usually made in the United States as an example of how hidden construction details affect comfort. "In France they make both legs as two separate units and the last seam is around the crotch and up the back, pulling the two sides together," she says. "In America the last stitch is up and down the inside of the legs. That's dramatically different. If you're sewing around the leg the machine will pull the fabric over so one side is a little off. If the last stitch is around the crotch you get a much better fit and the pants won't hurt in the crotch."

How seams are finished can also affect comfort. Says Emily Mann, who runs her own New York designing and trend consulting firm, "Seams that are turned and stitched or that have a marrowed [looped overstitching] edge will be softer and more comfortable than unfinished seams."

Elastic waistbands are another important element of comfort, but how the waistband is constructed can make a big difference in the way a pair of pants looks and feels. "Elastic that floats through a waistband is more comfortable and attractive than sewn-down elastic," says Loverde. The reason: the elastic can expand and contract more freely, you can arrange the material to fall in the most flattering way—usually, smooth in back, gathered in front.

Shape

To a large extent, the shape of clothes has more to do with fashion than it has to do with comfort. Clothes can be comfortable whether they're slim and body-conscious or loose and oversized. And just as too-tight clothes can be uncomfortable, so can too-baggy ones.

"Shaped clothes can be comfortable," says Anne Klein II's Assatly. "If they're darted and seamed comfortably there's no reason they should be uncomfortable." Also, says Emily Mann, the more fitted and shaped something is, the softer and more pliable the fabric should be. "Knits that are body-conscious but also move are a way to merge the idea of comfort and good looks," she says.

Says Gayle Dabal-Potter, "I've never been a real big fan of oversized clothes. I've always been more body-conscious without being skintight." One key to making comfortable yet body-conscious clothes, Dabal-Potter says, is in the cut. "Armholes and rises are the most important. You can drop an armhole on a jacket or make it a little deeper without making the jacket humongous. You can cut the rise on pants more generously without making them baggy in the seat. These are little things that can be improved on without changing the major look."

"In our design we like to keep shapes that fall away from the body a little bit, even if it's a tighter silhouette," says Sue Marx of Nancy Heller. "Also, we don't go in for darts or heavy, fitted fabrics or a lot of interlinings or facings that can make clothes stiff and less comfortable."

Whatever the shape, uncomplicated clothes with no fussy details tend to be most comfortable. "It's silly to put collars on clothes that don't do anything but get in the way," says Don DelCollo. "The collar may look great but the person who's wearing it is always trying to put it somewhere. Clothes shouldn't get in your way, you shouldn't be always pulling down or up on your sleeves or trying to keep a skirt in line."

How to Buy Comfortable Clothes

Now that you know the inside story of how designers build comfort into clothes, here's how to give those concepts the real-life test . . . in the dressing room:

Move Around—You can't truly gauge a garment's comfort by standing still and looking at yourself in the mirror; you've got to move around in the dressing room. In a jacket, top, or dress, raise your arms over your head to make sure the sleeves move with you, the wrists don't pinch, the underarms don't tug and pull, the body of the garment doesn't hike up. Cross your arms over the front of your body to check that the garment doesn't pull across the back. In a scoop-necked or wrapped blouse, bend over to make sure the front won't gap. With a slim skirt, take a large stride and also raise your leg as if climbing onto a bus to ensure that the skirt won't hamper your movements. Also with a skirt or pants, sit down to check that the waistband isn't too snug, the fabric isn't too tight across your stomach or thighs.

Try on a Garment as You Would Wear It—If you wear pants with socks and not hose, try them on that way to check that they're not itchy against bare skin. If you'll wear trousers or a skirt with an overblouse, don't try them on with a shirt tucked in; you won't get an accurate feel of the waistband. Always try on a jacket with the kind of blouse you'll wear it with: long sleeves can protect your arms from an otherwise-itchy wool; with a short-sleeved or sleeveless shirt you'll need a smoother-feeling jacket—one that's lined or made of softer fabric. If you'll wear a jacket or cardigan with tops of varying sleeve lengths underneath, try on with the barest possibility.

Consider the Time of the Month—Many women gain up to two sizes when they're premenstrual, a factor to consider when you're buying clothes for comfort. If it's your "thin" time of the month, buy clothes slightly large. Right before your period, go with things that fit more exactly.

Shop for Comfortable Clothes Late in the Day—"Gravity and water make your body expand throughout the day so your clothes actually are tighter in the evening," says Pat Mulready. That's why the clothes that felt fine all day can suddenly become unbearable once you arrive home from work. Also, when you're alone, your attention is focused on yourself (and the comfort of your clothing) in a way it isn't when you're out in the world.

How to Dress Comfortably Without Looking Like a Slob

Now that you've bought clothes that will make you feel good, you want to put them together in a way that will make you look good. In other words, comfort without sloppiness.

The right fit is a prime component of dressing comfortably without looking like a slob, say the experts. That means, obviously, not too baggy and not too tight. The ways in which too-tight clothes can be uncomfortable are evident, especially if you've ever suffered through an evening in jeans that were one size too small and shoes that cut into your toes. When clothes are too big, they can slip off shoulders, bag and bunch up in a way that can be uncomfortable.

Being creative with mixing color and fabric and shape can help pull off a look that's both comfortable and flattering.

"One problem a lot of people have is that they're afraid to mix colors," says Don DelCollo. "They're afraid they'll look stupid and in reality color helps them look better. Women who aren't fat but wear oversized pants and shirts in matching dark colors tend to look frumpy and larger than they really are."

"Putting shapes together can be a way to feel comfortable and look good," says Sue Marx. "The kind of things we look for here are a great-looking sweater with a real easy pant or a nice short skirt and if you want to dress it up maybe throw a linen jacket over it. For fall we'll take some cashmere and layer it: a short cashmere sweater and full elasticized cashmere pants with a long cardigan."

Dabal-Potter believes in wearing ultra-comfortable weekend pieces with dressier ones. "You can wear a black cotton turtleneck with a silk jacket," she says. "The key to making comfortable weekend clothes appropriate for work is choosing pieces in conservative colors like black or blue and mixing those with a Hermès scarf, textured stockings, gold or silver jewelry and flat, dressy shoes."

Comfortable shoes are, in fact, an essential element of feeling comfortable all over. "You should dress from the toes up," says Emily Mann. "The first priority for comfort should be your feet, because they hold up your whole weight. More and more flats are very stylish."

Attitude and self-knowledge can be the most important components of making you both look and feel your best. "All styles have their limitations and everybody looks good in different things," says Don DelCollo. "Your attitude and knowing what looks good on you plays an important part in the way you look and how comfortable you feel."

"The first thing that makes clothing uncomfortable is putting on someone else's idea of who you are," says Mimi Loverde. "The fashion world has encouraged this, has encouraged a woman not to know who she is and what to wear. It's given her all these rules of how she should look rather than encouraging her to develop her own individual style."

• *Style Analysis* •

JUDY NEWMARK *is the editor of the Sunday magazine of the St. Louis* Post-Dispatch *and the mother of two little girls. Newmark's all-cotton turtleneck, $12, and striped cardigan ("That was expensive; that was $30") are both from* Fashion Gal, *a discount chain; her pants are* Units, *$25; her suede booties were bought in a St. Louis shoe outlet three years ago for $30.*

HOW DOES YOUR STYLE COMPARE TO THAT OF THE TYPICAL ST. LOUIS WOMAN?

I'm certainly not a typical St. Louisan, and that's not just my imagination. People always ask, "Are you from New York?" or they think I shop in New York or Chicago. I shop in St. Louis, but I guess I'm looking for different stuff. The typical St. Louis style is rather conservative and Southern, not too showy, not too ostentatious, not by any means fashion-forward. Talbot's is received around town as being perfection. That holds no appeal for me whatsoever.

What was so wonderful about the past? Why on earth would a forward, modern woman choose to dress like a Victorian lady of leisure? I dress for the twentieth century. In the twentieth century women cut their hair, started showing their legs, began wearing less-confined styles, wearing trousers. All of that to me signifies wonderful things for women.

WHERE DO THESE FEELINGS COME FROM?

My grandmother came from a very unusual background. She was a wonderful, warm, adorable pharmacist and her sister was a lawyer. This was in Romania in the early twentieth century when most women couldn't read. My grandmother would use "old-fashioned" as a pejorative, meaning dated, repressive, superstitious garbage. To me also, modern is better; I wear pants all the time; I have my hair in a bob. All of it reflects a cultural system and intellectual outlook that I feel very comfortable with.

HOW DO PEOPLE AT YOUR JOB REACT TO HOW YOU DRESS?

I sit in a lot of meetings where I'm the only woman. I know the standard advice is to try to look like a fella in that real drab uniform, or they say you can soften it with femininity, which is saying that you should look like a Junior Leaguer: that's the volunteer mentality. I figure they're gonna know that I'm a woman, and I don't want them to mistake me for a wife. I want to be seen as someone who is creative, aggressive, not afraid to speak my mind, willing to take a chance, and I think I make that statement more effectively in a very contemporary red pants suit.

I believe that much of the advice women get on how to dress isn't true. One is that the way you look is more important than what you say. I honestly believe that if I'm on the ball I could go in in jeans and torn sweatshirts and it would still pay off in the end. I do much better to be myself, to let other people accept or reject me as I am. What's my percentage in misleading people? I see none. I'm on much better ground if I'm me. I have integrity: how I talk and how I look and what I think all fits together.

DO YOU DRESS PRETTY MUCH THE SAME FOR EVERY OCCASION?

I don't dress that differently for anything, to go to school, to work, or to a party. I might save a better fabric, my crepe pants, for going out, but I have the identical thing in knit that I wear to the office.

Maybe to some extent that's because I'm a child of the sixties, when you wore blue jeans everywhere. There's something principled about that, that you're one person, that you should spend your life in something comfortable and easy and that you really like. I like the idea that whenever you see me, you're going to see me as myself.

I do a lot of speaking, and I used to think you had to look like a charity lady to do this. I no longer believe that. They're asking me because they want me so I should just be me. I have red pants that I wear with a big black top and a long coat with no sleeves which is red and big red earrings, and the reception to that is very good. The whole thing of the right wing of fashion is that warmth and motherhood belongs to them and that's bullshit; you don't own certain feelings because you wear flowered dresses or serious suits. The mom of tomorrow who's wearing aluminum foil will feel the same way about her kids as Betty Crocker does.

I KNOW YOU HAVE STRONG FEELINGS ABOUT HOW MUCH CLOTHES COST . . .

I once saw in *Harper's* a pair of Bermuda shorts for $800. I would not spend over $10. I think if you start spending around $80 for shorts they're, like, to wear to your own wedding.

I believe if you start spending $800 for shorts you're not just rich, you're stupid. I look at the prices of the more moderate stuff and I am floored. Something to wear to the office and it costs $200?

HOW DO YOU GET GREAT STYLE CHEAP?

I really really know what I want. I love knits, and you can find knits that are not expensive. I shop at discount places a lot: Marshall's, Target, Fashion Gal. I love Units. I don't expect clothes to last forever; if it wears out, replace it. People justify expensive clothes by saying they'll wear it forever. I say, "Baloney, what are you going to do when you spill coffee on it? What are you going to do when you gain five pounds?" Nothing lasts forever. I buy futuristic materials, that are strong and you can take care of easily. My purse, as always, is ripstop nylon. I wear a lot of black, a lot of red; I wear gray; I'll wear sometimes a grayish blue. I do find I can put things together real easily. You can find a top, find a bottom, and you're dressed.

DOES YOUR HEIGHT AFFECT WHAT YOU WEAR AT ALL?
[Newmark is 5 feet 3 inches.]

*N*ot much. One time I was shopping with a friend who was my height and we were both admiring this real big necklace. My friend said, "Oh, Judy, you buy it. You can wear it and I can't." And I said, "You know why I can wear it and you can't? Because I do and you don't." That's all there is to it. We have all been inundated with these meshuga fashion rules and we have these very good empirical laboratories—our bodies. If I were taller, that would be swell, but I have never not worn anything because I wasn't tall enough for it.

AT WHAT POINT DID YOUR STYLE BECOME WHAT IT IS NOW?

*T*he current style came after the birth of my second child. I was pregnant from when I was thirty-two until I was thirty-six. I tried to improvise a little because I hated maternity clothes, and I hated the idea of spending a lot of money on clothes I'd wear for a short period of time. After I had Denny and got back in shape I decided that I would think about being modern, and that was when I really started wearing pants all the time. The knits I started wearing in pregnancy for obvious reasons and I thought, why do I have to give that up? I sort of evolved this current new woman phase after my pregnancy and I expect to wear it the rest of my life.

YOUR STYLE IS VERY INNER-DIRECTED. WHAT'S THE KEY TO THAT?

A lot of it is rooted in your childhood, in the kind of support your parents or your school gave you, in growing up with an inner-directed authority on any issue—fashion is the least of it. I love fashion magazines—I read five a week—but that doesn't mean that I want to do it all. I am sorry to say that if you grew up feeling incompetent, you're going to look for outward direction on fashion, you're going to want somebody else to run your life and your closet for you. Sure, stores will tell you what to do—they want to sell you something. Fashion gurus are not necessarily the brightest people you've ever met; it's not like their judgment is infallible. One thing they don't know is you. I'm very skeptical of the fashion industry and I think if anyone just thought about it for a few minutes she would be skeptical too. If you look on fashion as a personal art that's fun, that is agreeable, and that has some relationship to how you want other people to pick up on you, then you have to look a little more into yourself and less into what's going on around you.

A LOT OF WOMEN SAY, "I REALLY LIKE LONG SKIRTS BUT THEY'RE NOT IN FASHION. CAN I STILL WEAR THEM?"

There are two things going on. One is this really pervasive evil notion that only one style is beauty: here is beautiful, a handful of well-paid white women, mainly blue-eyed and blond, and maybe once in a while we'll let Naomi Sims through. It's an intolerant rigid standard that you have to be this tall and this thin, and no one else gets to look good. Then we end up with remedial fashion: what to do if you're human. That is just garbage. The human standard of what is beautiful is much broader than what we'd guess looking at the pages of *Vogue*.

The other reason women ask this question is this notion of rules of what we can and cannot do. We get a lot of bad information. We have to keep testing. If something appeals for whatever reason, for God's sake put it on in the store, and if you can't afford it buy a cheaper version. If you love it, if you decide your style is long velvet skirts or knit components, then wear them. You can make the worst clothing mistake imaginable and nothing is going to happen. We're talking about one of those very rare fields of human experience that is deliciously inconsequential.

The Best: Cashmere Sweater

100 Percent Pure Cashmere—Stay away from cashmere blends: the cashmere will be lower grade, the blend may include anything from cat's hair to newspaper.

Made in Scotland—Some good cashmere sweaters (especially designer ones) are made in Italy or Hong Kong, but the best and most classic still come from Scotland.

"Full-Fashioned"—Full-fashioned sweaters are those that are shaped and joined with

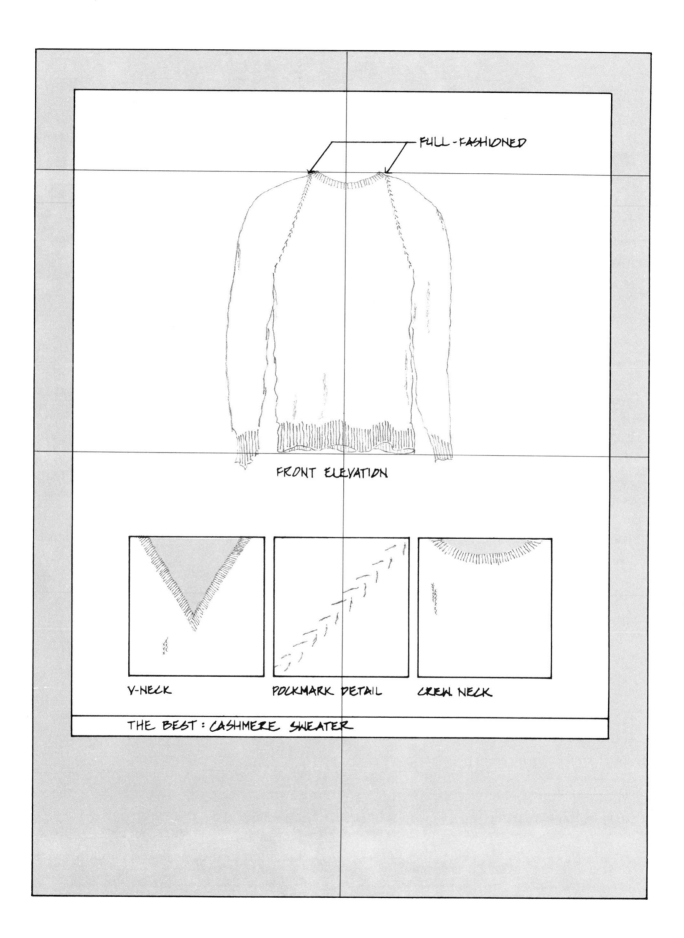

FULL-FASHIONED

FRONT ELEVATION

V-NECK

POCKMARK DETAIL

CREW NECK

THE BEST : CASHMERE SWEATER

knitting, not stitching. The earmark of full-fashioning: "pockmarks" at the shoulder, wherever the sweater is shaped. Full-fashioned sweaters are more classic, tend to fit better, have smoother seams, and can last longer than sweaters that are sewn.

One Ply/Two Ply—Ply refers to the number of strands of yarn twisted together for knitting. Two-ply cashmere is thicker, stronger, and more durable than one-ply, but is used most often in men's sweaters (which you may want to consider). Women's sweaters are more often one-ply, which is finer and more delicate.

Not Too Tight!—No matter what the fashion, a cashmere sweater looks best when it's roomy. Also, cashmere can be itchy and almost always pills: a looser fit will be more comfortable, look better longer.

Stretchy Ribbing—Ribbing at the cuffs and waistband should spring back into shape after being stretched. Go ahead, stretch it.

A Note on Style: If you pay for a top-grade cashmere sweater, buy a style and color you'll wear for years. A V-necked cardigan—neither too big, too small, too short, or too long—is one good choice. In pullovers, a crew neck is not as subject to the whims of fashion as a turtle or cowl or a V neck. A neutral dark color like black, navy, or gray is a better choice than white or beige (which can show stains) or a color color (which can become dated, isn't as versatile). It's heartbreaking to have to retire an expensive and wonderful cashmere sweater after a year or two simply because it's gone out of style.

EMOTIONAL ISSUE:
EMOTIONAL-COMFORT CLOTHES

You come home from work after a harrowing day during which your biggest client hung up on you and your boss yelled at you and your boyfriend broke your dinner date. The first thing you do is tear off your clothes and put on your softest, baggiest sweatpants and your brother's old sweater. Instantly you feel more relaxed, happier, both comfortable and comforted.

Certain clothes have an unmistakable power to provide emotional comfort, to cheer you up when you're down, to make you feel safe or self-assured or loved when the rest of life tells you you're not. But how can a sweater embody peace? A pair of pants esteem? A jacket security?

"One of the things I've found in my research is that a lot of clothes have a mnemonic quality: they have the ability to remind people of things they were associated with," says Michael Solomon, Ph.D., an expert in the psychology of clothing.

There are two basic kinds of emotional-comfort clothes, according to both Dr. Solomon and Arlene Kagle, Ph.D., a New York psychotherapist: those that comfort you when you're out in the world and those that comfort you from it. What both kinds have in common is what Dr. Solomon called that mnemonic quality; they're associated with good feelings.

In a study Dr. Solomon did for Levi's jeans, he found that "when people wear or even look at their favorite jeans they're reminded of special times when they had them on. It's often

superstitious: the lucky jeans you were wearing when your fiancé proposed."

As emotionally comforting clothes can be ones that remind you of good times, so can they be pieces that remind you of people you love. Many women say their most comforting items are a husband's shirt, an old friend's scarf, a grandmother's sweater. "People do use clothing as symbols of continuity," says Dr. Solomon. "Essentially clothing embodies the person that it left. When something's not new part of the spirit, so to speak, of the person who wore it is contained in that item." Many women say they're comforted by a loved one's clothing because it smells like that person, an association that's both powerful and direct.

Old clothes, your own or someone else's, can be emotionally comforting because of their very faithfulness. "We need a few touchstones in our lives. Something like a bathrobe and old slippers that you wear every day begin to have some ritualistic and carryover affect," says Maryland psychotherapist Stephanie Miller. "You need a few talismans in your life and clothes can become that."

The good feelings can be physical as well as emotional, which is why private emotional-comfort clothes are also often physically comfortable. "Clothes can literally influence behavior by being very constricting or very loose," says Dr. Solomon. "When you're conscious of your clothes you're on your best behavior; when you're not conscious of them, they won't inhibit you in either sense of the word."

This freedom can harken back to childhood: "I have two pairs of very thick cotton socks that no matter what else I'm wearing if I put on those socks they make me feel better," says one woman. "I also have two enormous cardigans that I wore every day when I was pregnant and that I loved, but I don't find them comforting anymore. My pregnant clothes remind me of my adulthood and responsibilities; my socks let me feel like a little kid."

Another reason physically comfortable clothes can provide emotional comfort, says Dr. Kagle, is that "they're clothes that are very forgiving: forgiving of the fact that you just had a whole pizza or a quart of Häagen-Dazs."

For some women, even when they're alone, emotional-comfort clothes have to look good as well as feel good. "Flannel nightgowns don't do it for me," says one woman. "My mother used to wear a lot of flannel nightgowns and I've never equated them with peace and love. I like luxurious long silk nightgowns that really feel great—nonrestricting, no elastic, soft fabric. When I know that I look good, it makes me feel good."

Out in the world, this look good–feel good equation becomes a more important factor in what makes clothing emotionally comfortable. "The public kind of emotional-comfort clothes are those we feel certain we look our best in," says Dr. Kagle. "Maybe it's a dress that we feel we can wear to any party and look good or an interview outfit—something that no matter who we're meeting will look good."

The one danger, endemic only to these "public" comfort clothes: sometimes, you can become so attached to the comfort they provide that you're blinded to how they actually look. "I had one dress that looked good in every situation," says Dr. Kagle. "I wore it to a college reunion and to an interview with CBS and then one day I looked at it and realized it was no longer the right length. One can become so comfortable that one becomes oblivious to the fact that the piece is no longer in fashion."

The Best: Terry Cloth Robe

Shawl Collar—Generously cut and double weight—thick enough to turn up and snuggle into.

Hanger Loop—For the back of the bathroom door.

Fullness Under Arm—Tends to rip here if too tight—you should be able to lift arms comfortably over head without the fabric pulling or tugging under the arm.

Dolman Sleeve—For fullness.

Double Stitching at Shoulder and Armhole—For strength.

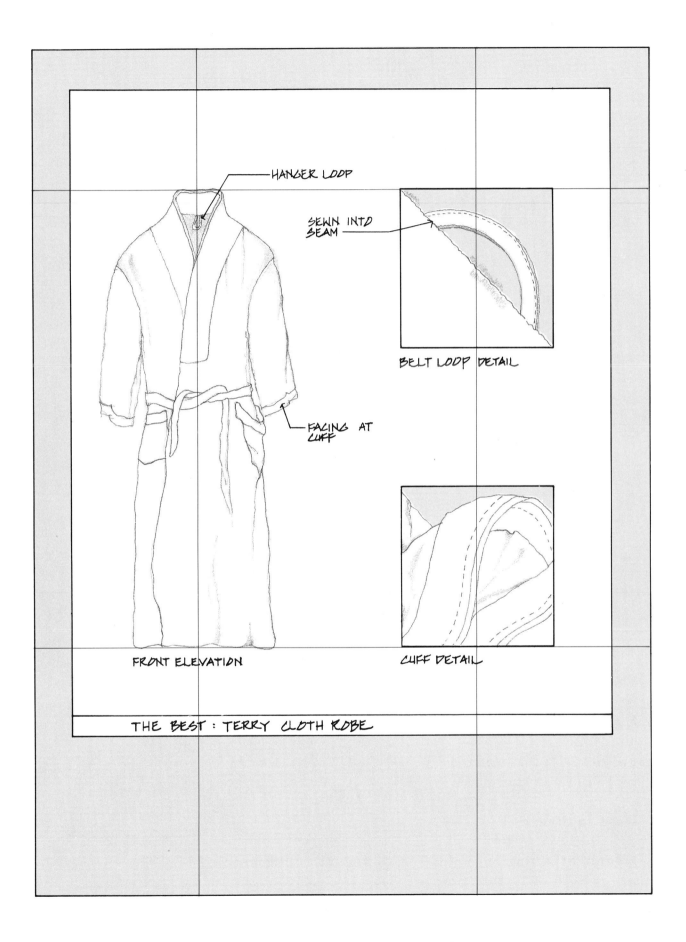

HANGER LOOP

SEWN INTO SEAM

BELT LOOP DETAIL

FACING AT CUFF

FRONT ELEVATION

CUFF DETAIL

THE BEST : TERRY CLOTH ROBE

Sleeves Taper in to Wrist—Shouldn't be too tight, but neither so loose that your sleeve catches fire when you reheat the coffee.

Facing at Cuffs.

Full Facing at Front, Stitched Down.

White—Most classic, purest next to skin.

Generous Cut.

Finished Seams—They don't have to be French seams, but they should be stitched at the edges.

100 Percent Cotton—Most comfortable, absorbent.

Two Belt Loops.

Belt Loops Sewn into Seam—Stronger.

Two Patch Pockets.

Calf to Ankle Length—Shouldn't drag on floor.

A Note on Terry Cloth: Terry comes in all manner of weight and texture. Very heavy terry cloth may feel luxurious, but it can break all your hangers and take three hours to dry. Too light, however, and it won't keep you cozy. If the fabric has big loops, they can catch and pull; if the nap is too short, it may not absorb water well. What you should aim for is something in between—choose a terry that's closest to your favorite, most durable towel. A few washings after you first buy will make it softer and more absorbent; a good terry cloth robe should feel and look better the more you wash it.

Sensible Shoes

Is there such a thing as a shoe that's both comfortable and flattering? That looks as good as it feels and feels as good as it looks? You bet. It may not be easy to find, but knowing what to look for, and how to know a comfortable and flattering shoe when you try one on, can help.

What Makes for Comfort—One key to comfort, many shoe designers say, is leather: a shoe that's not only made of real leather but has a leather lining and sole tends to be more comfortable than a shoe in which some or all of the components are synthetic. Of course, depending on your foot and the design of the shoe, it can be possible to find comfort in fabric or man-made materials, but in general, all-leather is the best bet.

What makes leather so comfortable? It's soft, for one thing, and it's also pliable. To some extent, it "gives" to accommodate your foot—although shoes as a rule don't truly stretch. Leather also breathes—in all-leather shoes, your feet won't get too hot or too sweaty, and leather soles provide a sort of air cushion under your feet.

Another important component of a shoe's comfort is the heel. What's more important than the heel's height is its balance: when you try on a shoe, the heel should feel solid under your foot—it shouldn't be wobbly or pitch you forward.

Further evidence of a shoe's comfort is in its feel. You should be able to flex the sole, and both the outside and the lining of the shoe should be soft to the touch. In most shoes, the upper and the lining are bonded together, but there shouldn't be so much glue that the shoe feels stiff and hard.

Rough edges and unfinished seams that can rub on your foot can cause discomfort. One shoe manufacturer says to look carefully at the details you can see—stitching, glue marks, how the lining's put in—as an indication of the amount of care and quality put into the parts of the shoe that you may not be able to see.

The shape of the toe is not an absolute indication of the shoe's comfort: "If the shoe is made well, how long or pointed the toe is has little to do with where the foot is," says Jamie Luwenda, a shoe designer for Evan Picone. "The point of a toe should happen after your own toes."

A Walking Revolution Afoot—The fact that working women all over America are wearing running shoes for comfortable commuting isn't news, but Norman Engle, a shoe engineer at U.S. Shoe, is determined to do something about it. He's spent a year and a half developing the "Easy Spirit Dress Shoe"—which combines the look of a classic pump (complete with high heel and pointy toe) and the comfort of a walking shoe.

When Engle started in the shoe business, round about 1950, comfort wasn't an issue. "The toes were so pointed that the podiatrists had a booming business. There should have been some rebellion but there wasn't." The rebellion came after the New York transit strike in 1980. "When women started wearing athletic shoes to work, they were telling us something," says Engle. "What they were telling us was that footwear wasn't comfortable."

What makes the shoe Engle has developed comfortable is what you can't see: two layers of "shock foam," of the sort in football helmets and astronauts' suits, hidden under the insole; a lining made of Coolmax, the stuff of professional running clothes, designed to draw heat and sweat away from the body; and a synthetic sole so flexible it can be folded in half. The shoes' uppers are kidskin, and Engle admits that there has been some validity to other shoemakers' claims that all-leather shoes are more comfortable, "up to this era." However, he says, "these materials were specially developed for walking and this construction eliminates a lot of the cement that can block the passage of air in leather shoes."

Another essential component of the Easy Spirit pump is a last (the mold on which a shoe is made) designed to accommodate the movement of a foot. "When you walk you strike first on your heel and then roll around the outside of your foot," explains Engle. "The weight transfers across from your little toe to your big toe—your power toe. There's a small depression in this last that your first metatarsal can relax into, so the shoe doesn't put a strain on your foot."

As research, Engle studied the walking patterns of dozens of people, and tried test shoes on anyone he could grab. The final comfort test: he's making another pair of pumps . . . for himself.

What Makes for Flattery—All right, you've got the comfort part down, but what about flattery? How do you get one without giving up the other?

If you feel you need to wear heels to look good, you can do so and still feel comfortable. While 2½ inches is the most popular heel height, heels that are 2 to 2¼ inches will probably be better for walking and will still be flattering to your legs, says Jamie Luwenda. "If you go higher than 2½ inches you're not talking about a serious walking shoe." Slightly thicker but still curvy heels will give you a better base of support than stilettos can.

Non-clunky flats and low-heeled pumps can be as flattering as heels. If you plan to wear them with a skirt, wear a skirt when you shop to avoid ugly surprises.

Some details that can be slimming to legs and make no sacrifice of comfort: an asymetrical strap or pattern on the shoe, "low-cut" pumps that curve down at the side of your foot, a classic Chanel pump—beige with a black toe. Sandals with straps across the toe-line only are likely to be more flattering than those with straps higher on the instep; ankle straps are usually unflattering on even slightly heavy or slightly skinny legs.

If you're petite or want to make your legs look longer, avoid very high-heeled shoes that will throw your body out of proportion—only emphasizing what you want to overcome—and aim instead for medium-high heels in the same tone as your hose.

In general, however, subtle differences can make one shoe flattering, another anything but. Don't necessarily give up on a style you like just because one version made your legs look awful; another model that looks exactly the same on the shelf may look infinitely better once you put it on your foot.

How to Buy Comfortable Shoes—If comfort is important to you, you can't just buy your shoes any old way. The first thing you should know is that some manufacturers' shoes will be more comfortable on you than others'. That's because each manufacturer works with its own lasts, which vary in size and shape and can be more or less comfortable on you depending on your foot. If you've found comfort in a certain brand of shoe in the past, chances are you will again.

The second thing you should know is that some styles of shoes fit better per se than others. The more straps a shoe has, the harder it will be to fit. "Strappy sandals are the hardest because feet vary so much," says one manufacturer. "You can have two models with perfect size 6 feet and the straps on a sandal will fall completely differently on each."

What makes one pair of shoes comfortable on you and another, similar pair uncomfortable may be a very small matter. "A lot of times it's millimeters that make the difference in comfort," says Jamie Luwenda. "If the measurement of the back of the shoe is slightly different it can throw the comfort off completely."

Are expensive shoes always more comfortable? "Expensive shoes that are made to be more comfortable are more comfortable," says Luwenda. "But sometimes you're just paying for style."

Shop for shoes after you've been on your feet a while, but not at the end of the day when your feet are at their biggest. Wear the kind of stocking or sock you'd wear with the shoe so you can get an accurate gauge of fit. Walk around, and take your time. Shoe experts advise walking on both carpet and uncarpeted floors, if possible, to see how the shoes feel on each.

If the toes pinch, if the heels slip, if all your weight is on the ball of your foot, if the shoe is altogether too snug or too loose, don't buy it. Salespeople may tell you that shoes stretch: they don't, at least not enough to make a perceptible difference in comfort. If you want to take a chance on special pads or grips the salesperson says will make the shoe more comfortable, that's up to you. In general, though, the way shoes feel after a five-minute walk around the shop is a good indication of how they'll feel once you're out on the street. If they're uncomfortable after five minutes, they'll be a lot more so after five hours.

The Best: Pumps

No Side Seams—Only seam is at back of heel.

Back Seam Straight and Centered.

Rolled Topline—The technical term for when the outside leather folds over the top of the shoe, joining the lining about an eighth of an inch inside. This is the smoothest and most comfortable construction, and also keeps the lining hidden.

Small, Even Stitching.

No Raw Leather Edges! No Seam Edges! No Errant Threads!

Leather Lining.

Suede Quarter Lining—Hugs your heel, keeps it from slipping out of the shoe.

Padding Under Leather Sock Lining.

Non-Black Sock Lining—On some people's feet, black linings can "bleed" and stain stockings.

Toe Should Be High Enough to Accommodate a Pencil—And not incidentally, your own toes.

Oval Toes—Neither too pointy nor too round, not squared off.

1⁴⁄₈ to 2¹⁄₈ Heel—Standard measures of heel height, these are roughly equivalent—depending on your shoe size—to 1¾ to 2½ inches, the optimum range for both flattery and comfort. These have the look of classic high heels without being too high.

Covered Heels—Simply, the heel is covered in the same material as the shoe. More classic than "stacked" heels, which are or look like wood.

Sole Wraps from Inside of the Shoe's Heel to Toe.

Leather Soles—By law, must be marked as such.

Hand-Painted Soles—Evidence of care in shoemaking. Soles are sometimes painted in two tones purely to show you that they're hand-done.

Edge of Sole Perfectly Even with Edge of Shoe.

Scored Plastic Heel Lifts—Scoring helps keep you from slipping; plastic lifts wear longer than leather.

A Note on Materials: Leather shoes are best because they breathe and give with the foot, footwear experts agree. But kid, calf, and suede can all be equally good-looking, high-quality, and long-lasting. Touch for softness, smoothness; look for sheen and even coloration.

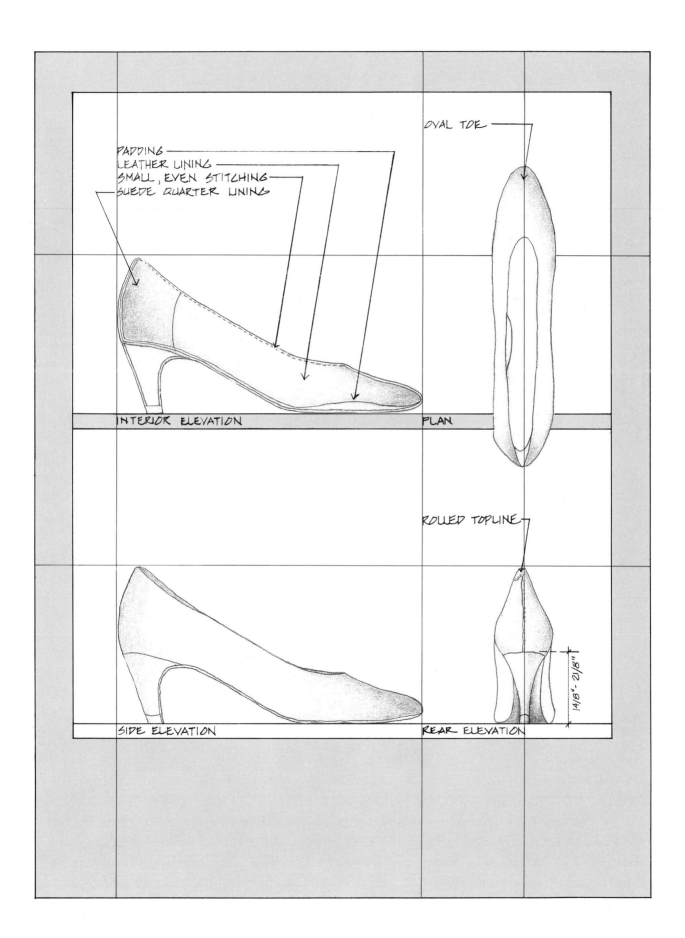

PADDING
LEATHER LINING
SMALL, EVEN STITCHING
SUEDE QUARTER LINING

OVAL TOE

INTERIOR ELEVATION

PLAN

ROLLED TOPLINE

14/8"- 21/8"

SIDE ELEVATION

REAR ELEVATION

GOOD LOOKS

12

Elements

·

How to Survive a Cold Front in Style

Monday, January 25. Ten degrees. Wind chill of ten below. You know the style in which you'd like to deal with this deep freeze: wearing long underwear and an enormous sweater, cuddled on the couch under an afghan and in front of a roaring fire. But you can't. You've got to go to work. And you've got to look good. Here, from women who live where it's frigid half the year, tips on dressing for a cold front without looking like the Abominable Snowman, from the outside in:

Coats—To fur or not to fur? That is the ultimate question for women in far-northern cities. Fur devotees are adamant: "The number one essential is that you have to own a fur coat," says Alice Bruce, an account executive at *Boston* magazine. "You basically never look good when it's freezing unless you're wearing a fur." Buying a raccoon coat two years ago changed her life, claims Bruce. "I don't have to wear seven thousand layers under my coat," she says. "I admit I bought the coat for style, but when it's minus four, I'm really really really not cold. It's a great fringe benefit."

"I'm not promoting the slaughter of animals, but there's nothing like a nice fur coat for looking great when it's cold outside," says Chris Daniel, a women's wear buyer for Dayton Hudson in Minneapolis and former trend expert for that store. "The problem is traveling with them: you can't leave them just anywhere and you always have to be so careful."

"I'm so torn about fur," says Kate Broughton, who runs her own Boston advertising and public relations agency. "If someone gave me one I'd certainly wear it but I feel guilty about buying one and I'm paranoid about being mugged. I don't know how comfortable or safe I'd feel walking around in a fur."

Instead of a fur, Broughton wears a full-cut dolman-sleeved wool coat loose enough to accommodate many layers underneath. Like Broughton, other women who choose a wool coat over fur—for moral, aesthetic, or financial reasons—say big is the only way to go.

"This year I bought myself a black long wool coat that's almost to my ankles," says Theresa Nix, an account executive at Golin/Harris communications in Chicago. "I'm wearing shorter skirts, but a long coat is the only way to stay warm and still look professional."

What about down coats? "They make a lot of sense," says Broughton. The trick is finding one that looks both stylish and professional. Norma Kamali's enormous "sleeping bag" coat is a favorite with many women in New York, but down jackets and longer quilted down coats often don't make it. Shorter coats are for weekends and not practical with skirts in sub-zero temperatures, and "most long down coats look very dated," says Janice Locascio, an image consultant at Carson Pirie Scott's Corporate Level in Chicago.

Thinsulate—a paper-thin insulator that's now used in classic wool and trench coats—is popular in Minneapolis, says Dayton Hudson's Daniel, and a smart solution to warmth-without-bulk.

Hats—I know, I know, I should wear one, say many women. But it's hard to find one that looks good and doesn't flatten your hair. A fur hat, with hair pulled back in a style that's already "flat" beneath, is one option for some women. Earmuffs are another. "I wear these things called Samurai earmuffs," says Kate Broughton, "that are two individual flat pieces of felt that hook over your ears." Says Daniel, "Here I am killing more animals, but dark mink earmuffs on a black velvet band are a very nice option."

A big beret or tam can also do the trick, advise both Broughton and Janice Locascio. Another good choice, a big wool challis scarf to wear around your neck, pull up over your head if it's windy or freezing, use as a shawl in a drafty office.

Still, many women feel good looks are worth what they sacrifice in warmth when they don't wear a hat. "I do nothing about hats because I haven't found one I don't look like an onion in," says Karen Faul, president of Cypress Robes, headquartered in western Massachusetts. "In my next life I want to have a face that looks good in a fur hat. That's the real solution to the hat problem: reincarnation."

Gloves—There is a single solution to warm, good-looking gloves: long leather ones. Alice Bruce wears cashmere-lined leather that reach up to her elbows. Mitzi Berry, a former legislative aide at the Wisconsin State Assembly in Madison and now a law student in Hartford, Connecticut, wears fur-lined leather. Silk-or Thinsulate-lined leather gloves can also be a good-looking and warm choice. Unlined leather, however, may not be warm enough when it's really freezing, say the women.

One no-no is mittens: they may be warmer than many gloves, but "snowflakes and Icelandic knits just don't make it for grown-ups going to work," says Daniel.

Kate Broughton, besides wearing full-length gloves, has decided to revive the muff. "It's a bygone piece of clothing that could be very functional in the cold weather," she says. "I'm making myself a funny-looking leopard one with a little wrist strap." Another warming trick of Broughton's: leg warmers . . . on her arms.

Boots—Boots that are slip-proof, water-proof, and truly warm usually have one major problem: they're ugly. Most women say they opt for functional boots over shoes or "fashion" boots in the deep winter, but say the boots that conquer the weather are so ugly they refuse to even describe them. Better-looking boots—to-the-knee flat leather ones, say—are not really an effective compromise, say the women. Outside, they don't keep feet warm and dry, and they're too hot in the office. "Fashion boots are really only an option in Atlanta when it's fifty degrees," says Daniel.

Short, lined (with pile, fur, Thinsulate, or down) boots are a better option than knee-high ones, say most women. "You're warmer with an ankle boot, leg warmers and a long coat than with a long boot," says Broughton, "and you can whip off the short ones in a second."

Still, there's ugly and there's ugly. "I tried wearing duck shoes with leg warmers and a long wool coat but I looked so stupid," says Theresa Nix. "It was just the ticket for warmth but I realized if I had seen a client when I was dressed like that it would have been the end of my career."

Instead of carrying shoes in a plastic bag, in addition to a purse and a briefcase, Janice Locascio recommends one large nylon or leather tote in which to consolidate all hand baggage.

Legs—Pants are admittedly warmer than skirts, but not a work-worthy option for many women. The alternative: layered legs. Mitzi Berry wears thigh-high socks over tights when the temperature dips below zero; other women choose leg warmers over opaque hose (often brands designed to withstand cold weather). The outer layer comes off once inside.

Clothes—If you don't own a fur, what you wear underneath your coat can be more important to warmth than the coat itself. Again, the solution is layers. For her Corporate Level clients, Janice Locascio recommends wool knit separates: "a cowl-neck sweater and knit skirt with a jacket, for instance." Broughton also opts for wool jersey, for both comfort and warmth.

"I never wear just a plain blouse," says Mitzi Berry. "I always wear a sweater, even if I have a jacket on top. I never know whether it's going to be hot or cold in my office, and I need to be able to peel pieces off or put them back on."

Medium-weight fabrics—from wool crepe to cashmere to gabardine to heavier cottons—have gained tremendously in popularity as opposed to bulkier materials designed for frigid weather only, says Daniel. "Women have gotten more sophisticated about layering, and medium-weight pieces are more functional: you can wear them through several seasons and you don't get so hot in the winter once you're inside."

Most women also choose long skirts over short for winter, no matter what skirt length they favor in warmer months. "It's a real contradiction when you wear a short skirt in cold weather," says Janice Locascio. "You don't want to look like a breath of spring when it's zero."

What's underneath your clothes can also be important. Silk camisoles or full slips are the undergarments of choice: "Silk keeps me warmer and feels nicer," says Theresa Nix. Daniel recommends silk knit camisoles, turtlenecks, and even long johns: "Silk knit is incredibly warm, you barely know you're wearing it, and it keeps you from itching under wools."

Extras—Psychological warmth can boost spirits during long, gray winters. Karen Faul gives herself and her cold-weather wardrobe a lift with brighter, richer colors for both outer garments and clothes. One slightly offbeat accessory—fur-lined lace-up boots or a paisley scarf—can also make winter dressing more fun.

"When it gets cold and everyone's bundled up, people tend to lose their individuality, which can be depressing," says Daniel. "Anything you can wear that sets you apart a little bit will make you feel better."

When there's a foot of new-fallen snow on the ground or it's thirty below, however, many women say they give up on trying to look good . . . which is not all bad. "It comes to a point where you can't care, and everybody's in the same boat," says Theresa Nix. "When there's a killer snowstorm all the little rules go out the window," Kate Broughton says. "Then, everyone is in great spirits because they drop their defenses and stop worrying about how stupid they look."

Which Fabrics Keep You Warmest?

"I wish there was an easy answer to this," says Gret Atkins, a textile expert at Cornell University in Ithaca, New York, where they know what cold is. "But warmth depends not only on the fiber content but the type of yarn, how the yarn is spun and knit or woven, the construction of the garment. You can't say that wool is warmer than acrylic or cotton, period. A cotton or an acrylic sweater can be much warmer than wool."

Bulk—the thickness of a sweater or a jacket—can be some indicator of its warmth, says Atkins, but not an absolute guideline. "It depends on the weather, too: if there's a lot of air movement you need a windproof layer," says Atkins. "A tightly woven fabric that's not bulky would provide wind protection."

Often, according to Atkins, "design is more important than what a garment is made out of. Elastic at the sleeve is better than a straight cut or, God forbid, a belled sleeve. A storm flap over the zipper and a tight fastening at the neck will keep you warm. If it's a jacket it should be snug at the bottom. What you want to do is warm up the air around your body and keep it there."

Is fur the ultimate cold-weather protection many women claim? Again, it depends. "Fur can keep you warm because air gets trapped around the hairs," says Atkins, "but if it's windy, fur will keep you warmest on the inside of a coat. In general, a thicker fur with crimped hairs—like shearling—will keep you warmer than a fur with long straight hairs."

As both a fabric expert and an inhabitant of a frigid climate, how does Atkins herself keep warm? "With layers," she says. "A lot of the buildings at Cornell are overheated, so with layers I can peel stuff off when I'm inside and put it back on when I go out. Also, the more of your body you can cover, the better. I wear pants instead of skirts, for instance, and I wear tights under them. If I had to wear a skirt, I'd wear stockings, woven acrylic tights and snuggies on my legs."

How to Survive a Heat Wave in Style

Thursday, July 25. Ninety-eight degrees. In the shade. You know how you'd like to cope with this heat wave: by laying naked in the bathtub with the air conditioner running full blast. But you can't. You've got to go to work. You have five appointments today, plus a business dinner, which means twelve transitions from the sweltering streets to the often-frigid indoors. Here's how to dress for a heat wave with style, from women and fashion experts in tropical cities:

Go Light, from the Skin Out—Women who cope with very hot weather half the year start talking about fashion by talking about beauty: summer means a lighter fragrance and moisturizer, less makeup, hair pulled off the neck.

This skin-out approach extends to underwear: preferably cotton or lace, as minimal as possible.

The big debate is whether or not to wear stockings. Many women don't, but most say going without is a mistake if you work in a professional setting.

"A lot of women down here kick hosiery in the summer, but I think it's a big mistake," says Molly Mackenzie, an image consultant and owner of The Hall Closet, a boutique in Fort Lauderdale. "When you've been down here a while you don't notice the heat as much so stockings really aren't uncomfortable."

Monica Davidson, co-owner of Kajun Kettle Foods in New Orleans, agrees. "When I first moved down here from San Francisco, I couldn't understand how women could stand wearing pantyhose in the summer. But my body got used to the heat. Now I can wear hose and even silk and not feel as hot."

Women coping with a heat wave in a northern city or traveling to the south—who don't have the advantage of being acclimated to constant heat—have no choice but to suffer through pantyhose in formal settings, or wear clothes that don't demand hose, such as pants or long skirts.

Fabrics—Wearing the right fabrics is one key to keeping cool when it's boiling outside, say the women and the experts. Natural fabrics are preferable to synthetics, they say, and some natural fabrics are better than others.

"Fabric is the most important factor in keeping cool," says Brenda Rosenberg, vice president of fashion marketing for Burdine's, based in Miami. "Cottons and rayons are good choices. Rayons are very lightweight, they have a nice soft feel, and they really don't wrinkle. I love the look of linen but you have to decide if you like to look richly wrinkled, and not everyone feels that way. I like silk but it tends not to breathe as well as cotton and linen and rayon."

"The first thing I do in the summer is pack away my silks," says Peggy Landers, a fashion writer for the Miami *Herald*. "In the heat and the humidity, they just get ruined." Landers also forswears linen—she has a low tolerance for wrinkles—and relies instead on cottons and lightweight wool gabardines, which she claims can be as cool as linens.

"The key thing in the summer is very light fabrics: cottons and linens and seersucker," says Monica Davidson. "People down here don't wear silk a lot because it's too hot."

Echoes Kitty Ryan, who owns Broward Liquors in Fort Lauderdale, "Silk is way too hot. You can't wear anything polyester or even [contradicting Rosenberg] rayon. I stay with cottons and sometimes cotton blends."

Naturally, unlined clothes are preferable to those with lining. "About half the clothes made today don't require lining because the styles are unstructured to the degree that certain pieces will fit better without lining," says Mackenzie. "A little cotton batiste slip may be cooler under a dress or skirt than an acetate lining."

Colors—Looking cool, say the women, can go a long way toward feeling cool, and that means light colors.

"In the summer I switch to a lot of whites and pinks even though they're not practical," says Nanette Wiser, editorial manager for Copley News Service in San Diego. "If I'm feeling hot and I look at myself I cool down immediately."

A lot of white is also an essential component of Southern style. "When I think of hot-weather dressing here, I have an image of a woman with her hair pulled up wearing a short-sleeved white linen dress and white or off-white shoes," says Monica Davidson.

"I do try to wear light colors. White and beige make me feel cool," says Peggy Landers. "You can also get away with brighter colors down here—it's something about the light—than you can in the North. But I do still wear a black skirt throughout the summer with a big white shirt, sort of like a uniform."

This white-and-black palette can be a good solution to packing for travel to a hot climate. Linda Nicholas, a New York hair and makeup artist who travels to the South and the Caribbean on fashion shoots throughout the winter, packs only "white, black, and a little blue." In these colors, she includes long skirts as well as minis, a lace-collared blouse as well as T-shirts, sweats along with dressier cardi-gans. Depending on the weather and where she's going, everything can potentially work with everything else.

The disadvantage of light-colored clothing is that it's harder to maintain, especially through summer grime and pollution. "You need more summer clothes down here," says Molly Mackenzie, "so you always have something nice and fresh and crisp in your closet. But of course summer clothes can be quite a bit less expensive than winter ones."

Style—The most essential style component of summer clothes, say the women, is to keep pieces loose, not binding. For many women, a simple dress with no defined waist is the ideal solution to work-dressing: "Sometimes, even the waistband of a skirt is too much," says Peggy Landers. When she has an appointment that demands she wear a jacket, Landers carries an unlined one along, puts it on when she enters the air-conditioned building.

"I like big, unconstructed jackets," says Nanette Wiser. "I always wear something with sleeves underneath so I can take off my jacket. I don't feel comfortable in sleeveless tops; it's too casual a statement in the office."

Landers also feel sleeveless clothes are too casual on even the hottest days, and prefers long, loose sleeves that she can roll up.

Women who must wear business suits in the tropics "have to get away from the concept of a structured suit," says Mackenzie. "A suit with an unlined flyaway jacket is lighter and easier to wear, more comfortable and cool."

In the extreme heat, professional dressing can accommodate less formality, more sensuality than is acceptable in northern cities.

"You don't see anybody wearing high-necked bow blouses here," says Burdine's Rosenberg. "There are a lot of women here who do wear suits, and under jackets women often wear barer tops. You see more soft dresses and two-piece outfits here, and career clothes are in lighter and prettier colors."

One factor mitigating the heat is the intense air-conditioning in many southern offices. While a lined jacket may be "impossible," says Mackenzie, a lightweight jacket or cotton sweater, or a non-fashion-statement shawl, may be a necessity for coping with temperature changes.

Again, how air-conditioning and temperature changes affect you has a lot to do with whether you're used to the hot/cold contrast. "When I first got here I used to bring a jacket everywhere because of the air-conditioning," says New Orleans's Davidson. "Now I find I don't need it and would never wear anything long-sleeved."

If you're traveling to a hot climate, however, you may find you need long-sleeved sweaters and jackets for air-conditioned buildings as well as lighter-weight pieces for the heat.

Accessories/Shoes—Whether you wear more or fewer accessories in the summer is mostly a matter of taste: a bracelet is not likely to make a significant difference in how hot or cool you feel. Kitty Ryan, for example, says she prefers wearing more accessories in the summer, because she's wearing fewer clothes. The real issue seems to be not more or fewer but different: looser, lighter in both weight and color—pearl stud earrings as opposed to gold hoops, an ivory or tortoise bangle instead of a metal cuff.

Most women say that, to the office, they wear closed shoes rather than sandals. The big change in summer is to flats instead of heels. "High heels are a pain. They're too tight and hot here in the summer," says Peggy Landers. "I still wear black and brown shoes in the summer, and cream, but never white. White to me is tacky Easter shoes."

Ten Hot Weather Lifesavers

In the dead of summer or in tropical climates—whether you're a traveler or a full-time resident—the following items can save your fashion life:

1. **A LOOSE, UNLINED, DARK, ALL-COTTON BLAZER**—It should be good-looking, but doesn't have to be the height of chic or cost a fortune. Ideal for pulling together a tank and skirt, for throwing over a dress in a chilly restaurant, for making anything look more formal on the spur of the moment. Why dark? So it won't spend every other week at the cleaners. Why unlined and all-cotton? It will keep you the coolest with the least wrinkling.

2. **LIGHTWEIGHT, EASY-CUT BLACK PANTS**—These should be casual-looking enough to roll up and wear to the beach, formal enough to pair with a good top and wear to a restaurant. As with the blazer, black will help keep them handy when all your whites have gone to the cleaners.

3. **AN UNOPENED PACKAGE OF MEN'S PLAIN WHITE T-SHIRTS, SIZE LARGE**— In case of an emergency, break the plastic. What kind of emergency? You need something to throw over your bathing suit, you spilled ketchup on the shirt you were going to wear with your shorts . . . or your suit, the night's turned cold and you've got to wear something to bed.

4. **A PAIR OF INEXPENSIVE, PLAIN, FLAT ESPADRILLES**—Any time you see classic espadrilles—and classic means canvas and completely flat, not wedged—for $10 or less, buy them. Then wait for the first time you need something to get across that rocky path to the beach, the first time you realize your heels don't look right with that long, gauzy skirt, the first time you're too lazy to tie your sneakers when you just need to run to the store for milk. Want to bet your $10 espadrilles you thought you'd never wear are worn out by the end of the summer?

5. **A LISLE COTTON-KNIT CARDIGAN**—A classic style in a large size is best, to throw over everything from a bathing suit to a linen dress to a nightshirt, when you feel chillier or more exposed or even fatter than you expected.

6. **A SHORT, SLIM WHITE SKIRT**—If you're an unreformed slob or have tiny kids, forget this one. If not, it's the kind of thing you'll turn to again and again for occasions from the most businesslike to the most festive. The right cut can be surprisingly slimming worn with a long top—shaped or loose.

7. **A LONG, LOOSE, PRINT SKIRT**—Even if you're devoted to short, even if you never wear prints, this sort of skirt can save your fashion life like nothing else in hot weather. It looks good over bathing suits, with plain T-shirts, in the country or city, by day or night. And there's nothing cooler or more comfortable to wear on bottom.

8. **AN UNSEAMED SKIN-TONE ALL-COTTON KNIT BRA**—The coolest, most comfortable, least visible option, for when you can't get away with not wearing one.

9. **THREE PAIRS OF SHEER, BEIGE-TINTED PANTYHOSE**—For business meetings or shoes that pinch, keep not-quite-nude pantyhose on hand.

10. **AN INCREDIBLY COMFORTABLE DRESS RIGHT FOR ANYTHING FROM A JOB INTERVIEW TO A WEDDING**—This should be an unadorned fabric and style—black or tan linen, say, and straight-cut to the knee—that transcends fashion. The kind of thing you can keep in your closet for about five years, trot out every time you need something presentable and the thermometer reads ninety-eight. In the shade.

STYLE

Part V

STYLE
13
Style, Fashion, Fads, and Trends

•

You are confused. What is this thing called style, anyway? Is it the same as fashion? Is fashion the same as trends, and are trends fads?

No to all of the above, but describing what makes style different from fashion different from trends different from fads is a very tough job. The differences are subtle, and telling one from the other is often impossible except in retrospect. Nevertheless, we'll try.

"Fashion is what's happening in the world of clothes at any given time, and trends are a component of that," says Tracy Hayes, a fashion writer at the Dallas *Morning News.* "Fads are things that arrive out of nowhere that everybody wants to jump on, and style is something else totally."

Any clearer? Let's try again.

"Here's a little formula to help the layperson differentiate," says Mary Gallagher, Paris-based commercial director of Promostyl, the international fashion forecasting agency. "Style transcends trends, trends transcend fashion, fashion transcends fads."

Perhaps it would help to deal with them one at a time.

Style—We are not talking here about style as synonymous with fashion, as in "I hear short skirts are in style this year." The kind of style we're talking about is, by nature, individual. It's the particular way one person dresses to suit her own taste, satisfy her own needs, flatter her own body and coloring, create her own comfort, express her own personality.

"A person with style may have clothing in her wardrobe from the current fashion, but she's not dictated to by what's in fashion at the moment," says Mary Gallagher. "She knows how to put together pieces—old, new, high fashion or flea market—to create a look that's purely hers."

While style is "not genetic, it obviously comes from somewhere," says Tracy Hayes, most clothing experts agree that style emanates from within. Whether consciously developed or unconsciously evolved, true style is determined only by the individual, remains consistent—but not static—over time.

To understand style, says Miami *Herald* fashion writer Peggy Landers, "you have to understand fashion and know the point at which style and fashion merge and where they diverge." Landers cites this example: "There are women who've always worn their skirts at or about the knee, and they're never thrown by different skirt lengths. When skirts get really long they will be comfortable keeping their skirts at the same length or buying a longer skirt if they feel like it. Because they're aware of the cyclical nature of fashion, they know that if the length they're wearing is not absolutely of the moment it will be at some point, and it will always be right for them."

Fashion—There is one element of fashion that never changes: It always changes. That's because fashion is a business, catering to—and often creating—a collective lust for novelty.

"Fashion is born of change and is, by nature, continually renewed and modified from season to season," says Mary Gallagher. "When a person is described as fashionable, she is usually wearing the latest designs, fabrics, accessories, or colors."

It follows that looking fashionable is not the same as having style, or even as looking good. It takes neither mental gymnastics nor self-knowledge to wear what's in fashion; it's for sale, head-to-toe, on the mannequin in the window of the nearest store. Hence the term "fashion victim": the woman who wears whatever's been decreed "in" at the moment, without regard to what's practical, what looks good on her, what she wants or needs.

But it's possible to view fashion with an overly curmudgeonly attitude. Yes, some fashion is ridiculous; yes, many women spend too much money because they feel they have to listen to designers' dictates; but fashion can also be liberating and just plain fun.

"When you're aware of the history of fashion you know how to use it, you know what will stick around and what won't, and what works for you," says Peggy Landers. "Fashion is great for accessories, for fun items. I don't like these women who are so into style and basics that they're boring."

Also, it's becoming easier to play with fashion and still create an individual look. "Over the past decade, there has been a many-things-go approach, where several looks are in fashion simultaneously," says Mary Gallagher. "A person can change her image or stay with her own style and still be in fashion."

Trends—Trends are large forces, going beyond the seasonal adjustments of fashion and the personal considerations of style. "Trends are what lead to the current fashion, and also affect architecture, interior and industrial design, visual images such as photographs, music and even food," says Promostyl's Gallagher.

Where do trends come from? According to Gallagher, "They evolve from what people are interested in and attracted to culturally, socially, and intellectually, and can also spring from news events, from politics and economic factors." Promostyl and other trend-forecasting services keep track of such non-fashion happenings in order to predict their influence on fashion over the next few years.

In fashion, says Gallagher, "long-term trends have short-term variations. For example, a long-term trend could be retro, but tailored to the current fashion it may appear as thirties Hollywood, American fifties campus, or British country squire." These fashionable looks are all variations of a trend toward nostalgia, which sprang not from fashion but from the social mood that followed the sixties and seventies emphasis on the future.

A trend, then, is not equivalent to a fad, but rather an overall direction that influences clothing over a long period of time. It can be difficult, however, to tell the two apart initially. Knit pants, for instance, are a prime example of something that could have been a fad—come and gone in the space of a few months—but rather were part of a trend fortified by a return to comfort, to staying home, and to dispensing with pretense.

Fashion insiders say that, with time, they develop a sixth sense for which trends are really trends, which are mere fads. "Over the seven years I've covered fashion I've developed some instinct," says Peggy Landers. "That whole cycle of clothes getting shorter and barer felt wrong to me, and then there was the stock market crash. Now that the Reagan years have come to a close and with the economy shaky and with even people who have a lot of money not spending it as freely, I see clothes becoming not quite as outrageous, more sedate, more serious, in beautiful fabrics with fine lines."

Fads—The pouf. Oversized buttons. Football player shoulder pads. Hair bows. Slides. The Kelly bag. Leopard chiffon scarves. Crucifix earrings.

It's easy to see a fad for what it is in looking back, but not always so easy to spot when it's at its height. That's because fads somehow capture our collective imagination; when they look good, they look very, very good, and when they look bad, they look horrid.

"Fads tend to be jokey and disposable or, to borrow a British expression, cheap and cheerful," says Mary Gallagher. "They are usually so short-term that the wildfire is snuffed out almost as immediately as it catches on. And if you're caught wearing the item next season, you're hopelessly out."

Jeanswear is a fertile breeding ground for fads, says Gallagher, as are accessories and costume jewelry. What ignites a fad? Sometimes simply a design that is the quintessence of a fashion or a trend. And often, a fad will take hold when it's sported by a high-profile person or a movie character; Madonna's single black cross earring, for instance, or Crocodile Dundee's hat.

How, then, to develop that internal instinct of which real style is born, tuning into trends, taking what's best of fashion and fads, turning a blind eye to all that's disposable, wrong for you?

The first step is learning to pay attention to what you want to wear, ignoring all the voices (mom, friend, advertising, magazines) that tell you what you "should" wear. If you love long black velvet skirts, big brightly colored sweaters, and earrings, then go for that, even if *Vogue* is telling you to wear short skirts, your mother always said you look better in pink than red, your husband wants you to show off your figure with tighter tops, and the saleslady at the local shop keeps nudging you to expand your wardrobe with scarves.

It's near impossible for someone with style to look awful, if her style is truly determined by what she likes and feels great in. Where some people run into trouble is adopting a style—because it looks wonderful on their best friend, because an image consultant advised it for them—that isn't really what they'd choose on their own.

How to avoid the sirens of fashion and fads, which are, after all, so seductive? It may help to know how people in the fashion business do it, which is something like how some people who work in bakeries stay slim.

"There comes a point in fashion reporting where you're sick to death of the hype and you feel as if you're caught in a massive manipulation," says Peggy Landers. "Once you've been around the cycle once, you become aware that these designers need the hot, extreme statement to generate news value and excitement, that while the clothes may be tighter or looser or a different color or a new fabric, it's all pretty much the same."

Outsiders who visit the fashion department of any national magazine are often shocked by how "boring" everyone looks. While many fashion writers and editors may get excited by new fashions and trends, there's usually little evidence that they embrace them for their own wardrobes. The reason? The fashion press is always one season ahead of the general public; they know, even as a new shape or color or accessory is everywhere in all the stores, that it will be nowhere to be found the following season. And, as Landers pointed out, they also know that fashions come and go, but clothes stay pretty much the same.

That's not to say you'll never spot a fashion expert wearing a trendy item like an animal-print scarf or an alligator belt or cowboy boots. You will. But again, it may be smart to do it like they do: buy it cheap, wear it for fun, cast it aside the minute you're tired of it, and don't jump on any fashion just because everyone else is.

Wear it because you want to, and you'll never (okay, rarely) go wrong.

Six Earmarks of a Classic

"Classic" seems to be a favorite word of advertising copywriters these days, translated to, "This is something worth blowing a lot of money on." But clothes that are truly classic transcend fashion, look and feel good over a long period of time. They are, by definition, not fashionable; wonderful, maybe, but not exciting. How do you spot a classic? Look for these earmarks:

1. **MINIMAL DETAILS**—No fancy seams, contrast stitching, geegaws or doodads. A classic is usually itself—a sweater, a jacket—plain and simple.

2. **MIDDLE-OF-THE-ROAD STYLING**—A true classic ignores the swings of fashion: it is not oversized, nor body-hugging, nor pinched in at the waist, nor boxy. It does not have wide nor narrow lapels or legs, it does not flare or billow. Classic styles do not exaggerate the body, or mask its natural characteristics.

3. **FINE FABRICS**—If you're buying something to look good over time, it's essential that you choose top-quality fabrics: not just wool but the finest wool, not just lamb's wool but cashmere, not just velvet but silk velvet.

4. **NEUTRAL COLOR**—Not whatever is being trumpeted as a "new" neutral—be it hunter green or red or pale blue—but a true neutral: black, navy, gray, beige, white, and sometimes brown.

5. **STURDY CONSTRUCTION**—A flimsily made classic is a contradiction in terms. For a classic to really hold up like one, it must be well sewn, with edged seams and fast buttons and lining where appropriate.

6. **STYLE THAT'S SURVIVED THE TEST OF TIME**—Before a classic can earn its name, it's got to keep looking good over a number of years. How many years? Hard to say, but a lot. A hacking jacket qualifies, for instance, while a short knit jacket does not. A straight knee-length skirt can be classic; a miniskirt isn't. Stirrup pants are not classics; but jeans, at this point, deserve the status.

STYLE

· 14 ·

The Personal Image

·

You love black. You wear black a lot; in fact, almost always. But someone—maybe it's your mother, your best friend, or your shrink—thinks the fact that you wear black all the time means something. Something bad. It means that you're depressed, that you don't like yourself, that you want to disappear. You argue that you wear black because it's easy, because it's slimming, and because you like it, period. But still sometimes you wonder: is your attraction to black clothes a sign that something's wrong?

There's no question that the clothes you choose reflect your self-image, that they say something about who you are and how you feel. Wearing dark colors all the time, for instance, may indeed be a sign of depression. "Many depressed people feel more comfortable in darker clothes because it makes them less visible," says Philadelphia psychiatrist Ellen Berman. "When people feel better about themselves, they tend to dress in more colorful things."

But clothes as a reflection of personal image is a complex issue, making any simplistic or general interpretations questionable. Clothes can convey messages on a person's attitudes toward class, conventionality, mood, money, age, and sexuality, but what exactly they're saying is often idiosyncratic, difficult to read. You may favor black clothes, then, not because you're depressed but because you want to look slimmer and hate to diet, because you don't like spending money on dry-cleaning, and because you want to look sexy without being obvious about it.

"I don't think you really know most of the time what a woman is trying to say with her clothes unless you ask her," says Dr. Berman. "You can have somebody who dresses very sloppily because she doesn't think she's worthy, or you can have someone who dresses very sloppily to prove that she doesn't have to follow the norms but can still get what she wants. A woman who dresses in a very sexy way is trying to say something about her sexuality, but you don't know whether she is trying to say, 'I am a sexual person,' or whether she is trying to fake being a sexual person."

Clothes express something about where you fit in the world, where you've come from and where you want to go, and they may also express basic feelings about your body and your femaleness, says Dr. Berman. But again, exactly what they're saying may not be clear.

"Women who terrifically don't like their bodies may dress very primly and conservatively and not put any money into clothes," Dr. Berman says, "but a lot of women who don't like their bodies cover them with very expensive clothes, so it's not a one-to-one correspondence. There is always some connection between clothes and the inner self, but the connections may be very subtle."

Often, clothing choices and preferences are unconscious, which is one reason they may be difficult to interpret, even for the person doing the choosing and wearing. "We unconsciously go to what we like, but the liking is dictated by the way we feel about ourselves, by who we think we are," says Stephanie Miller, a therapist and executive director of the Women's Counseling and Psychotherapy Service in Columbia and Towson, Maryland.

New York psychotherapist Arlene Kagle likens clothes to dreams: "We study dreams," she says, "because in a dream anything's possible. Someone's wardrobe makes a dreamlike statement, because women can choose from a range of clothes—from sexy to demure to tailored to sporty to romantic—and then wear them in individual ways."

The interpretation of a wardrobe can be as individual, as personal, and as multifaceted as the interpretation of a dream, according to Dr. Kagle. Some clothes express a woman's "inner vision of her public self," Dr. Kagle says, citing the example of a corporate lawyer who, for work, "dresses like an armored tank—her clothes say 'beware.' " But, says Dr. Kagle, "the same woman may wear $80 French couture bras and have a lot of fun with that. And her inner vision, when she's alone on a rainy Sunday, may be a sex kitten who dresses in very sexy lingerie. One of the nice things about fashion is that it's possible to express multiple personalities."

Whatever your clothes are saying about your inner self, it can be important for you to understand the reasons behind your choices and to be aware of the messages your clothes send to others.

"Clothes can be a means of understanding yourself and getting feedback on how others see you," says Susan Kaiser, Ph.D., author of *The Social Psychology of Clothing*. "Because we often make clothing decisions unconsciously, they enable us to understand ourselves, to look back and see why we're concerned about dressing a certain way."

When your clothes send messages that are inconsistent with your stated intentions—when you want to be seen as sophisticated and sexy, for instance, but wear puffed-sleeve pink dresses, or when you wear sloppy clothes to an interview for a job you say you want—it can be evidence of a deep ambivalence. Interpreting and coming to terms with such a misalignment may lead you to change your style . . . or your life.

Sheryl Spanier, a vice president of Fuchs, Cuthrell, who counsels executives in career transitions, tells the story of a woman on her way to a job interview at a top cosmetics company: "She stopped into my office dressed very casually; she didn't even have her hair done. Now she had lost her job three times, and it wasn't because she wasn't capable, and I said, 'You're not going to the interview like that.' I personally took her to the store and bought her an oufit and took her to get her hair done and took her to the makeup counter of the company where she had the interview and had her made up and she looked fabulous. She went and got the job. She lasted six months."

At that point, the woman returned to Spanier, "obviously for some help." "The whole thing broke loose—that she wanted to be accepted in spite of how she looked, that she was very rebellious," says Spanier. "It was her way of trying to express her individuality, but she was hurting herself. It was really a fear of success."

Beneath that fear, however, was a more complex issue, says Spanier, and a very specific wish. "Over and over again she was using the way she put herself together as a way of not confronting her own sense of self," Spanier says. "The whole real issue there was the issue of career versus family. What she really wanted to do was have a baby."

While clothes can signal personal, often hidden, fears and wishes, there is a crucial third link in the personality–clothing chain: the interpretations of others. If feeling good about yourself can lead you to dress well, then dressing well can make other people respond to you more positively, which will make you feel even better, and so on. Conversely, feeling unhappy or ambivalent can lead you to dress sloppily or inappropriately, which can lead other people to ignore or criticize you, which can make you feel more unhappy, downward in a vicious circle.

Most people are not aware of this complicated link between personal image and clothing and the world's response, says image consultant Joyce Grillo, "at least not on a very high awareness level. People may say, 'I'm depressed today and I don't care how I look,' but they don't realize the full impact: that by letting themselves go they will get more depressed."

But which comes first: feeling good or looking good? "It's a process," says Elaine Mack, personal shopper at Bergdorf Goodman, who guides hundreds of women through style changes. "You can't separate a change in style from a change in self-image. If people can get themselves to change the way they look on the outside, it sometimes helps them to begin to change how they feel about themselves on the inside, because they get much more positive feedback. And then some people have to make themselves feel good first, before they can attempt a change in the way they dress."

The best of the personal image consultants are aware of this connection between self-image and clothes, and see their mission as helping their clients express themselves with dress. "One thing that bothers me about being an image consultant is that I hate the name," says Vicki French Morris of French-Haines. "I feel like more of an interpreter than an inventor. I'm not making a mask; I'm interpreting the personality and taste of the person. The reason it works is that the person that's really there is coming forth and the communication feels very honest. You don't get that funny feeling of 'Something's wrong here.' "

What counts as dressing better or more confident or more consistent with one's personality can vary with each individual, say the experts.

"Usually you'll see that when people gain more confidence, they'll wear clothes that express more confidence, but again, you never know what expresses more confidence for that person," says Dr. Berman. "It may be that they're wearing something that's more expensive. It may be that for the first time they say the hell with it, and they put on slacks. You have to look at where the person's starting from."

Several years ago, says Dr. Berman, she had a patient who was "very uptight." "She was the kind of person who ironed her jeans," says Dr. Berman. "And finally one day she came in with a pair of jeans she'd worn the day before, and she'd been out running around in them, and she hadn't washed them. And you know, we clapped and congratulated her; I told her she was wonderful and she should be proud of herself. For her, the issue wasn't dressing what most people would call better, its was allowing herself to relax and not iron her jeans."

• *Style Analysis* •

KIM BONNELL *is the senior editor for fashion at* Glamour *magazine in New York. For her picture, Bonnell wore her black silk Comme des Garçons wedding dress, which cost $700 ("It was so expensive I wanted it to be something I'd wear more than once"), black suede shoes— her ideal pair—from Stephane Kelian bought at a discount shoe store for $150; and earrings purchased at an open-air market in Nairobi for $8.*

WHAT WAS THE FIRST BLACK THING YOU EVER BOUGHT?

I remember it very well. It was a really sleazy blouse, but the point was it got me started wearing black. I tried it on and I was surprised at how good it looked, because I'd never owned anything in my adult life that was black.

This was back in Chicago, and when I actually started making a conscious effort to buy black things, there weren't very many black things around. Then I discovered this store called Ultimo; it was a very expensive store with all the Italian designers and Japanese clothes—they had a lot of black clothes, but they were really expensive. That's when it started to dawn on me that black had this chic about it that I wasn't really conscious of before that. I was pretty old to be discovering this—I was about twenty-seven.

WAS THAT WHEN YOU FIRST BECAME INTERESTED IN CLOTHES?

No, I think I was always interested in clothes, particularly more critical of clothes than most other girls or women that I knew. More particular. I have a feeling it was probably boarding school, the uniform. My uniform was a navy blue bolero—I think it was all made of rayon, because it would get really shiny after a while—white Peter Pan collar blouse, narrow blah skirt. I wore that for seven years.

IF YOU HAD TO WEAR SOMETHING OF WHAT YOU HAVE NOW FOR THE NEXT SEVEN YEARS, WHAT WOULD YOU CHOOSE?

I would choose my Romeo Gigli jacket—it's sort of between black and blue, and it's long, and it has high buttons—and these four-year-old Yohji Yamamoto pants I have that are baggy but real tight at the cuff, so when you put the jacket over it you see this very lean jacket and these very lean pants. The pants are really comfortable, they have an elastic waist, they're made of lightweight gabardine, and I really like how perfectly they end—they snap actually—at the ankle. The top would be a sleeveless cotton mock turtleneck, which I'd want to alternate between black and white. The jacket buttons all the way up so only a little bit of the neck shows. It's really like a priest.

WHAT ABOUT ALL THIS CATHOLIC STUFF? IS THE BLACK AND WHITE FROM UNCONSCIOUS CHILDHOOD FEELINGS?

It's a very practical way to dress. It makes getting dressed a lot easier. The older you get you realize life is a process of elimination. You start taking away all those things are are irrelevant, that you don't like, that don't have any meaning for you. I know that yellow is not even a factor in my life. Never will I want yellow clothes. It's like, never do I want to go hear Elton John, never do I want to read Jay McInerney. It's nice to have it set and to want few enough things that you can afford nice things. You can have the best of your own selective judgment. I really bask in that.

HOW MANY BLACK JACKETS DO YOU HAVE?

All seasons? Work jackets? Black and navy? Twelve or thirteen, and about half of those are navy.

WHEN YOU WERE A TEENAGER, AFTER YOU LEFT BOARDING SCHOOL, WOULD YOU GO SHOPPING BY YOURSELF?

I did, and I had to pay for my own clothes, movies, and records from an allowance of $5 a week, so I couldn't really buy very much. Usually I would get one major thing, coat or boots, for Christmas or my birthday, and I had to buy everything else. This was in a pretty affluent town. All my friends would go out every August and buy eight new Villager outfits, and I would buy one sweater. A lot of my attitude about being particular developed because I had to be particular about what I bought, because I was buying so little.

I remember one occasion, when I was about fourteen, when I needed a dress for a dance.

I must have gone, on four successive Saturdays, to about fifty stores, looking for the perfect dress. What keeps me doing that, even now, is knowing that out there is the perfect thing, and that if I just look hard enough I'll find it.

WHAT MAKES SOMETHING PERFECT?

At this point it has a lot to do with the fabric, and the detailing is very critical. I notice the size of the buttons, if there's an unnecessary decorative seam somewhere, if the size of the lapel is just a little bit off, or if the notch is too low, which can make something look cheap. If something doesn't fit quite right but I love it, I'll sometimes buy it.

DO YOU HAVE ANY IDEA HOW MUCH YOU SPEND ON CLOTHES?

I spend a lot on shoes; I probably spend $800 a year on shoes. On clothes, I probably spend in a year $1,000. I buy everything on sale, because the clothes I like cost a lot of money and I'm not willing to compromise on what I want. I don't even start looking at fall clothes until November, when they go on sale.

HOW CAN YOU BE SO PARTICULAR AND STILL GET IT ON SALE?

Once the sales start I become very feverish about going around to the stores. In the course of a week and a half I'll go to four big stores, because the clothes in the big stores go on sale before the clothes in the little stores, and I'll scope out what's there and what I like and what I want to buy, and a week later I'll go back to it, and I'll keep going back until they're marked down enough to buy.

WHAT'S THE MOST EXPENSIVE THING YOU EVER BOUGHT?

An Armani jacket for $500. It wasn't worth it. It would have been worth it for $300. It's not as versatile as I hoped it would be. It's shaped to be fitted in the hips and that makes me self-conscious.

I would love to have more money to spend on clothes. I would avoid that whole sale routine and just go out in August and buy all the great stuff and not worry about it. I would buy more Comme des Garçons, not the weird stuff, but her fabrics are unbelievable. I would buy more Armani. I would buy a cashmere coat. I'd buy more shoes. I really do feel self-indulgent about shoes, but even so I've resisted so many that I'd like to have.

WHAT WOULD YOU DO IF YOU HAD LESS MONEY? IF YOU HAD YOUR TASTE AND YOU WERE STARTING FROM SCRATCH?

I could get a certain amount from secondhand shops. One of the neat things about black is that if it's cheap it looks less cheap than other colors. I could buy a black sweater reasonably cheap, stuff from the Gap. I think I could do it, maybe not happily.

When I broke my leg it was an interesting challenge, because I had to adapt what I liked wearing to a whole different set of physical realities. In the beginning I wore a long, full black skirt all the time. For black tie I went to the secondhand store and bought a tuxedo, and had the pants tailored a little bit, and had new buttons put on the jacket and wore it with a satin blouse.

AT WHAT POINT WAS YOUR STYLE FIXED IN THE WAY IT IS NOW?

About eight years ago, since I stopped being married to my first husband. People who wanted to understand my style would try to find reasons why I wore black all the time. First they'd say, "Well, your mother died. You're in mourning." Maybe that is a reason, but I was never able to really make sense of that. After I broke up with my first husband, guys would see me three times and I'd be wearing black every time and they'd say, "Are you sad about something?" I'd say, "No, I'm okay, I just like black." People don't really accept that you can just like black, there has to be more to it than that. I think it has a whole different set of reasons of making your life easier.

DO YOU HAVE ANY COLORS AT ALL IN YOUR WARDROBE?

I have a pink T-shirt. Running clothes, you're really limited, so I have a blue-and-purple windbreaker. I have a red sweatshirt. In the summer I have tan, but no real color color.

What happens to me now is that I look at these things—like this purple coat—and I try them on and I think, Yeah, this is a beautiful coat, and then I think, I can't wear this. It can look great on me, and I know that, but I just feel wrong, I feel uncomfortable, I physically cannot abide it. I would want to wear a big sign that said, "I'm wearing this purple coat but it's really not me! It doesn't have anything to do with me!"

ARE THERE SOME SHAPES YOU FIND YOURSELF LIKING NOW THAT YOU DIDN'T LIKE BEFORE, OR SOME WAYS OF PUTTING THINGS TOGETHER THAT ARE NEW FOR YOU?

For Christmas my husband gave me a jacket and a skirt that never in a million years would I have bought. They're in the right colors, but we're talkin' sexy. It's a jacket that comes in at the waist and curves out at the end, and this skirt that's jersey stretch and real tight. It looks fabulous; I look at myself in the mirror and go, "Wow," and then, "I can't wear this!" My husband says, "Why? You look great," and I say, "If I walk down the street in this people will look at me." This is my husband's vision of who I am. He knows I'll only wear it if it's black, but he wants it to be sexy black.

TELL ME ABOUT YOUR WEDDING DRESS.

*W*hen we decided to get married Michael said, "You can't wear a black wedding dress," and I let him know I wasn't agreeing to that. I told him not to worry, it wouldn't be depressing; it could be black but it wouldn't be deadly. I looked at a lot of stuff. I went to Matsuda, Charivari, Saks, Bergdorf's, Norma Kamali, Bloomingdale's, and I'd look at dress-up things, at suits, at sporty things, to really get a sense of what are my options. After looking at colors and at white and at cream, I decided I didn't want to spend all this money on something that I'm never going to even wear again. I saved Comme des Garçons for last, because I just knew that I wanted to get married in a Comme des Garçons dress, and there it was, black with a white jacket. I figured Michael would not have any problem with this because it presents itself as really more white than black, but I could live with it too because it was really black. I'm traditional enough that I wanted the dress to be pretty and happy, but it was important to have a wedding dress that was expressing me.

EMOTIONAL ISSUE:
CHANGING STYLES IS HARD TO DO

You've gotten a new job. Or you've quit your job. Or you want to dress in a more grown-up way or in simpler styles or in clothes that are more adventurous. Why, then, given the desire and the money, do you walk into a store, determined to buy something more grown-up or simpler or more adventurous or more professional or more casual, and walk out with something that looks just like everything else in your closet?

In theory, changing styles should be as simple as choosing a tailored purple dress, say, over a loose-fitting black one. Take it off the hanger, put it on your body, and presto: a new style. In reality, however, changing styles is anything but simple, say psychologists, image consultants, and women who've been through it, calling up such deep issues as self-image, lifetime habits, your standing among your loved ones and in society.

Part of how difficult a style change will be depends on how much you want to make the change. But changes you initiate yourself—to upgrade your wardrobe, to start looking better—have their own inherent problems.

"When you're talking about changing clothing style, you're usually talking about becoming more flamboyant, more out there, wearing brighter colors, a lot of jewelry, that kind of thing," says Ellen Berman, M.D., a Philadelphia psychiatrist. "You don't hear women agonizing over whether they're going to wear quieter clothes. The discomfort comes with a change in style which makes you more visible."

For women in particular, says Dr. Berman, "clothes are really like taking up space in the world, because you know people look at you, and you know they're making a judgment about you. And so the question is, How much space do you want to take up? That's the hard part, because most women have been trying not to take up too much space."

Indeed, women say the adjustment to being more visible is the most difficult part of a style change that takes you from conservative "safe" clothes to ones that are brighter, prettier, more fashionable.

Barbara Kasman, who metamorphosed from a self-described "beige person" who wore glasses and Red Cross shoes to a woman of style when she left a corporate job to start her own public relations agency, says, "It invites comments, because when you look so different people have to say something. That's what's scary, drawing attention and inviting judgment."

Trading in her glasses for contacts, says Kasman, was like "shaving off a beard." Now, says Kasman, when she thinks of people telling her they liked the way she looked in glasses, it seems as if they were saying, "I like the way you look with a bag over your head."

Mastering the details of a new style—from learning to put in contacts to choosing the right shoes for a new dress—is part of the problem involved in making a style change, says Kasman. But what's ultimately a bigger problem is adjusting to seeing yourself, and being seen, in a different way. "In the beginning I felt like the old me dressing up," says Kasman. "It was very scary. But people responded positively and now I feel I couldn't walk out of the house dressed in my old clothes, I really couldn't."

Another reason changing styles can be so

difficult, says psychologist Stephanie Miller, is that it can signal to the world other, more essential changes.

"The clothes may represent a change in class, which may only be from lower middle to middle middle, but that's a large shift," says Miller. "Or you may want to stand out, where you once wanted to fade into the woodwork, and that's a big adjustment: are you going to be noticed, accepted?"

Many women who claim to want to make sweeping changes in their style nonetheless pull back at the moment of truth, say experts. Vicki French Morris, owner of French-Haines wardrobe consulting in Chappaqua, New York, says that most women who hire her say they want to simplify their wardrobes and clear out their closets. However, says Morris, "they say they want to get rid of things and after item number two they start getting very nervous and by the end of the session they're grabbing things out of my hands."

Why do so many people say they want to change their style, and then have trouble doing so? "People are very ambivalent about what they want, so the part of them that wants something says it, and the part that doesn't want it keeps wearing the same clothes," says Stephanie Miller. "Clothes can be evidence of hidden emotions."

When your life or your looks have changed, your old clothes can be the last vestige of the old you, a way to hang on to a self-image or a set of values that have otherwise passed away. For instance, says New York psychotherapist Arlene Kagle, "people have a lot of difficulty changing clothes as their bodies change. If they always had a great waist, when they see belts

they always think, That's for me. They've got two or three grandchildren and they're not Scarlett O'Hara anymore, but it's hard to shift."

Not wanting to spend money can be another reason people refuse to change styles when it's appropriate or desired, says Dr. Kagle, as can following a set of internal style rules passed down from mom and dad. And, says Dr. Kagle, some people want to be judged on the basis of their inner qualities, not on the basis of their clothes.

If changing your style is difficult at best, and often impossible, in many cases it may not even be desirable—at least not all of a sudden, in a major way.

"It's best to change as a slow gradual process, like that guy in the commercial who colors his hair slowly, rather than an overnight boom thing," says Atlanta image consultant Susan St. Charles. "If you change quickly, it's too much for everybody: spouses get nervous, kids get nervous, peers get nervous, employees get nervous. In the corporate sector, if someone walks in one day all decked out, it almost looks like she's being a traitor. A partner can feel like she's being deceitful. We think, You're not the same person. How am I going to relate to you?"

According to Dr. Ellen Berman, how other people react to changes in your appearance depends on what those changes are, what they mean, and how much the person has invested in your staying the same. "For some people another's change is a sheer, unadulterated pleasure. The person looks better, and it either doesn't matter or it's just really nice," Dr. Berman says. "However, if the other person is a husband, say, who married his wife because she would stand in his shadow and he wouldn't have to worry about competition, then he's not going to like it. If the woman looks remarkably better and other men start looking at her, the husband will be either delighted or horrified, depending upon how much he trusts her and their relationship."

Then, too, if you change your style dramatically, you have to be prepared for the changes it may spark in your life. "I've seen several women get married and several women get divorced," says Susan St. Charles. "I've seen people get promoted too fast. One woman came to me because in six weeks she was up for an 8 percent increase and wanted to dress for that, and she ended up getting a 12 percent increase, and then was promoted again in a short period of time and transferred. Sometimes

people aren't ready for that kind of increase and movement."

But most women who weather the difficulties of a style change to arrive at a look with which they become comfortable find the concurrent changes in life and attitude only positive. The prime reason: it's a chicken-and-egg process, with changes in the way you feel making you ready for changes in the way you dress which make you ready for more changes in the way you feel.

"It takes time to adapt, but now I have a totally different self-image," says Barbara Kasman. "I know people react to me differently, and I also know I literally feel differently when I'm dressed in more stylish clothes, even when I'm sitting in my office all by myself."

Small Changes That Can Make a Big Style Difference

Maybe your style needs a lift, or you want to make a change without overhauling your entire wardrobe. Where to start? With what you love most. How to proceed? Consider these small changes that pay big style dividends.

IF YOU LOVE . . .	TRY . . .
Classics	Breaking the mold with detail and/or color: a perfectly plain scarf in pink chiffon, for instance, or a simple navy jacket to which you add tortoiseshell buttons.
Skirts and blouses	Adding a wonderful belt.
Beige	Mixing it with dark neutrals: charcoal, navy, black.
Loose-fitting clothes	One body-hugging piece (you might be surprised how many people ask if you've lost weight).
Bright colors	Mixing two you never thought would go together—red and purple, for instance, or green and orange—or mixing brights with strong pastels, such as orange and coral.
Jeans	Wearing them with dressed-up pieces, such as a starched white blouse, a fitted jacket, silver jewelry.
Jewelry	Building a trademark collection: silver hoop earrings, for example, or enamel bracelets, or jeweled animal pins. The narrower your focus, the more interesting variations you'll find.
Jackets	Finding a way to make all your jackets distinctive: with silver buttons, with antique pins on a lapel, with an alligator belt cinching the waist.
Sexy clothes	Wearing sexy lingerie under everything—a black lace bra under a navy T-shirt, a teddy under a suit—for a sexy feeling even when you can't be obvious about it.
Black	Wearing it with navy.
Shoes	Eliminating the competition by wearing simple, neutral clothes and stockings, minimal jewelry, letting your shoes be the sole standouts.

EMOTIONAL ISSUE:
LIFE CHANGES/STYLE CHANGES

Your husband has been transferred from New York to Los Angeles. Although you've lived in and around New York your entire life, you're excited about the move and even more thrilled when, one month after you arrive, you land a great job at a local public relations agency. To celebrate, you buy a new dress: a tailored linen dress that, by New York standards, looks chic and professional. After several weeks of wearing this dress in L.A., however, you finally catch on that it's sending off a very different message. This dress, which in New York says "high-powered yet creative businesswoman," in California says "Beverly Hills matron."

Making a major life change—moving to a new place, going from school to job, switching careers, leaving the corporate world for a creative job or to stay home with a baby—often means making a major style change. In theory, this is easy: trade in your wools for linens, throw out your suits and buy jeans. But that's just considering the practical changes you have to make in your wardrobe when you change your life. More important, and more baffling and more far-reaching, are the inner changes and societal reconsiderations that usually accompany a major life change, spark a change in the way you dress.

"When I first moved to L.A., I had no idea what to put on any morning. I didn't know where to take my cues from," says Susan Gordon, who recently moved from New York to Los Angeles. "I could read the different uniforms in New York, but here it was easy to misinterpret what people were wearing. I really felt quickly like I was in big trouble."

Gordon's first move, spurred by California's warmer climate, was to invest in more summery clothes. "The first month I bought three pairs of shorts," she says. "I wore shorts in New York but here you need a whole shorts wardrobe: longer shorts and beach shorts and shorts you can wear to the dentist's."

Other changes were prompted by the overall difference in California style. "I went on a rampage and bought pastels I never would have thought of buying before," says Gordon. "I always thought peach or mint green would look horrible on me. I don't know if it's the light here or the climate, but I can get away with it here while I would never wear those colors in New York. And shoes—people wear white shoes here in a way they don't in New York. I have to focus on different parts of my body and figure out where I have gaps."

The corporate culture is different too in California, Gordon, now features editor at *California* magazine, has discovered. "What I bring to my expectations of what's appropriate for the office are fourteen years of working in New York in a semi-corporate situation, but in general L.A. is less formal and there's a very wide range of options that are acceptable," Gordon says. "You see people in white linen and people in brown wool suits and people in jams, orange T-shirts, and paint-splattered espadrilles."

If Gordon hasn't completely mastered the California style, neither does she any longer have one fashion foot in New York. "Last year I wasn't fully committed to the idea of staying here forever, so I thought how could I buy clothes appropriate to here and not home," she says. "Now I see that this is home. Now if I'm going to visit friends in New York I don't have any New York clothes."

Often, making a major life change—changing careers, for instance, or going back to work after staying home with a child—is accompanied by major internal changes that can work to propel a change in style.

Paula Golden, who went to law school after her two children were in school, says that going from any-old-thing mom clothes to the structured clothes required by a job in state government was an unpleasant, if ultimately enlightening, change. "I was very uncertain about how to move through professional society," she says. "My dress reflected my insecurity and conformity. It really caused me to go through this period of what was right and wrong. What changed it back was a rejection by my superior. I left state government and the day I left I threw out my entire wardrobe and started buying new clothes."

Throwing out all the clothes in her closet, says Golden, made her realize that, "I could do anything I wanted. I decided that if I ever did anything again it would be on my own terms." Including, says Golden, her own fashion terms.

Now the executive director of the Massachusetts Seatbelt Coalition, Golden loves dresses, bright colors, and standout jewelry for work. "I really have an aversion to suits now," she says. "When I look at a two-piece suit I look at an iron maiden."

Another woman, who went from the corporate world to working at home part-time when her child was an infant and now recently has moved back to a corporate job, says she finds the changes in her style symbolic of her changing feelings about her career.

"Before I worked at home, my attitude was that I was going to spend my whole life working in an office and I'd be damned if I was going to dress any particular way," she says. "I was into dressing for comfort, even at the office, in jeans, sneakers, that kind of thing."

That trend intensified once she started working at home. "There was something about going to my desk barefoot that I really relished," she says. "I can remember having a few business conversations when I was half-dressed and feeling a little uncomfortable, but for the most part really enjoying not having to think about how I looked."

Now, however, at her new job, this woman says she finds herself wanting to dress up more. "The clothes I bought before I started this job don't reflect the amount of ambition I realize I have," she says. "They're more unobtrusive than I want to be. But I feel conflicted because while I want to stand out in my job, I have the same feelings toward my free-lance work and I feel an intense pull toward my son. I haven't found a way of dressing that suits all three ambitions. A white Chanel suit with a plastic cover?"

Most often, style changes that accompany life changes are happy experiences, evidence that a metamorphosis, however difficult, has taken place.

Fifteen years ago, Judy Patrick, now an Atlanta-based executive for a corporate relocation firm, was "still married, in church every Sunday and every Wednesday night. I couldn't look nice because you were a sinner if you did."

In 1974, Patrick got divorced and started working for the first time in her life, initially as a receptionist and secretary to support her two children. Where her religious life had been a barrier to dressing up before her divorce, a lack of money hindered her style in the early years of her career.

Gradually, however, Patrick moved up in the business world, began to make more money and "became much more style and quality conscious."

"My friends have teased me because this past year I've spent more on clothes than I have in my entire life," says Patrick, "I've had so much fun. Clothes can make you feel completely differently about yourself."

Or, more accurately, clothes can confirm that you already do.

• *Style Analysis* •

SUSAN ROGERS is a senior associate for a New York marketing firm that specializes in nonprofit corporations. Rogers bought the Norma Kamali suit she's wearing in her picture for $240 at a Dallas department store three years ago, soon after the birth of her son, "because I needed a lift and it's a very forgiving shape." Her sweater, from Adrienne Vittadini, was $90 five years ago, and her flowered scarf is mail order, from J. Crew, $53. Her pendants: Waterford crystal, a gift from her sister, and an antique sterling-and-ivory pendant— that actually functions as a tiny note-pad—from a small Manhattan shop.

WHAT DO YOU USUALLY WEAR TO WORK?

Sometimes I dress up, in a silk blouse, a skirt and heels, but not always. I've got this one thing that I wear that I call Sweetheart of the Rodeo. It's got pink brocade cowboy boots and a denim skirt and this sweater that I bought in London. I wore it one day and the owner of the company popped into my office and I said, "Oh, no," thinking he would say something to me about what clients want to see and instead he said, "Wow, you look great! Where did you get that sweater?" That's the nice thing about working in a place like this. You're supposed to be creative.

HOW DOES THE WAY YOU DRESS HERE COMPARE TO HOW YOU DRESSED WHEN YOU WERE A NEWSPAPER REPORTER?
[Rogers worked on the Dallas Morning News *and the* Miami Herald.]

When I was a reporter I used to have these disguises, different outfits I wore for different people. I tried to look not too opulent; you can really offend people by looking too opulent. I wouldn't wear a fur coat, for instance. I'm uncomfortable with furs. I carry a leather purse, and I wear suede shoes, and I eat meat, but I have a problem with fur coats. It's just too too too too much attention.

I go back and forth between thinking people should wear blue jeans and T-shirts—all of us, exactly the same thing—and wanting to go over to Harry Winston's and fill up both hands. It's kind of more of a problem in New York, because every day you get both extremes when you walk down the street. It's hard for me to justify spending $3,000 on a fur coat when, (*a*) I have to put my kid through college at some point and (*b*) I should be giving it to somebody who needs it more. I have the same problem paying retail. I almost never do.

HOW DO YOU SHOP?

Rarely. I'm a real believer in basics. The shirt I'm wearing [a green silk one, on the day of the interview] is older than my relationship with my husband; I've had it since I was in college. The scarf I'm wearing came from a mail-order catalog—I just recently discovered scarves, because in Dallas it was just too damn hot to wear them.

I like to shop in the weird stores in Brooklyn that don't have any signs outside and you go inside and there are all these Perry Ellis shoes lying around and you don't know where they came from. It's very strange, but you can find stuff there you wouldn't imagine. I like Ann Taylor because whenever I can't find anything and I'm really stuck I know if I go in there I'll find something. I like Unique Clothing Warehouse—you can buy all kinds of basic stuff there. I like the Gap. I went to the outlet malls in Dallas, and there are some great boutiques down on Greenville Avenue in Dallas. I shop a lot in catalogs: T-shirts from Lands' End; I really like Honeybee, although it's sometimes too kicky.

Actually, I do most of my shopping when I travel, and I often buy on impulse things that I really love—my birthday cake sweater from London, my gray-and-black shoes with the planets and stars from Paris, my piano shawl scarf from Wales.

I hardly ever buy a whole outfit. I buy a lot of white shirts, a lot of black skirts—black skirts in weird shapes. I'm a big proponent of the shoulder pad—small shoulder pads are God's gift to people with hips.

DID GROWING UP IN THE SOUTH INFLUENCE YOUR STYLE?

*M*ore than place, what influenced the way I dress was my parents. My father loves clothes, and he would tell my mother how to dress us. He used to pick clothes out of the stores. I was a very picky little kid, things had to match; I would only wear certain kinds of socks—I remember being desperately unhappy if I had to wear a kind of sock I didn't like. To my parents, appearance was very important. They were married when they were very young—fifteen and seventeen—and so they were more obsessed with clothes and much more hip about clothes than other parents might be. My mom and my two sisters and I buy each other things.

HOW DID THE MOVE TO NEW YORK FROM DALLAS AFFECT YOUR WAY OF DRESSING? TO ME DALLAS HAS A REALLY DISTINCT STYLE, AND VERY DIFFERENT FROM THAT OF NEW YORK—IT'S COLOR AS OPPOSED TO BLACK, IT'S MAKEUP AS OPPOSED TO UNDERSTATED . . .

*I*t's hair that can stand on its own and walk around the room! I have elements of that in my wardrobe. I can't help it; I just like that sometimes. But I also find it somewhat in bad taste. I'm from Dallas right now, but I was from a lot of other places before.

I really try to not buy stuff that I won't wear; that's the non-Dallas part of my personality. My mother has a closet that's as big as my child's room. I love to go home and look at her stuff, but I just can't deal with that much. I don't own that many clothes, and I try to really love the ones I have. I wear them until they're falling apart. If I buy something I don't love, I try to get rid of it immediately.

CAN YOU THINK OF SOMETHING YOU BOUGHT RECENTLY THAT YOU DIDN'T LOVE?

I bought these really beautiful pants. They were brown, and they had black and red and blue threads. I'd put these pants on and I just looked wrong. They came out of my desire to be a New York person when I first got here. I looked around and nobody looked like me. Well, you know these women who look incredibly classic, with cameos and pearls, and they looked like they walked out of a Ralph Lauren ad. These pants were just so tweedy; they were never right for me.

DO YOU HAVE A POINT WHERE YOU SAY, "I WOULD NEVER SPEND MORE THAN X AMOUNT FOR A SKIRT OR A JACKET"?

*T*he cutoff point for me is $100. I have a hard time spending more than $100 for a single item of clothing. I don't think you have to spend that much money to look good, if you have a clear idea of what appeals to you. For me, it's black, it's navy, it's pants with tapered legs, it's something that has some shape around the shoulders. I remind myself of women who date men and if they're not immediately marriage material, that's it. I don't try out clothes.

I like catalog shopping. You can look at things and there are some pretty basic rules about how it will work out. If it makes the model look fat, you are not going to look thin in it. If they're giving you stupid names for colors, like tealberry blue, that's a hint that it might really be green, not blue. If it's clear from the picture what color it is, that's a good buy. Sizes are trial and error—you get to know a brand or a catalog. I used to be able to buy completely out of catalogs, and then I had a baby. I usually take my measurements now.

HOW MUCH DO YOU SPEND ON CLOTHES IN A YEAR?

I'm scaling it down a little bit. I have this fear about getting old and looking ridiculous. I used to dress in this wildly dramatic way, and I don't do that anymore, although my husband would disagree. I probably spend about $1,000.

IS THERE ANYTHING ABOUT YOUR FIGURE THAT YOU DRESS TO HIDE?

Yeah, my hips. Today I'm wearing a tight, short, knit black skirt, but I'm wearing it with a wide black belt. If you wear a wide belt slightly above your waist, it can make your hips look smaller. I wear tapered pants, not even straight legs. Dark colors.

ANYTHING YOU HAVE A PASSION FOR?

Suede, silk, black, brilliant brilliant blue. Really nice leather things but not leather pants. They feel too stiff and crunchy, and they seem sort of ostentatious. Textures in general are very important to me; how something feels is important. I'm quite partial to hand-knitted things because I like the way they feel.

I love watches. I have four: a black rubber Mickey Mouse that I bought for my son; a silver bracelet kind of watch; a thin gold watch on a gray snakeskin strap, and an all-gold watch.

I also treasure high heels. Two and a half inches is exactly the right height. It puts me at eye level with most male clients. And I love pantyhose. I've got them in every color.

ANYTHING YOU WOULDN'T WEAR?

Yellow. Most greens. Everybody says no polyester, and that is just not true. If people look at their clothes they'll find they have some polyester in there. I have a beautiful blouse that my husband's grandmother gave me—it's cream color with tucking—that I wear with a pretty silk crepe skirt, and it's as polyester as it can be. It's comfortable and it drapes beautifully and people stop me in the street and ask me where I got it, so I think it's stupid to be a snob about polyester.

IS THERE ANYTHING YOU'RE A SNOB ABOUT?

I'm a kind of reverse snob. I hate women who look so perfect, that high-WASP kind of perfection. They're like people out of a J. Crew catalog. At least the models in J. Crew have that kind of haunted, melancholy look, looking at the ground like, "May have to, sob, go into capital." I do own turtlenecks, but they're all black.

I have to admit to being obsessed with clothes to a certain degree. Clothing is a good way to express your desires to be artistic. If you appreciate color and form and line and shape and have definite opinions about what you like and don't like, clothes are a way to get that out of your system. I've always thought your clothes should be really, truly part of you.

Old Clothes:

How to Weed,

What to Save,

What to Toss

•

You've tried to get rid of them. Really you have. You've torn your closet apart, hardening your heart as you toss everything that doesn't fit, doesn't flatter, or isn't in style anymore to the side. Maybe you've even bundled all your rejects and looked up the Salvation Army's phone number. The problem, though, is their little voices, crying out to you from the garbage bag: "You can't throw me out! You paid $200 for me and you wore me only once!" and "How could you get rid of me? Your mother gave me to you for Christmas!"

Getting rid of old clothes—even those you're sure you'll never wear again—can be a difficult task. Why can it be so tough to part with what are, after all, just pieces of cloth?

Because it's tough to see your own clothes as "just pieces of cloth." "It's a struggle to weed out your own closet," says Atlanta image consultant Susan St. Charles, "because there's much emotion attached to your own clothes. You remember what you paid for each item, where you wore it, who gave it to you. Getting rid of things can be extremely liberating but you need someone to tell you how to do it."

Indeed, it's many a woman's fantasy to leave the task to someone who will make objective and not emotional decisions, to hire a professional to weed out and reorganize her closet. How do the professionals do it?

Before they even open the closet doors, most wardrobe consultants will talk to you for at least an hour about what you like, what you need, where you want to go with your style. This is to get a handle on your ideal theoretical wardrobe before they tackle your actual one.

Next, they go through the items in your closet one by one, making decisions about what's in, what's out, what might be possible. The key, of course, is how they decide which is which.

Are there any things that are always out? "Clothes that are faded, torn, that are in a color that goes against you, or a silhouette that's inappropriate," says Los Angeles image consultant Andrea Sells. "If you're large-busted and you've got a blouse with breast pockets and dolman sleeves, I say, 'Unless you're ready for a breast reduction, forget it.' "

French-Haines's Vicki French Morris's criteria for what to toss: "If it doesn't fit, if it's unflattering, if it's unlikely to ever be flattering or to fit in the near future, if it's an unflattering color, or if it's so much of a period piece that it will always look dated, such as a blouse with muttonchop sleeves."

Joyce Grillo of Impression Management, who teaches a course in closet cleaning, advises students to spend an entire day each season weeding and reorganizing their closets, accompanied by a full-length mirror and paper and pen with which to list every item you're certain you'll wear, everything you need to buy.

However, it's not always easy, even for the experts, to practice what they preach. "My personal criteria for getting rid of something is, if I haven't worn it in three years or if it's totally not me anymore," says Joyce Grillo. "But I have a hard time getting rid of things because I always know I'll want them the next month. I have been known to go back and pull things from the incinerator room."

How Grillo deals with this in her personal life, and what she advises clients who have trouble parting with clothes: "I have a box where I put all these things I don't really wear but I'm not ready to get rid of. I want them visually out of my way so I can make sense of what's in my closet. After something's been in the box for a while, it's easier to throw out."

Creating a halfway house for old clothes can be a good technique for handling the ambivalence of getting rid of things, say women who've devised their own effective closet-cleaning methods.

"I have a container that's a giveaway box stuck at the back of my closet," says Boston advertising and public relations writer Kate Broughton. "If I try something on and it doesn't fit, or I see something hanging up and think I'll never wear it, I throw it in there. Once the box is full, I go through it real quick to make sure there's nothing I tossed in there in a fit of insanity."

One advantage of this system, says Broughton, is that if she later wants something back, it's still there. "I'm glad in a way that I have a hard time getting rid of stuff," she says. "I had a Vittadini cotton knit sweater dress that had nothing wrong with it except that it had stretched out, and when I was pregnant I rummaged around, found it, cut it off at the thigh and it was perfect."

Keeping a castoff box makes it easier to toss things aside, says Broughton, even if she's worn them only once. "If I've worn something and I'm constantly adjusting the shoulder pads or always rolling up the sleeves because they keep sliding down, I realize there's no way I can ever change that and I get rid of it," she says.

The payoff: a closet that includes only clothes she likes and wears. "My working collection of clothing is limited but I'd rather not have to comb through a closet full of stuff that doesn't appeal to me, and most often if something doesn't appeal to me at one point it never will."

Other women have their own version of Broughton's giveaway box, quarantining unwanted or iffy clothes in a suitcase, an extra closet, or in the back if they have a single closet. The point is, always, to keep the clothes that fit, that are flattering, that you like, and that you wear in one place, and to keep anything that makes you feel fat, foolish, or guilty in another.

One thing that can help you finally move out those things you're sure you're ready to part with is knowing they'll go to a good home. Makeup artist Linda Nicholas says it's easier to get rid of clothes she doesn't like but that are in good condition because her mother wears the same size she does. Other women give unwanted clothes to an appreciative sister, friend, cleaning woman, or charity.

But even those women who have their recycling systems down pat say there are some things that are just impossible to throw away. "I have a pair of the most beautiful pants that I paid $10 for that I'll never wear but I may never throw out because they're such good quality and they were such a bargain," says Nicholas. "And I have trouble throwing out all-cotton sweatshirts or sneakers even when they have big holes, because they're so comfortable that I love to wear them even if they're falling off. It's easier for me to get rid of something that I've worn three times and don't like anymore than something I passionately love that's worn out."

Carolyn Gutjahr, a St. Louis urban planner, has an easy time getting rid of old T-shirts or the interview suit she never wore after she got the job, but finds it difficult to part with clothes that she's made herself. "Even if I feel that they're out of style or that they don't suit my style, there will be something about those pieces of clothes, the fabric or the buttons, or that I think I did a good job with the sewing, that makes them very hard to throw away," she says.

Sometimes, people keep things they don't wear out of pure sentiment. "I have one closet I use every day that holds that season's clothes and one in the back of the house with all my other clothes, and when I switch closets that forces me to throw things away," says Lisa Amos, a management consultant in New Orleans. "But I have a few things I know I'll never wear again that I just can't throw away, such as the dress I wore to go away on my honeymoon."

Lots of stuff you can't bear to part with and little room to store it? One woman's solution is to take Polaroid shots of her favorite clothes, keep those in place of the real things. But for some people, it takes a catastrophe to realize that old clothes are often best put out to pasture.

"I used to be much more acquisitive," says Kate Broughton, "and then once when I was moving I had a car fire and all the clothes I owned burned up. The next month was so incredible because all these habits I'd gotten into—a special way of laundering something or worrying about what I was going to wear—just fell away because I literally had no clothes."

Rather than feeling devastated, Broughton found the experience "eye-opening." "I realized you can get so enslaved to your clothes that they take control of you. I have never gone back to that level of accumulation, and whenever I'm tempted to all I have to do is sit back and remember what a wonderful feeling I had after the fire," she says. "It's not that I'd want all my clothes to burn up again, but I know it's better to live slim."

Six Things to Save

What, when you're weeding through your closet, should you absolutely, positively save, even if you haven't worn it recently? The items below:

1. **CLASSIC EVENING WEAR**—Silk pants, an embroidered kimono, a charmeuse tunic—anything that still fits and is in good shape, even if you had a baby three years ago and haven't been out after midnight since. The next time you have to attend a once-every-five-years formal event, you may not have to buy new clothes.

2. **COMFORT CLOTHES**—It doesn't matter if the wonderful alpaca cardigan you bought in Paris looks as if it were chewed on by moths the size of bats; if it makes you feel that you are once again strolling by the Seine, keep it.

3. **SENTIMENTAL FAVORITES**—The sleazy lace nightgown, size petite, your husband gave you for your first anniversary. The sweater your mother knit you when you went to college in North Dakota. The jeans you embroidered and wore to everything from rock concerts to your roommate's wedding. Don't throw out important memories because of any silly rules. Hey, but let's not get ridiculous. The patchwork-print skirt you wore the first time you made a perfect souffle doesn't count—unless it launched your career as a cook.

4. **THE SKIRT THAT MAKES YOU LOOK TEN POUNDS THINNER, EVEN IF IT'S OUT OF STYLE**—A supremely flattering item is always a keeper, even if it looks dumb or dowdy for a few years. You never know, fashions may change. And then again, so may your body.

5. **HIGH-QUALITY CLASSICS IN GOOD CONDITION**—What I'm thinking of are things like tweed blazers and cashmere sweaters that one year may fit a little too tight for the style, or may have a cowl neckline when everyone's wearing turtlenecks, or may have lapels that are a little too wide or too narrow. For a short time, these so-called classics may look awful to you—but if they're in good shape, hang on, because the style standing of these sorts of details always changes, and they'll look good again someday.

6. **THE SKIRT OR PANTS THAT FIT LAST YEAR, BUT NOW ARE A LITTLE TOO SNUG, OR A LITTLE TOO BIG**—Whenever I gain or lose ten pounds, I tend to think this is it forever, and out with everything that reminds me of my former shape. But if your weight fluctuation is recent, and if you tend to go up or down a size consistently over time, it's smart to keep items that fit in your normal range, even if they don't fit right now.

Ten Things to Toss

When you're cleaning out your closet, what to save is usually more obvious than what to toss. But hanging onto useless items can blind you to the real gaps in your wardrobe by giving you what I think of as the "illusion of plenty"—clothes, clothes everywhere, and not a thing to wear. Here, a list of all those items that finally and absolutely deserve to die:

1. **THE THIRD, FOURTH, FIFTH, AND SIXTH SET OF OLD CLOTHES YOU'RE SAVING TO WEAR WHEN YOU PAINT THE HOUSE**—Yes, it's smart to hang onto tattered T-shirts and jeans for sloppy jobs around the house. But do you really need an entire house-painting wardrobe?

2. **STRETCHED-OUT, HOLEY, OR SAGGY SOCKS, HOSE, UNDERWEAR**—Out, once and for all, with those droopy drawers, baggy bras, worn-out socks, and tights with the crotch that always ends up at your knees.

3. **THE SKIRT OR PANTS THAT ONLY FIT THE SUMMER YOU TURNED VEGETARIAN AND FELL IN LOVE**—Do you really need a constant reminder that for one brief shining moment you actually wore a size 4?

4. **WHITE SHIRTS WITH YELLOWED ARMPITS, BROWN CUFFS, AND RING AROUND THE COLLAR**—If you love white shirts, it can be hard to admit when one has met with terminal dinge. If you're having trouble facing facts, give them one last hyper-thorough laundering. And if that doesn't work, say good-bye.

5. **SHOES THAT HURT**—Maybe your toes will get shorter. Maybe one day you'll suddenly feel comfortable in high heels. Maybe you'll wear them with Band-Aids and heavy socks. Maybe you should give them to the Salvation Army.

6. **THE INCREDIBLY BEAUTIFUL SILK BLOUSE WITH THE BIG GREASE STAIN ON THE FRONT**—Wonderful, nearly new pieces that have nevertheless been ruined are probably the most difficult things to part with. Still, if you keep the silk blouse, you'll feel terrible every time you look at it. Better to throw it out, save up for a new one, and wear a napkin around your neck in restaurants.

7. **THE ITEM YOU BOUGHT WHEN YOU WERE DERANGED AND HAVE NEVER SEEN FIT TO WEAR**—We all make mistakes. But if a few years go by and your mistake still seems entirely like one, let it go.

8. **OLD PURSES**—I'm not sure why this is, but purses are the one thing that seem to never, ever come back into style in exactly the same way.

9. **GIFTS THAT WERE NEVER YOU**—We all get them, the well-intentioned lacy blouses or lavender polyester dresses that we'd try to avoid wearing if they were the last clothes on earth. And yet we keep them, thinking we'll put them on when the giver comes to visit, or that if we throw them out, the giver will be angry. Do this if you must, but after a year or two, you can safely get rid of such items, claiming if you're questioned that you "wore them out."

10. **THE PERFECTLY NICE PIECE THAT NEVERTHELESS MAKES YOU FEEL FAT OR UGLY**—Perhaps the color is wrong, or it's just the wrong style for you. This kind of clothing is like the perfectly nice boyfriend who nevertheless makes you feel angry and depressed. Better give it to someone else who will appreciate it, and move on to a perfectly nice piece that makes you feel terrific.

•16•

The Evolution of Personal Style

•

Everybody's always telling you how great you look. Not just when you wear your wonderful new dress, but when you wear the same skirt and sweater you've been wearing all winter except with a different pair of shoes and a pin at the neck, or when you throw on a pair of jeans and your husband's sweater. How, they all want to know, do you do it?

You don't know.

Did someone teach you how to put clothes together in such a wonderful way?

Not that you're aware of.

Do you have secret fashion tips and techniques?

Not really.

Do you shop at one special incredible store?

No, just wherever's cheap, or handy.

Many of your acquaintances will no doubt think you're lying, or at least holding back, playing coy. They're wrong.

Women who have that ineffable thing called style, who always look terrific in their own wonderful way, usually have trouble explaining exactly how they do it. Call it a talent, an art, or an instinct; the fact is, style is something that usually springs from an early fascination with clothes, is matured by a keen visual sense and a strong measure of self-knowledge.

That's not to say that style is genetic, or inborn, as unattainable as long legs or broad shoulders. While many women credit a clothes-conscious parent, or a job in the fashion business, with nurturing their sense of style, neither are necessary ingredients of style, nor are money, a sophisticated upbringing, or an urban life. Rather, what does seem essential is a highly tuned sense of what's right—meaning what's most practical, most flattering, most appealing on some elemental level—for you, as well as the conviction to wear it. Some women seem to have full-blown style before they get their first Barbies; other women develop and refine it over the years. The bottom line: style can be acquired, but it can't be bought.

To discover something about a woman's style, it doesn't help to ask her where she buys her clothes or how she puts them together—the methodology is often beside the point, even unconscious. What's more pertinent is how a woman grew up, how she lives now: the interplay of life and style. Here, the stories of six women, and how their styles evolved:

Vicki French Morris, owner, French-Haines wardrobe consulting, Chappaqua, New York

When I was a child, my great-aunt took me to the dime store and said I could buy anything I wanted, and I bought chartreuse socks. My taste ran to the frilly. I used to make doll clothes when I was a little kid, and I remember stitching down the rickrack so that it wouldn't curl.

My mother has always been interested in clothes, and has very definite ideas about style. She thinks that color is not really very nice, that one should only wear black, navy, beige, and wine, so I always get a kick out of wearing red when I see her. She was a very unsophisticated Italian girl from Philadelphia who was also very observant. Now she's in her seventies and is just so chic. She volunteers at the Sloan Kettering thrift shop and it doesn't occur to her not to buy something if it's secondhand. She took a Chanel couture suit out of the garbage.

My dad was president and chairman of AMC (a department store fashion buying office) when I was a teenager, so I could buy things wholesale and traveled all over Europe and got *Women's Wear Daily*. So I was very interested in fashion, and in art, which relates very much to fashion, and I went to Manhattanville College and in the summers worked at *Harper's Bazaar*. When I got out of college I worked at *Mademoiselle* and *Vogue*.

I married a banker, and we left New York to move to Cambridge in the sixties when Harvard was having the strikes and people were hippies instead of the clean-cut Catholic girls I knew at Manhattanville. I started dressing in a more counterculture way but I was never really counterculture. Then I became a mother and for a number of years dropped out of anything related to chic, but I continued to love clothes and would always help my friends shop and pull outfits together.

I just fell into this business with a friend. We practiced on everybody who would let us in her closet until we felt we had it perfected. For a couple of years we did men, but when I bought out my partner I didn't feel comfortable with that; I like women's clothes.

One thing I love consistently, not only in clothes, is texture. I adore cashmere, partly because I'm always cold but also for its texture and drape. I also love linen; I don't mind the wrinkles. In Thailand I bought things because of the beautiful weave of the fabric. I love jewelry that has a sculptural quality.

The colors I like are black and white and red and bright blue and silvery gray or lavender. I love all different shades of white. In my closet, you'd see a big range of functions, but you would know one person liked those clothes: there's a consistency, clean lines, and interesting textures. Each season I probably wear for business three outfits more than any others. I have no hesitation if I'm tired of something to get rid of it, but I also can keep something forever if I'm still wearing it. I spend a lot on clothes each year, probably about $8,000.

For fun I love shoes that have something whimsical, like buttons, or mock Chanel shoes with striped tips. I love that kind of thing in accessories. I love my ceramic dog pin, my silver chain with the little spy glass and the toothpick case hanging on it. That's where the chartreuse sock person hangs out.

Tracy Achor Hayes, fashion writer, Dallas *Morning News*

I've always been one of those girls who loved clothes. I've subscribed to every fashion magazine from the time I was ten. I fell into this business through the back door; I was a history major at the University of Texas, and when I got out of school I moved back to Dallas and got a job in the advertising department at Neiman Marcus. I discovered that what I liked wasn't the ads but the products being advertised.

Then a job opened at the newspaper, and I bluffed my way in. People of style are good bluffers. Newspapers are not citadels of stylishness, and it was 1979, and they just didn't know what to think of me. I had this real real real short hair, and one of the people thought how brave I was to be coming to work while undergoing chemotherapy.

I do still love this business. I can still get excited enough at a fashion show to cry. It's probably skewed my perspective: I tend to look around me and generalize that the rest of the population is on the same level, that I'm not outrageous. When I go to a restaurant, I say to my husband, "People are looking at me," and he says, "Of course they are," and I say, "I'm not weird," and he says, "Of course you are."

I feel like I'm a chameleon that runs from one trend to another: if it's the newest thing I want to have it. I've always felt that I was totally a trend slut but other people have always told me certain clothes "looked like me," so somehow from this mishmash my style remains consistent, but I couldn't tell you what it is, except that I dress to hide my figure problems.

I think I'm one of those people who can smell what's happening before it does. All of a sudden something starts looking good to me and then, oh my God, here it comes. I have a trunk saved with a quintessential outfit from each period, and I've been looking at these things from college, from the late sixties and early seventies, and thinking, Gosh, these Indian prints look kinda good again, and I like these silver and turquoise bracelets and this necklace from Afghanistan. I've been seeing scarves tied Rhoda-style—that was my sign in the sixties—and I'm getting that feeling. And then we go to Christian Lacroix and here we go Rich Hippie. But in a way it's bad because as soon as it's validated, then it's a trend and it will go out, so I'm not even going to get to enjoy it. '

Barbara Kenerson, stockbroker, Providence, Rhode Island

I've always been a clothes horse, even during the sixteen years I was a schoolteacher. I have four brothers, but my father was always a very sharp guy. One of my aunts is very sharp—she and I were real buddies; I was the daughter she never had. My mother still wears bell-bottoms.

I like to shop if I'm in the mood; I find it very relaxing. I hate to be with anybody else. I go to Loehmann's. I don't always find things, but every now and then I'll find a beautiful dress and a suit. Armani is great; I love that look. I buy $300 blouses for $120, and to me that is a bargain, while most of my friends want $80 blouses for $40. I hardly ever feel desperate. It's not as if I've got to go out tonight and find a black dress for a party tomorrow night.

I wear a lot of dresses, beautiful wool dresses. I like something that's not tight but has a small waist and looks good with a belt. I'm never afraid to try something new. When minis came in the first time, I started wearing them before other people did. In my office here a lot of people wear suits, but I started wearing dresses.

I have dressed this way my whole life, even when I was a poor college kid and had a job in a department store. When I was a teacher, the kids always knew what I had on, even if they didn't understand the math I was teaching. If you're a creative person you don't have to spend a lot of money to look great.

Joyce Grillo, president, Impression Management, New York

As a child I watched old movies and I'm still fascinated by the dress of the thirties and forties.

I love that style, that very tall, classic dress look. A lot of my sense of style comes from that, looking at these women and wanting to look like them—elegant and great, tall and powerful, sexy and pretty yet tailored.

At a very young age I was allowed to pick out my own clothes. I wore uniforms to school until I was thirteen, and I hated my uniform, I was so tired of it, and now it's funny, but I love navy and white, and gold buttons.

When I really started to buy a lot of clothes was when I started working, when I was seventeen. I was a stenographer in an insurance company and made $58 a week. The first thing I bought was a copy of a Chanel bag; I used it for a long time and I never threw it out.

I didn't really start to buy quality things until about ten years ago. I began to realize I looked and felt better in more expensive clothes. I learned a lot from my first roommate—for instance, to have one pair of good pumps.

In the eight years I worked at Citibank, I never wore a little suit. It never occurred to me that if I didn't wear a suit that it would work against me. When I first started working at the bank, I bought a brown forties-looking suit that came in at the waist. I put a pin in the lapel, wore it to work and got a lot of compliments.

When I first started my business I tried to make a lot of statements with my clothes. I'd give presentations wearing a floral dress or creative earrings or a teal jacket and purple shirt. I don't really do that anymore. I've gotten very, very conservative. I'm feeling more confident and understanding my business more, so I don't have to prove anything with my clothes. And I got tired of those things; they wear on you after a while.

Also, I've been spending more and more money, and I've started to buy less, and when you do that you want clothes that are classic. I never wear anything out, and I keep my clothes forever. I have a bag I bought in Saks when I was twenty-five, a black bag I paid $25 for and still use. Up until this year I had a pair of navy wool pants I bought eight or ten year ago that I loved. My husband put them in the washing machine and they shrank. I wanted to kill him.

Kate Broughton, advertising and public relations writer, Boston

Part of the reason I dress the way I do is wearing Catholic school uniforms for twelve years. I never knew what it was like to have lots of clothing, and while I hated the uniforms, there was a simplicity in having a limited selection. In college I was a hippie and didn't need clothes, so I was a late bloomer in being interested in clothes. It's ironic that I wound up getting involved in fashion and working in upscale magazines [Broughton was an editor at *Boston* magazine].

The look I'm most comfortable with is sparse clothes, hair really short, and intricate earrings. The earrings take the place of both a froufrou hairdo and elaborate clothes. I don't like to fuss and primp. I like stuff to be really functional. I dress almost like my school uniform—oversized blazer, no makeup, earrings the only jewelry allowed.

I went through what I thought of as my Madison Avenue high-fashion look, in which I sewed a lot of clothes by designers like Geoffrey Beene. Then I went through my preppy stage because, being from West Virginia, I had never seen preppy stuff before. It looked so neat and well-kempt, I fantasized about wanting to look that pulled together but that was too straight-laced for me.

I came into a comfortable period when the Annie Hall look started. I never liked to dress butchy but I like funky man-tailored stuff. It was comfortable and it looked good on my shape, and I've not veered too far away from that. Since I sew more than I buy, I would sew what took the least amount of time—a simple jersey something that I could wear with a belt.

The temptation when you wear loose baggy things is to not be in the best shape and I would like to wear more form-fitting clothes. I wore a lot of stretch pants and baggy sweaters when those were big, and I like ankle-high boots. I have never moved into the ultra-accessorized look, scarves or any of that.

I will play around with color, though. One Christmas one of my sisters bought the *Color Me Beautiful* book for another sister, and we all sat around and analyzed each other. It's really made a difference. I've eliminated certain colors that I'm drawn to but that make me look washed out—like teal and jade green and pumpkin. I've limited my colors to grayish blue, like a postman's blue, soft pink, watermelon red, mauves, chalky whites. The book said I should not wear black but I do. I used to get so overwhelmed when I walked into a store, and now I feel it's better to shop by color first and then go to style because if it's not a good color it won't look right no matter how good the style. I wouldn't say I've bought into that whole Color Me Beautiful thing but it has saved me from a lot of mistakes.

Mary Gallagher, commercial director, Promostyl, Paris

As a child, my Air Force family moved quite often and I learned very early the virtues of packing light to get around more easily. These days, moving and traveling are part of my life and I'm so often schlepping around presentation panels, portfolios, and dossiers when I'm traveling that the last thing I need to worry about is what to pack.

I prefer simple clothing where the design element comes through in a few details or in the fabric. I tend to wear solid colors, with black being the major color in my wardrobe. I enjoy adding other fashion colors to black, but I do rely on black and white when traveling. I bring a few black pieces, mix them around with a few other pieces, and I have a week's worth of different looks.

Where I really go wild is with shoes and socks. I have my favorite shops in different cities where I make my pilgrimages to find the most unusual or fun footwear. I only wear flat shoes because they're so comfortable and I love the way they look. Tokyo is the best place to find great socks.

Working in the field of fashion forecasting can be frustrating when it comes to buying clothes. When Promostyl anticipates a trend eighteen months ahead of season and our designers sketch the style in our trend books, I'm dying to wear it. But, of course, it hasn't been manufactured yet and by the time it is, I'm on to the next trend.

When I'm buying clothes, I don't think, What do I have in my wardrobe to go with this? I imagine myself in a scene, wearing the item: Won't this pullover be perfect walking along the beach? Never mind that there's no romantic beach walk in the near future. I'll still be imagining the beach scene when I'm wearing the pullover on an airplane.

Index

W

Waistbands, elastic, 215
Wardrobe, assembly of, 114–16
Washed and prewashed garments, 214
Watches, 125, 273
Weather concerns. *See* Cold-weather dressing; Hot-weather dressing

Wedding dresses, 261
    nontraditional bride, 144–45
Weddings, clothing to wear to, 131
White shoes, 87, 241
Wiser, Nanette, 128–29, 240
Women's groups, discussions about clothing in, 64
Wool coats, 235
Working mothers, inappropriate clothes for, 173

Y

Yamamoto, Yohji, 258
Yellen, Sue, 163

About the Author

Pamela Redmond Satran is a former fashion editor of *Glamour*, where she was also fashion features editor, a job which she created. While at *Glamour*, Satran originated the columns Smart Shopper, Clothes Strategies, and Style, and produced numerous stories dealing with the practical and emotional side of fashion. Satran is the co-author of *Beyond Jennifer and Jason: An Enlightened Guide to Naming Your Baby* and the author of a novel, *Balancing Act*. She writes a nationally syndicated column on working parenthood, and her articles have appeared in *Glamour, Elle, Mademoiselle, Self, Working Mother, Working Woman*, the Village *Voice*, and the Washington *Post*. At New York University, she taught a course called "How Clothes Become Fashion," and has also taught writing at Parsons School of Design and the Pennsylvania Governor's School of Excellence.

Satran lives near New York City with her husband, Richard, an editor for Renters, their daughter Rory, and their son Joseph.